SIEGFRIED SASSOON: POET'S PILGRIMAGE

BY DAME FELICITAS CORRIGAN:

GEORGE THOMAS OF SOHO
(*Secker & Warburg*)

TO ANY CHRISTIAN
(*Burns Oates*)

IN A GREAT TRADITION
(*John Murray*)

S.S. to F.C. 24.5.61. 'Wiggin's photograph looks rather awaitful of whatever may be coming to me. In the library with Webster's dictionary on the table, and in that chair I wrote and revised most of my three vols of autobiography, and wore the paint off the elbows.'

SIEGFRIED SASSOON: POET'S PILGRIMAGE

Assembled with an Introduction

by

D. Felicitas Corrigan

LONDON
VICTOR GOLLANCZ LTD
1973

© Stanbrook Abbey, 1973
ISBN 0 575 01721 X

Printed in Great Britain by
The Camelot Press Ltd, London and Southampton

CONTENTS

Acknowledgements	
Note	11
Introduction	15
Part I: 1886–1914	43
Part II: 1914–1934	73
Part III: 1934–1957	119
Part IV: 1957–1967	171
Index	251

LIST OF ILLUSTRATIONS

S.S. to F.C. 24.5.61. 'Wiggin's photograph looks rather awaitful . . .' (*photo Maurice Wiggin, Sunday Times*) *Frontispiece*

	facing page
At the Press Bazaar, 1898, aged 11	30
At Algeciras, *c.* 1931	30
Garmisch 1929	31
S.S. and his son George	96
Malaga, March 1934 (*photograph by Hester Sassoon*)	97
Sic sedebat—1952 (*courtesy George Sassoon*)	128
March 1959: 'resting in Mother Church, as it were' (*photograph by George Sassoon*)	128
Unveiling a tablet to Walter de la Mare in St Paul's Cathedral, 1961 (*photograph Central Press Photos Ltd*)	129

ACKNOWLEDGEMENTS

My warm thanks are due first of all to the poet's son, Mr George Sassoon, for the use of photographs and for his kind interest in the publication of this book; and then to Dom Hubert van Zeller for his personal recollections, enlivened still further by two inimitable cartoons; to Father Alec Robertson, Sir Alan Lascelles, C.M.G., and Mr Edward Lindley for their letters; to Miss Judith Masefield and Mr Richard de la Mare for copyright material; to the librarian and staff of St John's College, Cambridge, for their ready assistance in checking references; and to the following publishing houses for permission to quote from books issued under their imprint:

Faber & Faber Ltd, Siegfried Sassoon's publishers
Constable Ltd, Siegfried Sassoon: *Meredith*
Rupert Hart Davis Ltd, *The Best Of Friends* edited by Viola Meynell
Holt, Rinehart & Winston Inc., for the use of Dom Hubert van Zeller's caricature entitled *Siegfried*
Sheed & Ward Ltd, William Langland: *The Vision Of Piers Plowman* trans. by H. W. Wells, 1935
Barrie and Jenkins Ltd, *On A Calm Shore*: Poems by Frances Cornford. Designs by Christopher Cornford, 1960
Oxford University Press, *Wilfred Owen: Collected Letters* edited by Harold Owen and John Bell, 1967

NOTE

THIS IS NOT a critical edition of Siegfried Sassoon's letters. Discretion has demanded the omission of certain passages and a pruning of irrelevant matter. No letter has been quoted in full, and while the text has not been altered, extracts on the same subject have occasionally been combined. *Something About Myself*, included among the juvenilia (p. 52), has been reproduced in the abridged form of the story that Stanbrook presented to S.S. on his eightieth birthday (p. 243). With the sole exception of the quotation dated 1949 (p. 132) all the excerpts from Sassoon's diary have been drawn from that kept when he was writing *Sequences* between 1951 and 1954. The diary opened upside-down on the last page of a cheap paper-covered exercise book containing jottings for his study of Meredith, and it continued backwards interspersed with notes, in microscopic script at every possible angle, crammed into every inch of space. As far as possible, specific dates of entry have been given, but as it has been impossible to check references, a few extracts have had to remain undated. Along with the first rough drafts of *Sequences*, Sassoon wrote some forty other poems which he rejected for publication. These have been rifled and provide the bulk of the unpublished poems scattered throughout this book. Sassoon's punctuation has been rendered consistent throughout, but his idiosyncratic spelling, particularly obvious in juvenilia, has been retained.

D. F. C.

INTRODUCTION

'MY REAL BIOGRAPHY is my poetry,' Siegfried Sassoon once wrote to me. 'All the sequence of my development is there. For me, it is the only thing that matters, and was my only path in the bewilderments and inconsistencies of existence. And all my best poems expressed an element of experience. Blunden has sometimes said that I ought to have exercised my imagination more, but I think I have been true to my natural abilities. The art of poetry belongs to *life*; one lives for it just as other people live for their essential vocations of whatever kind they may be. It is one's earthly home, and the other poets, dead or living, when masters of the art, are one's housemates.'

The poetic record of Sassoon's life, from the age of ten-and-a-half to eighty, is unique in English letters. The long journey was a spiritual as well as a poetic one, and this book attempts to chart its course. To the poems have been added passages from his various writings, especially from his letters. These have been chosen with a specific purpose in mind—to sketch the background of a poem, deepen the reader's awareness of its significance, supply biographical links, and wherever possible to project poet and poem as it were on a three-dimensional screen. It was Siegfried Sassoon's declared wish that the present editor should deal with the spiritual aspect of his poetry from youth to old age. 'I agree to *anything* you do,' he wrote, 'as you are the only person in the world who bothers to write about my religious poems. The childish poems do come out better than I'd realized. In the context of my career I suppose they are significant. And you seem the only one likely to illuminate that career by understanding and sympathy.' Possibly, perhaps necessarily, the picture will appear limited.

As will be seen, Siegfried Sassoon did not enter the orbit of Stanbrook until October 1959, a good two-and-a-half years after the crucial episode in his life which led him to the Roman Catholic Church. The emotional stress preceding his action has been sufficiently set forth by the poet himself in *Lenten Illuminations* and in his long letter of retrospect; anything further would lie outside the scope of this book. *Poet's Pilgrimage* is not a conversion story, still less a doctrinal thesis. Save for the Introduction, the poet has been left to speak for himself throughout, with as few editorial interruptions as possible.

Of all the figures on the literary stage during the first half of the twentieth century, perhaps few can rival Siegfried Sassoon as the outward embodiment of 'the perfect English gentleman'. Born in the Kentish Weald, educated at Marlborough and at Clare College, Cambridge, he became in turn aspiring young poet, cricketer, golf enthusiast, winner of point-to-point races, and devotee of fox-hunting. He enlisted at once on the outbreak of war in 1914, and achieved fame as 'Mad Jack' for his courageous exploits, as the Angry Young Man who hurled his Military Cross into the Mersey, and as the satirist whose savagely realistic poems from the Front sent eyebrows up and temperatures soaring. The tall commanding figure of Captain Sassoon with his abundant reddish brown hair, his tawny deep-set eyes, his Ivor Novello profile, and general air of 'an offended deerhound' soon became a legend. 'England's Young Soldier Poet' was to find it impossible in later life to alter his public image.

That he was a 'gentleman', no one has ever called in question; a soldier, one of the bravest; a poet, one whose work will endure, but . . . was he English? On his mother's side, undoubtedly. And for many years, in this not unlike Wilfred Owen, he tended to see himself solely as his mother's son. His mother, Theresa Georgina Thornycroft, was the grand-daughter of John Francis, sculptor (1780–1861), the daughter of Thomas Thornycroft, sculptor, the sister of Sir John Thornycroft, naval architect, and of Sir Hamo, sculptor of the statues of Gordon in Trafalgar Square, Gladstone in the Strand, and Cromwell at Westminster. Traditionally, the Thornycrofts were Cheshire farmers, wedded to the English soil. From them Sassoon was to derive his love of the countryside, of field sports and cricket, and his power of chiselling thought into lapidary epigrams.

As he grew in self-knowledge, Sassoon became increasingly

aware of the driving force of his Jewish ancestry, 'I sometimes surmise,' he admits, 'that my eastern ancestry is stronger in me than the Thornycrofts. The daemon in me is Jewish. Do you believe in racial memories? Some of my hypnagogic visions have seemed like it, and many of them were oriental architecture.' Alfred Ezra Sassoon, Siegfried's father, born in England, was the first Sassoon to be born in Europe at all. Almost incredibly the enormous family of Sassoon, 'the Rothschilds of the East' as they were called, new immigrants from the commerce and market-places of Baghdad and Bombay, men who wrote their invoices in Hebrew characters to emphasize their Jewishness, had within a single generation so firmly entrenched themselves in English life, that they were to be found playing a prominent part in county and country, in the arts, in royal circles, and in Parliament. The history of the founder of the dynasty, David Sassoon, Siegfried's great-grandfather, has been admirably recorded in Mr Stanley Jackson's study, *The Sassoons*.* Alfred, second son of Sassoon David Sassoon of Ashley Park, was an accomplished violinist. To this father and to his patriarchal forebears, Siegfried almost certainly owed his love of music, his poetic gift, and his idealism. Mr Jackson has observed that in the 1960s the two outstanding Sassoons—neither remotely identifiable with their ancestral tradition of vast mercantile power and social grandeur—were both great-grandsons of David Sassoon: one, Rabbi Solomon Sassoon, President of the largest Sephardic seminary in the world, owner of a library at Letchworth which has attracted Jewish scholars from all parts; the other, the Roman Catholic Siegfried. In any study of Siegfried Sassoon it should never be forgotten that he was a Jew, outwardly perhaps different, inwardly strikingly akin to his rabbinical cousin.

It is debatable whether, during the greater part of his life, he would have accepted the designation 'Christian'. Probably not. His father had been the first Sassoon to marry outside the Jewish faith. This act so outraged Alfred's mother that she refused to admit his wife or children to her house at Ashley Park, and cut them out of her will. When Siegfried was five, his parents separated, and the upbringing of their three sons, Michael, Siegfried and

* Stanley Jackson *The Sassoons* William Heinemann Ltd 1968

Hamo, was left to the children's mother. Theresa Sassoon, a woman small of stature but great of soul, was a sincere Anglican. She saw to it that the children were baptized and, at sixteen, Siegfried received Confirmation in St Paul's Cathedral. The recollections of his childhood in *The Old Century* make it clear that prayer, Bible reading and church-going were accepted by the family as normal occupations. Small Siegfried had his own quaint way of imbibing the *Old Testament* from a family friend, Ellen Batty, who occasionally acted as governess. 'I had always liked hearing about the twelve tribes. "They all seem to have the right names," I remarked to Batty. "Abraham couldn't have been called Elijah, could he? If he had been he wouldn't have had that long grey beard." I had great respect and affection for Abraham, and I admired Elijah for calling down curses on those beastly priests of Baal. The word Pharaoh, for instance, suggested someone with a very beautiful voice standing alone at the top of a lot of stone steps with the evening star shining above him. Solomon, on the other hand, always appeared to be talking to a large buzzing crowd, possibly because I had heard that he had a million wives. Such names were like vanilla, which smelt the same as it sounded.' At Cambridge, Christianity vaguely permeated his serious-minded moments and, at his mother's request, he consented to discuss the Catechism with her friend, an Anglican canon, but could arrive at no clear understanding of the real meaning of religion. 'Only experience can teach that,' he adds. During the 1914 war he developed a hostility to 'parsons beating their drums noisily to the rhythm of the Warrior-Christ', and like many of his generation found institutional religion mortally boring. 'In all that war I never said a single prayer,' he wrote. Wilfred Owen spoke for both of them when he told his mother in a memorable phrase: 'I am more and more Christian as I walk the unchristian ways of Christendom.' All the same, Sassoon was never quite able to shake off the religious upbringing of his earliest years. Experience taught him as he later admitted that 'First-found beliefs remain'. When a child, he would stand in the garden of his home, Weirleigh, send his voice ringing over the Weald to God away out there at the other side of the infinite space across the valley, and then listen all ears to the silence, waiting for God to answer him, as He certainly would. It was a parable of his whole life.

There was never a time when he was not introspective, essentially religious; he was a born contemplative. By temperament and calling, a contemplative will always of course crave for solitude, but circumstances may make that solitude impossible to obtain. When occasion demands, he is frequently to be found in the front line, acting with a foresight and resolution that spring from his inner vision and deep reserves of strength and peace. A common fallacy imagines that the contemplative is necessarily a recluse, preferably seated on a mossy stone beside a crystal spring of water. The fallacy is disproved by fact, at least in the western hemisphere. Four, selected at random from a host of others, could scarcely find time to call their souls their own: Augustine of Hippo, prince of mystics and hammer of heretics; Bernard of Clairvaux, the honey-sweet doctor, who carried the twelfth century on his shoulders; Catherine of Siena, 'the greatest woman in Christendom', who dragged Pope Gregory XI back from Avignon to Rome; and Teresa of Avila, loved by all the world, yet accused in her lifetime of gallivanting round Spain with young men as she went about her seventeen Carmelite foundations. None of these arrived at their experience of the Absolute in a desert-like seclusion removed from all human anxieties. Their contemplation remained uninterrupted beyond all movement of body or mind in the secret place at the core of being, called by Catherine of Siena 'the Sea Pacific of the soul'. There, in the self's indivisible centre, they plunged into the mystery of God.

This is not to put Sassoon into their illustrious company—that would be absurd. But the widely accepted idea of Sassoon the man of action turning recluse as 'the Hermit of Heytesbury' in reaction against a world he no longer understood or approved is at least open to question. His solitariness was inborn. At eight years of age he could cheerfully leave his two brothers to the blissful enjoyment of their noisy games while he luxuriated in a tent all alone, independent and secure, listening to the melodious murmur of an Aeolian harp hung in a crab-apple tree. All the excitement he needed, he found in the exploration of his own thoughts. He dwelt alone in much the same way among throngs of men in the Gehenna of the Somme. When 'Mad Jack' captured a German trench with little more than a wave of his hand, his immediate reaction was to sit down somewhere, fish in his pocket, bring out a book of poems, and forget all about the Germans on the run. The gas and flames of diabolical warfare could not blast or consume his tree of life. So too during the Second World War when man, seemingly bent on self-destruction, refused to listen to him, he quietly went his way to ponder ultimate values, the human soul

> that world within an ignorant shape
> One with the solar system and the ape

hoping that one day someone might hear and understand.

In the *Observer* of 3 September 1967, Edmund Blunden, a friend of fifty years' standing, dismissed as nonsense the current notion of Sassoon as a rough and ready fox-hunting man, incapable of intellectual subtleties and grandeurs. 'Despite his solitariness,' he writes, 'he watched the world astutely!' The adverb is exact. Sassoon's judgements were astute. There is a revealing passage in *Sherston's Progress* where George Sherston is discussing his indebtedness to Dr Rivers. As a young man, he confesses, he had paraded scraps of information about people and things as if he knew much more than he actually did. Rivers faced him with this conversational dishonesty. 'Since then I have altered my procedure, and when in doubt I pretend to know less than I really do.' Sassoon was a master of understatement, and the reader would be rash to take his self-assessments at their face value. Beneath the disarming modesty, behind the smoking pipe, there was a first-class brain, ears that caught every inflection of a voice, eyes whose penetrating glance shot from under lowered lids missed nothing. He knew a great deal about very many things and his comments, always original, could be as devastating as they could be magnanimous.

Siegfried Sassoon belonged to that band of men and women to be found in every race, country and religion, who may be characterized as *homines religiosi*. They seem to be gifted by nature with a sense of the numinous, as lesser folk are with an ear for music or an eye for form. Among these 'men of religion' an even smaller class may be further distinguished, that of the prophetic type. In himself, a prophet is neither a politician, social reformer, thinker nor philosopher, much less is he a clairvoyant. He does not necessarily foretell the future at all. The *pro* in the Greek *prophetes* does not mean 'before' but 'forth'. The prophet is a forthteller rather than a foreteller. His predictions, always related to historical circumstances, may be explained as the result of a normal faculty of observation combined with an intensified insight into the religious and moral situation. Nowhere is this more evident than in the prophetic rôle as set out in the Bible. There all the prophets are involved in the historical process and are concerned with the course of events, not as passive bystanders, but as proclaiming what they have seen as critical observers of the national, social, and moral state of the people. It has already been said and will be said again that Siegfried Sassoon was a Jew. 'You have got it *right* about my Jewish blood,' he wrote to me. 'As a poetic spirit I have always felt myself—or wanted to be—a kind of minor prophet. I suppose most poets aim at being prophetic communicators. But the idea has always been very strong in my mind. And found utterance in the war poems of course.' In the face of that unequivocal admission, there is no need to apologize for placing Sassoon among the prophets.

As a forthteller, the prophet is a man with a message to proclaim, to announce for all the world to hear. He never keeps his experiences to himself, he must tell others what he has seen and heard. And that is exactly what Sassoon did from the battlefront. Writing enthusiastically to his sister Mary about the war poems in Sassoon's first published book, *The Old Huntsman,* Wilfred Owen tells her: 'My dear, except in one or two of my letters you will find nothing so perfectly truthfully descriptive of war. Cinemas, cartoons, photographs, tales, plays—Na-poo. *Now* you see why I have always extolled poetry.' Perhaps because Sassoon consistently belittled his own war poetry and generously praised Owen's, there has been a failure to realize how special his achievement was. He proved himself the unsurpassed spokesman for the common soldier. Filled with compassion and a sense of solidarity with his men, he gave literary expression to their feelings and personal experience, making audible and intelligible the fearful realities that the 'screaming scarlet Majors' and the politicians wanted to evade:

> I said it very loud and clear
> I went and shouted in his ear.
>
> But he was very stiff and proud;
> He said 'You needn't shout so loud'.

From the first, his revolt was essentially religious in character. Man was made for higher things than politics or even patriotism. ... 'O world God made!' 'O Jesus, make it stop!' Under his conviction that things were going from bad to worse and that civilization (one of his favourite words) had to be pulled together, come what might, he felt an inner compulsion to sacrifice everything, to sacrifice the very tradition of English poetry and his own ideals, to sacrifice his own reputation and life if need be, to prevent the destruction of the nation. It was the voice of the seer and the prophet calling to ears that, in biblical usage, were uncircumcised and would not listen. From the depths of his padded armchair in the Library of the House of Lords, Edmund Gosse raised his cultured voice to deprecate his young friend's 'savage disconcerting silhouettes' which, he was afraid, would 'tend to relax the effort of the struggle'. He might well feel afraid.

In 1917 his 'young friend', one of the bravest and noblest of the fighting men, unflinchingly faced the scorn of fellow-officers, the public taunt of showing the white feather, and possible courtmartial when he raised his solitary voice against the deliberate prolongation of human slaughter for ignoble political ends. He refused to fight any longer. In those days, the oddity was conscientious objection; in the age of protest that is ours, we wonder that anybody was ever persuaded to fight at all. For that reason, Sassoon's splendid gesture of defiance can be under-estimated or treated as mere eccentricity. The prophet Jeremiah had been through it all before: 'Then the princes said to the king, "Let this man be put to death, for he is weakening the hands of the soldiers who are left in the city, and the hands of all the people, by speaking such words to them"' (Jeremiah 38:4). Sassoon was not put to death; he was merely incarcerated in a hospital for the treatment of shell-shock at Craiglockhart, Edinburgh. There he made two of the greatest friendships of his life—with Dr W. H. R. Rivers and Wilfred Owen—and thus enriched, returned to the front line until a bullet in the head forcibly put him out of action. Edmund Blunden, who of all men ought to know, has repeatedly insisted that the emphasis of Sassoon's war poetry and his dramatic manifesto were essential: he swept away the illusions and the profusion of absurdity circulating in the first years of war. The mockery, disillusionment and despair of his war poems are simply variations upon the theme of longing—longing for the savagely annihilated joys of the past when nature and man were in peaceful harmony, for the spiritual intimacies of solitude, and for a dwelling-place for the spirit of man:

> I have no need to pray
> That fear may pass away;
> I scorn the growl and rumble of the fight
> That summons me from cool
> Silence of marsh and pool
> And yellow lilies islanded in light.
> *O river of stars and shadows, lead me through the night.*

As the years went by, Sassoon grew ever more impatient with the constant demand for his war poems—'war poems' usually meant only his most savage invective. No one seemed disposed to look at what else was there—equally good, but different from what they expected to find. 'Why can't they realize,' he asked, 'that the war poems were improvised by an impulsive, intolerant, immature young creature, under the extreme stress of experience?' In the light of Sassoon's self-depreciation, it is instructive to listen to Wilfred Owen on *The Old Huntsman*.* To his father, Tom Owen, he wrote:

> I think this work of Sassoon's will show you to the best possible advantage the tendencies of modern poetry. If you don't

* *Wilfred Owen: Collected Letters* Oxford University Press 1967, letter 543 to Tom Owen 26 August 1917

appreciate these, then it's Na-poo. There is nothing better this century can offer you. *The Old Huntsman* was put in as a title piece, to catch the hunting-people, and make 'em read the rest. 'The Death-Bed' is a piece of perfect art.
'Morning Express' is the kind of thing that makes me despair of myself; everyone says 'I could have done that myself!' Only no one ever did.*

The Old Huntsman (1917) was followed by *Counter-Attack* (1918) and *War Poems* (1919). In the minds of most literary critics and the reading public, these fixed his classification for the rest of his life. He was reckoned as having had his say. Anything further was measured up against these early compositions, and dismissed either because it resembled them or because it did not. 'Those clever people up in London', as Hardy called them, decided that Sassoon had proved himself a powerful war poet but was otherwise a trifling versifier. A review of Sassoon's *Collected Poems* in the *Sunday Telegraph* of May 1961, consigned the author to the limbo of those essentially minor poets with 'plenty of technical accomplishment and feeling' who could not rise above the conventional until some shattering experience removed the blinkers for a time: 'Then the hitherto stagnant depths of their natures are suddenly churned up.' This sentence became one of S.S.'s most cherished self-descriptions—he rolled it round his tongue like old port. The reviewer singled out from the few poems worthy of notice one, *I Stood with the Dead* which, he claims, is good because evoked by memory of war experience. This drew from Sassoon the dry marginal comment: 'Written in June 1918! Appeared in *The Nation*, 13 July, the day I was shot in the head.'

His war poetry ended on the triumphant cadence of *Everyone Sang*, his 'Innisfree' as he called it. He has described in *Siegfried's Journey* just how it came to be written. There is a kinship between prophet and poet in their common experience of inspiration under a feeling of necessity and constraint. Sassoon often referred to his consciousness of a kind of abnormal force compelling him to write. It came apparently unsought, and if it did not come, he was powerless. On analysis, it may be a purely natural process:

* For S.S.'s opinion of 'Morning Express' see page 203

when a poet has an idea to put forth, he must brood over it until it shines. It may then seem to come like a flash of lightning. Sassoon never worked rationally and methodically at anything. Yet once he had reached maturity this man, who could versify or parody at will, refused to write a single line that did not come as if dictated. He spent his youth mastering the arduous technique, and after that wrote only under the sense of a subject that made its own form, and of feelings which formed their own words, so that every phrase of his best poetry is a mystery of significance and music.

During the immediate post-war years, his mind was as chaotic as the world around him, a condition inevitably reflected in his poetry. The compassion and sense of brotherhood aroused by his years in the trenches led him to join the Labour Party, and to his mother's distress, he even undertook the editorship of the literary page of the *Daily Herald*. Satirical verse poured from his pen. At the top of his voice he damned Mayfair sybarites who lived in purple and fine linen while the miners starved, he turned heavy artillery against the rumour breeders of the popular press boasting of a circulation 'from big to vast, from corpulent to bloated', he castigated the political jobbers of the money market whose power of purchase 'Pays unemployment. Buys champagne, and builds new churches.' As experiments—which they largely were—the verses are linguistically interesting. The texture is closely woven, the rhymes extraordinarily inventive, the expression biting and vivid, yet the satires are too slick, too heartless, and somehow they misfire. He was shouting too loud and the fortissimo jarred on sensitive ears. He saw his mistake in time and decided to adopt 'a laconic, legato tone of voice' in a new style of 'realistic poems about everyday life'.

It was shortly after the war that S.S. met Wilfred Owen's brother, Harold. Mr Owen's pen-portrait of Sassoon in *Aftermath** bears the hall-mark of authenticity. No one who knew S.S. well could cherish any illusions: at no time could he have been an easy man to live with, and there were moments when unconsciously he made heavy demands upon his friends. Throughout the 1920s he seemed likely to become the embodiment of the

* Harold Owen *Aftermath* Oxford University Press 1970

eligible bachelor, financially secure, lionized in all the London drawing-rooms, the handsome young poet always in the public eye. Without family obligations, self-centred and probably selfish, he ran the danger of ending up as a thorough-going egoist in the finest Meredithian tradition—a fate he escaped finally, simply by his ability to see through himself. He had an inimitable way of catching himself out in a pose and suddenly exploding all his own nonsense. That came with maturity. In 1917 he had been able to look into Wilfred Owen's eyes and admire himself mirrored there as Keats plus Christ plus Elijah plus his colonel plus his father-confessor plus Amenophis IV in profile.* Wilfred's sailor brother Harold with his practical northern sturdiness was a rather more daunting proposition. Haughty Sassoon may have been in youth but boorish, never—he was too civilized for that, and in his later years his character was marked by extreme gentleness and courtesy. One thing is to be noted throughout Mr Owen's very honest strictures: S.S.'s rudeness towards him went hand in hand with acts of munificence. It was he who gave the struggling artist introductions to Glyn Philpot and William Rothenstein, and by his patronage secured welcome publicity for Owen's exhibition at the Claridge Gallery. By nature extremely shy, Sassoon dispensed bounty in a delicate, subtle way that the outward discourtesy was probably meant to disguise. But at least on one point Mr Owen is surely mistaken? He relates how the hall-porter at The Reform Club corrected his 'Mr Sassoon' to 'Captain Sassoon, sir!' and goes on to suggest that while S.S. repudiated war, he yet clung to empty titles. That would be completely foreign to the man. Undeniably he retained the title; to the end of his life the villagers of Heytesbury referred to him as 'the Captain'. In *Goodbye to All That* Robert Graves has supplied the likely explanation. Thomas Hardy asked Graves in 1920 why he no longer used his army rank. Graves explained that he had resigned his commission. 'But you have a right to it!' Hardy replied. 'I should certainly keep my rank if I had one, and feel very proud to be called Captain Hardy.' Hardy's approval would have been quite enough for Sassoon, as it proved to be for Graves and Osbert

* *Wilfred Owen: Collected Letters* Oxford University Press 1967, letter 557 to Siegfried Sassoon 5 November 1917

Sitwell. The use of the title maintained a precious link with the men that he loved, who had fought and laughed and suffered by his side.

Thomas Hardy, it is true, was one of Sassoon's heroes, but the two met as equals rather than as master and disciple. To find Sassoon's prototype and model one must turn back two centuries. He gravitated naturally to the Metaphysical poets, but of them all it was Henry Vaughan who claimed his whole-hearted veneration and allegiance. In 1924 he visited the poet's burial-place where he wrote his sonnet, *At the Grave of Henry Vaughan*. This was more than passing homage. It was a personal salute across the centuries from a fellow-poet treading, he felt assured, in the footsteps of one who had himself fought in war, endured toil and tribulation, and had yet managed to dwell in secrecies apart. With the seventeenth-century visionary more than with any other poet, Sassoon felt deep affinities—with his strength, simplicity, directness, his controlled imagery, his reticence and his serenity. In a lecture *On Poetry* given at Bristol in 1939, Sassoon says of Henry Vaughan that he had learnt from George Herbert the potency of the homely epithet, and shared with Donne an intense awareness of darkness and light. Nothing could better sum up Sassoon's own achievement. Poets like musicians have their signature tunes, their personal poetic idiom. Without being in the least derivative, the qualities of Sassoon's work inevitably recall Vaughan. Once he has found his true medium, the sense of the infinite pervades almost everything he writes. The world of nature and the simple things of everyday life take on a new lustre. The lamplight on the ceiling of his room shines like a strange flower, every petal of the bowl of white flowers at his elbow is transformed into a mystery of wonder. Yet the poet remains with his feet firmly planted on the earth he loves, aware of the ticking clock, the frost on the window pane, the rumble of late traffic. Certain ideas constantly recur—stars, secrecies, flowers wondrous white, and above all, angels. Angels may be a pretty poetic device—or they may not. Sassoon really believed in angels. They had lived in his mind from childhood, part of the furniture of his universe, as the Mamsy poems testify. He never swept them away. War, when it came, was a conflict against powers of darkness. If men were to attain to true peace, far more was required than the mere cessation of shooting one another. *The Power and the Glory*, written in 1925, rings with this challenge:

> Let life be God ... What wail of fiend or wraith
> Dare mock my glorious angel where he stands
> To fill my dark with fire, my heart with faith?

Fifteen years later, in the *Observer* of 23 May 1940, he published a war poem ending with this couplet:

> In every separate soul let courage shine—
> A kneeling angel holding faith's front line.

Judas Maccabaeus in the face of Nicanor had done precisely what S.S. was doing in the face of Hitler—raising men's morale by reminding them of the angelic support that is theirs. In *A Last Judgement* (1927) he spoke of 'the angel, whom his heart had lifetime long denied'; in *Earth and Heaven* (1937) he assured us that

> ... angels are about us everywhere
> In love's good deeds, in life's transfigured face,

and in *Lenten Illuminations* (1957) a poem 'full of cardinal allusions, signal experiencings', he put the question:

> How came it (ask your Angel—ask that vigilant voice) ...

Sassoon's skull as well as Vaughan's surely housed white angels

> and had vision
> Of daybreak through the gateways of the mind.

Cosmic speculations about heavenly beings are of course universal, and possibly as old as man's imagination itself. But a most important strand of angelology runs through the Bible from the Cherubim in Genesis whose flaming sword guards the gates of Eden, to the choirs of the heavenly host in the Book of Revelation. They convey the sense of the divine, speak as oracles of God, and with their powerful intervention in human affairs, they minister to man. Sassoon was a Jew. His angels may very well have been housed in that unchartable element, his inherited subconscious mind which, he was fond of asserting, knew a lot more than the conscious one. Within a minute of turning the light out, visualizations of angels as well as of automatic writing and oriental architecture often accompanied his falling asleep. In 1926 he would have called himself an agnostic. In that year he wrote a short poem to which he has given no title. It bears out the following argument: 'The poets themselves admit that in their best lines they discover meanings and metaphors of which they knew nothing while composing them. Technique had been instinctive; *thought* had been somehow uncensored. The brain-work was there, but it had been fundamentally mysterious' (*On Poetry*). The occasion of the poem was a walk in Kew Gardens, the metaphor of the 'flocks of silver angels' being suggested by the prunus blossom:

> As I was walking in the gardens where
> Spring touched the glooms with green, stole over me
> A sense of wakening leaves that filled the air
> With boding of Elysian days to be.
>
> Cold was the music of the birds; and cold
> The sunlight, shadowless with misty gold:
> It seemed I stood with Youth on the calm verge
> Of some annunciation that should bring
> With flocks of silver angels, ultimate Spring
> Whence all that life had longed for might emerge.

Unless the last two lines are meaningless, the poem is implicitly Christian, or at least Judaeo-Christian. For while pagan literature harks back to a Golden Age of the Gods, the *Bible* alone looks to the future, to a Messianic eschatological age in which all things will be restored. The best is yet to be. Kew Gardens becomes the new Eden, the transient loveliness of prunus blossom transformed into angels heralding a Lukan annunciation of saving redemption. In this mysterious shadowless dawn of final resurrection, man stands with the second Adam, *puer aeternus*, in a youth that will never grow old. On the purely personal plane, this together with so many other poems speaks with the same longing voice, the voice of one who from childhood had stood waiting for the moment when the answer would come, the gift be given.

With ever deepening awareness he began to look upon the activity and power of creation in terms of the divinity behind them, and while he continued to respond to nature, he was being drawn to concentrate on the riddle of man set in this riddle of a universe. The conscious process seems to date back to 1923 when, in *Conclusion*, he had tried to sort out his thoughts into some coherent pattern:

> I am so woven of sense
> And subtly uncharted
> That I must vanish hence
> Blind-souled and twilight-hearted.
> Soon death the hooded lover
> Shall touch my house of clay,
> And life-lit eyes discover
> That in the warbling grey
> I have been early waking,
> And while the dawn was breaking
> Have stolen afield to find
> That secrecy which quivers
> Beyond the skies and rivers
> And cities of the mind.

In the same year *Apocalypse*, a poem of packed brevity, humorously analyses the warring elements, the ins and outs of evolutionary man, that go to make up the imaginative experience of the writer:

> In me, past, present, future meet
> To hold long chiding conference.
> My lusts usurp the present tense
> And strangle Reason in his seat.
> My loves leap through the future's fence
> To dance with dream-enfranchised feet.

At the Press Bazaar, 1898, aged 11

At Algeciras, c. 1931. 'Looks in need of interior assistance'—S.S.

Garmisch 1929, 'Natural Religion, so to speak.
"At the end of all wrong roads I came
To the gates of the garden without a name"
Collected poems p. 216 (staying that summer in a queer old house
by the river, all very much the background of the poem'—S.S.)

INTRODUCTION

> In me the cave-man clasps the seer,
> And garlanded Apollo goes
> Chanting to Abraham's deaf ear.
> In me the tiger sniffs the rose.
> > Look in my heart, kind friends, and tremble,
> > Since there your elements assemble.

This poem marks the beginning of that dissecting process characteristic of his later poetry. He is at once his past, present, and future self, but past men are also part of him as he is part of future men. What then is meant by 'self'? This all-important question, propounded in 1924, was resumed only ten years later.

In the interval he turned to exhibit in prose both his semifictional and his historical self, now as George Sherston and now as Siegfried Sassoon. His six volumes of autobiography, published between the years 1928 and 1945, are marked by a deep and subtle sense of humour, a profound feeling for the innocence of youth, and a nostalgia for an English way of life destroyed by war and scientific advances. His was essentially a pre-machine mentality. He had no desire to travel 500 miles in a minute or reach the moon. He liked horses, he said, because they were so completely unmodernizable, so independent of fashion, and because like himself they absolutely refused to move with the times. It seems unnecessary to say that Sassoon was a superb rider, but perhaps it is necessary to remark that the pleasure he derived from a day with the hounds rose out of the aesthetic love for the English countryside of a young poet at the height of his physical vitality. 'To watch the day breaking from purple to dazzling gold while we trotted up a deep-rutted lane; to inhale the early freshness when we were on the sheep-cropped uplands; to stare back at the low country with its cock-crowing farms and mist-coiled waterways; thus to be riding out with a sense of spacious discovery—was it not something stolen from the lie-a-bed world? There were beech woods, too, in the folds of the downs, and lovely they looked in the mellow sunshine, with summer's foliage falling in ever-deepening drifts among their gnarled and mossy roots.'

No one has ever been found to suggest that the adventures of George Sherston, fox-hunter and infantry officer, had a religious basis. Yet at the head of the final book of the Sherston trilogy, there stands the curious epigraph: 'I told him that I was a Pilgrim going to the Celestial City.' The very title of *Sherston's Progress* leaves no doubt that the evocation of Bunyan's spiritual allegory is deliberate. Had the book been written twenty years earlier, the reader might have nodded knowingly and construed the text as a studied piece of sardonic mockery on the part of the author of *Counter-Attack*. George Sherston, come from the City of Destruction, wrestles with an Apollyon in the uniform of a British chief-of-staff, passes through the Valley of the Shadow of Passchendaele, and at the end of his pilgrimage finds a way to Hell from the very Gates of the Celestial City. Such an attitude might have been forgiven, for there is precious little throughout his *Memoirs* to identify George Sherston with Bunyan's Christian, no hint that he ever read the *Bible*, looked for guidance from any Evangelist, or hoped at the last to walk along the streets of the heavenly Jerusalem with a crown on his head and palm in his hand.* Somehow one assumes that the quotation is to be found on Christian's lips, yet a search reveals otherwise. 'Then they went on,' we read, 'and just at the place where Little-Faith formerly was robbed, there stood a man with his sword drawn, and his face all bloody. Then said Mr Great-Heart, "What art thou?" The man made answer saying, "I am one whose name is Valiant-for-Truth, I am a pilgrim, and am going to the Celestial City."' Siegfried Sassoon was nothing if not subtle. Does he mean to recall also that earlier pilgrim, honest Piers Plowman, who ploughs his half-acre and then, pack on back, sets out to find Truth?

> and love shall arise
> And such a peace and perfect truth be with the nations
> That Jews will wonder whether finally
> Moses or the Messiah has come among them,
> And wonder in their hearts how men are so true.†

---

* S.S.'s *Diary* 6 March 1954: 'Stayed in bed and read Part I of *The Pilgrim's Progress*. It is for all time, I think, in spite of its similitudes being outmoded. Its humanity will survive its being condemned by modern psychologists. It remains *alive*.' Note. Re-reading it in 1964, I found that in '54 I had understood nothing at all of the Gospel doctrine which pervades it. I read it with *new eyes*.

† William Langland *The Vision of Piers Plowman* Sheed & Ward 1935

INTRODUCTION

In 1936 when *Sherston's Progress* was published, from the peaceful retreat of his Wiltshire home, George Sherston watched the promulgation of the Nuremberg laws in Germany, and listened to the howling of the SS wolves as they branded his bloodbrothers with the star of David and herded them into gas chambers. It is not surprising that very little poetry issued from his pen during that disastrous decade. The little that came is significant. Three smallish collections were published, *The Road to Ruin* (1933), *Vigils* (1934), and *Rhymed Ruminations* (1939). This time the prophet spoke, not as forthteller but as foreteller. His agonized predictions of chemical and biological warfare, of death by fire, gas, and disease, are evident from the titles and a line or two:

At the Cenotaph: 'The Prince of Darkness to the Cenotaph
     Bowed. As he walked away I heard him laugh.'
Mimic Warfare: 'Troops on manœuvres, mechanized and masked.'
News from the War-After-Next: 'We launch tomorrow our great
     new Bacillus,
      And an overwhelming victory is
     expected.'
Asking For It: 'Grant us the power to prove, by poison gases,
     The needlessness of *shedding* human blood.'

Like one in purgatory, he said, he learned the loss of hope. No one wanted to listen. When the doom he had prophesied descended on Europe, he was already engaged on his prose writings. *The Old Century*, his own favourite book, was published on the eve of war and was followed by *The Weald of Youth* (1942), *Siegfried's Journey* (1945), and *Meredith* (1948).

Unlike Henry Vaughan, Sassoon did not engage in family feuds or lawsuits but these years, like Vaughan's, were far from unclouded. He had to find peace of mind in war, leisure to write amid crowds, fretted and frayed in spirit as he was by a hundred and one vexations. Upon the outbreak of war, his large house was requisitioned for evacuees. 'Our refugees had to be got rid of a month ago, owing to lice and skin disease,' he wrote to Sydney Cockerell in June 1940. 'They behaved very badly. We are now expecting another batch—this time, I hope, without mothers, & with responsible guardians.' The next consignment met with rather more approval, for at Christmas he again writes to Cockerell: 'George has had an ideally happy Xmas day, & has been singing & squeaking continuously. When I came in from walking off the plum pudding, he was having his Xmas tree with the refugee children; miniature fireworks were being let off and Hester's hair has been full of confetti ever since. It was a charming sight, & to me much preferable to a party of *rich* children!' In 1942 a Company of King's Royal Rifles with twenty Bren gun carriers bivouacked at Heytesbury House, 200 vehicles drove into the park, the brigadier and his staff were quartered in the dining room, and Sassoon found himself in the thick of army exercises once more. 'Odd to think of all those chaps lying snoring on the floor—overlooked by the Manet still-life & Reynolds's picture of Roman eccentrics making music,'* he commented to Sydney Cockerell. The following year a camp for 1,500 American troops was set up in the park, necessitating the construction of broad roads, and the installation of Nissen huts and the usual army equipment. No wonder that when his property was made over to such tenants, the owner preferred to converse with the buttock of the night rather than the forehead of the morning in order to secure the quietude essential for his writing.

Apart from the thirty-three poems of *Rhymed Ruminations*, Sassoon published no poetry during the Second World War. In 1950 he resumed with the eighteen of *Common Chords*, the twenty of *Emblems of Experience* (1951) and the twenty-four of *The Tasking* (1954). All these were privately printed until combined into the sixty-two poems of *Sequences*, published by Faber in 1956. For the most part, its publication met with the solid silence of non-recognition. If Siegfried Sassoon gives an impression of hyper-sensitiveness in the letters referring to *Sequences*, it must be remembered that no true artist in words submits himself to his arduous task without the hope of securing an audience to listen. However, from 1938 onward it had been made abundantly clear that understanding would become a less and less likely reward of

* *The Best of Friends:* Further Letters to Sydney Carlyle Cockerell, Rupert Hart-Davis 1956, pp. 86, 115

his labours. In a sentence worthy to rank with the 'stagnant depths', an American critic wrote of the author of *Sequences*: 'Like a decommissioned man-of-war, he rests quietly at anchor in poetry's mothball fleet.' One wonders whether the poems would have reeked so strongly of camphor had they been published ten or fifteen years later?

It is part of a prophet's vocation to encounter scoffing and incomprehension. In spite of that, he has sometimes been required —as were Hosea and Jeremiah—to become not only a speaker but 'as a mouth'. His words, his whole personality, his whole personal life, everything that he has and that is in him, has to become a speaker, a forthteller. And this, I suggest, was Sassoon's rôle during his 'purgatorial time'. After reading his diary and the poems consequent upon his experience, few would deny that his personal suffering throughout these years was extreme. There is a photograph taken in 1952 in his library at Heytesbury which he has labelled *Sic sedebat*. He is leaning forward, seated on the end of a low divan, his head illumined in a spurt of flame from a small, newly-fed log fire. A tiny teapot, relic of a solitary meal, stands in the kerb among the ashes, contradicting in its austerity the opulence of the well-stocked bookcase in the background. The hands are clasped, the dark thick hair ruffled, the eyebrows raised questioningly, the eyes lined and tired, the whole face havocked, and trenched with deep lines of pain and dejection. He might be sitting as a model for the prophet Jeremiah:

> Little enough you've learnt
> While being within you burnt,
> Consuming nights and days
> In brief oblivioned blaze: . . .
> Toward kindled flames to come
> Your divination is dumb:
> Little the mind remembers,
> Sighed the shifting embers.

His was certainly no quiet walk at eventide with a pleasant and communicative God in the beautiful Eden of his manorial home in Wiltshire.

One could indict the whole century out of Sassoon's mouth. From the first he had proclaimed that man unaided was incapable of saving himself. He had revolted against a series of false gods, against the war to end all wars, against science and technical progress set up as saviour and salvation, against the humanism that would substitute service of man for service of God. For all that, he could not hand out ready answers to the problems. He had to face them in his own person, to become the parable of twentieth-century man. The poet, according to Baudelaire, is the most conscious point of his age. What was evident of Sassoon in the First World War was not so evident in the Second. Today we live in a world of men whose deepest need is unsatisfied because God seems so far away. Who is He anyhow? God, they say, has become a dead language, a grandiose and ultimately unbelieved-in word. His inaccessible infinity has made man himself all the more finite and questionable. He no longer asks questions. He has himself become the question-mark. We call it the crisis of identity and fill books about it. Sassoon never studied philosophy, dogma or metaphysics. Intellectual abstraction was foreign to his concrete imaginative nature; brainwork was essential—so much he would concede—but it must always be accompanied by felt experience. In this he symbolizes the ordinary man who wants to arrive at his highest conclusions by means of his own perceptions. In the Hebrew fashion of the Bible, Jew in this as in so much else, Sassoon always wrote with his heart as well as his head, the heart being the seat of understanding, an understanding supported by conscience, imagination and will. As early as 1933, with a deep gravity underlying the gaiety, he had asked:

> That problem which concerns me most—about
> Which I have entertained the gravest doubt—
> Is, bluntly stated, 'Have I got a soul?'

Our contemporary existential approach claims that certainties, if such there be, are to be found solely within man himself. The beatniks and drug addicts are forcing upon the world the truth that man does not live by bread alone. There is in all men a human religious consciousness that hungers for the spiritual and transcendental. But that brings us back to the question—precisely what is meant by 'the soul'? It is this human condition of man as compounded of body and spirit that Sassoon sets out to explore in his sequence of questions and answers. The purpose of his questionings is not to acquire by analysis or learning; it is to strip away inessentials and place the soul in a condition where it can receive. On a mature level, it is the little boy calling out to God across the Weald, and expecting an answer.

His head, heart, soul, brain, spirit, sound at times like a medieval allegory reminiscent of Langland's

> While I am quick in the body I am called Anima;
> When I complain to God I am called Memory....
> When I flee from the flesh and forsake the body
> I am speechless spirit.

In *The Alliance*, for instance, spirit despising flesh, wants to sunder body from soul but is convicted of error and finally asks forgiveness of the brain. It all sounds curiously spatial, an almost geographical conception of man's incommunicable selfhood. But that does not greatly affect the poet's quest. He is not writing theology or psychology. As a poet he is portraying mortal man brooding upon himself and his destiny; he wants to know not what a man thinks about death and life, but what he feels about them.

Sassoon has himself called the poems of *Sequences* 'half-agnostic performances' which speak as though he had never heard of the Son of God. He finds little room in them for the *Bible* or Christian revelation although he frequently thinks in terms of the psalms. Yet in *The Making*, a poem written to compassionate a friend whose imprudence had brought upon his head hurtful publicity, Sassoon expresses a belief in what Christians would term original sin and divine forgiveness. Man comes into the world

> Flawed with inherited humanity,
> And fooled by imperfections wrought through race.
> This He first fashioned; this He can forgive
> When granting His unapprehended grace.

He has added an important pencilled annotation to *Resurrection*—the italics are his. 'This is the first "spiritual" poem,' he has written, 'of those in this book—by which I mean the first which "cried out for the Living God" *in me*.' In that brief sentence, he has drawn three fine distinctions. His poetry is no longer emotion of the heart as it was in *The Heart's Journey*: it is now wrung out of his spirit, a distillation of something rarer and much more subtle. No longer is God a pantheistic abstraction as so often in his earlier work. No longer is He Out There in starlit infinity, a Primordial Cause, unknown and unknowable. He is a living Person. And He is within a man's very self. When, to use Newman's phraseology, notional gives place to real assent and the all-important truth is grasped that the Kingdom of God is within, encounter with the living God at the inmost centre of being is surely man's most momentous spiritual discovery. To pass from the one conception of God to the other must involve a crisis in any spiritual life.

It is significant that when at last Sassoon was given the end of the golden string to lead him out of the labyrinth, he rolled it into a ball with texts from the *Bible*.

> While you were in your purgatorial time, you used to say
> That though Creation's God remained so lost, such aeons away,
> Somehow He would reveal Himself to you—some day!
> For Him, the living God, your soul and flesh could only cry
>   aloud.
> In watches of the night, when world event with devildom went
>   dark,
> You implored illumination.

And that was as far as he had got in 1957. Had he stopped there, at this introspective, purely personal religion, he would never have taken the decisive step he did. Being an honest Valiant-for-Truth he followed where the Spirit led, and it led in a direction clean contrary to all his previous journeying. The independent questioning self he had set such store by all his life had to acknowledge its nothingness before the All, had to see itself as it was, destitute of all power to help itself, in urgent need of God's free gift of grace. It had to go further still, and meet God's demands and conditions. At seventy years of age, the proud spirit of Siegfried Sassoon was being invited to bow in obedience and yield in faith to an outward inflexible authority. On the natural plane, the instrument of this vital change in his life was a nun, Mother Margaret Mary, at that time Superior of the Convent of the Assumption, 23, Kensington Square, London, W.8. She it was who, after the publication of *Sequences* at the end of 1956, wrote to the author and inaugurated a correspondence which lit a candle in his inward darkness. On 14 August 1957 he was received into the Catholic Church at Downside Abbey.

The almost abnormal self-awareness which had characterized Sassoon since childhood, colouring all he thought and did, now turned to his spiritual profit. For self-awareness is the natural substratum of any authentic contemplative experience. Only at this very centre of being, beyond all concepts and images, can man obtain a real glimpse of the central mystery of God. ' "Be still and know that I am God"—my most often repeated words from Scripture,' is S.S.'s pencilled annotation to *Renewals*. We ascend to God by descending into ourselves, where we must learn to be still and silent in His presence. 'The wonder is that one dares to say anything,' Sassoon writes, 'when contemplating that infinite silence and stillness from one's human near-nothingness.' Today, in the frightening whirl of contemporary evolution, when man has rejected the intellectual concepts which yesterday were his pride, the only place on which he can stand without losing his foothold and being washed away, is this central and fundamental experience. God is entirely other, yet mysteriously immanent within us, and the soul that enters into communion with God finds there its very self. There can be no crisis of identity. *Melius scitur Deus nesciendo*, St Augustine says—God is best known by unknowing. As Sassoon with theological exactitude puts it:

> O purpose of my prayer, breath of my being,
> Your inward light I share through sightless seeing.

This is the truth Sassoon discovered and set out in the few poems that mark the last decade of his life. Po Chu'i, a Chinese poet of Charlemagne's age, used to read his poems aloud to an old peasant woman and cross out whatever she couldn't understand. He asserted that every poet must become a sage before ever he embarked on the writing of poetry, since poetry involved the whole personality. The real problems of modern poetry are moral and spiritual. It is the achievement of Sassoon's later poetry that it expresses in simple language a genuine and true view of life. To say that his language is simple does not mean that as poetry it is readily assimilated, that there is little to ponder. It is the work of a sage, the expression of truths that form the rock foundation of human life lived in its wholeness—which is all that holiness means. There is no dislocation between the natural and the spiritual, between body and soul.

It was with the profoundest conviction that S.S. always maintained that poetry was most moving and memorable when it spoke the simplest language of the heart. When it does, 'the utterance may be magnificent, or it may be unemphatic; but there is never any doubt about its directness and humanity. I mean the true vocal cadence of something urgently communicated—the best words in the best order—yes—but empowered also by sincerity and inspiration' (*On Poetry*). The style is the man. His own poetry is always natural, wholesomely human and humanly interesting. Occasionally it undeniably falls flat. The reader chuckles with appreciative sympathy when Edward Marsh answers the unfortunate couplet,

> I am that man who with a luminous look
> Sits up at night to write a ruminant book

with

> I am the man who with a luminous nose
> Sits up at night to write voluminous prose.

Sassoon had little sympathy with many of the twentieth-century practitioners of poetry. The immense technical development in versecraft without any corresponding emotional development, the stress on the non-communicative aspects of poetry, the air of

INTRODUCTION 41

profundity produced by scientific method and experiment rather than by an expression of the human condition—all these he deplored as a harlequinade of intellectual activity manufactured by mannerisms and adroit tricks of style. He would have none of it, save by way of ridicule.

To mark his eightieth birthday, 8 September 1966, the Literature Panel of the Arts Council sponsored the private publication of eight poems. With the idea of a musical sequence still in mind, Sassoon aptly entitled them *An Octave*. These last poems leave no doubt that they were, as he said, his living heart. No superficial reading or consideration can plumb their depth. Here above all must Wilfred Owen's injunction to his sister be observed. They 'should be read seven times, and after that, not again, but thought of only'. For years Sassoon had ceased to look for sympathetic understanding of his work. His vocation was to be a poet. To the end he would be what he was, a seer, a maker,

> To carve the stubborn stone;
> With sense intense explore,
> And inward sight.

As early as 1917 in his first long published poem, a poem of essentially religious meditation, he had put into the mouth of the Old Huntsman the question:

> But where's the use of life and being glad
> If God's not in your gladness?

Half a century later the same voice answered the same question. The day after his eightieth birthday, Siegfried Sassoon wrote to the Abbess of Stanbrook: 'I almost dreaded the impact of all this acclamation which has exceeded my expectations. But I have prayed to be enabled to see myself as I truly am, and to be beyond it all in the sanctuary of Him who is my final refuge and rest.'

'I told him that I was a Pilgrim going to the Celestial City.'
                 Siegfried Sassoon: Epigraph to *Sherston's Progress*

Parable of a Pilgrim

'A man wished to go to Jerusalem and, because he did not know the way there, he asked another man who, he hoped, would be able to tell him.

'The other man replied, "Keep on your way and have no aim but to be at Jerusalem, for that is what you desire and nothing but that. In the spiritual sense Jerusalem is the vision of peace and represents contemplation in the perfect love of God. For contemplation is nothing else than the vision of Jesus, who is true peace. Put everything else behind you and forget it that you may have that which is best. Beware of enemies who will do their best to hinder you if they can. Always answer: I am nothing, I have nothing, I desire only one thing, and that is the love of Jesus. Hold on your way and fix your mind on Jerusalem." '

Walter Hilton *The Scale of Perfection*, translated by Dom Gerard Sitwell, Burns Oates 1953

PART I

1886–1914

Down the glimmering staircase, past the pensive clock,
Childhood creeps on tiptoe, fumbles at the lock.
Out of night escaping, toward the arch of dawn,
What can childhood look for, over the wet lawn?

Childhood 1934

The Old Century

Far off in earliest-remembered childhood I can overhear myself repeating the words 'Watercress Well'. I am kneeling by an old stone well-head; my mother is standing beside me and we are looking into the water. My mother tells me that it is 'a very deep-rising spring'; but I do not want to be told anything about it, even by her. I want nothing at all except to be gazing at the water which bubbles so wonderfully up out of the earth, and to dip my fingers in it and scatter the glittering drops.

Many a half-hour's pilgrimage we made from our house to Watercress Well which, after having been one of my 'favourite places to go to', now becomes a symbol of life itself in an opaque and yet transparent beginning. From that so intensely remembered source all my journeyings now seem to have started.

Again, from those lost years of childhood, I hear my voice. This time it asks a question. 'What will the seeds be like when they come up?' I am standing beside my mother, who is making a water-colour sketch of a man sowing. It is a bright dry morning in early spring and we are sheltered from the cold east wind by the catkined hazels of a little copse where I have been picking primroses.

'What will the seeds be like when they come up?' Recovered in my clear memory of that spring morning, the words now seem like part of a parable. And the purpose of this book is to tell whither the water journeyed from its source, and how the seed came up.

A Belated Discovery unpublished
('All our knowledge is ourselves to know'—Pope)

Admitting ignorance, comprehensive and uncharted
Of all that is beyond my localized concerns,
I come to the conclusion—cocksure though I started—
That *next to nothing known* is the last thing one learns.

This world, encyclopaedic subject, for my mind
Remains existent as an undiscovered land:
Therefore the apparition named myself I find
The only matter that I can hope to understand.

The Old Century

Had I been writing my own story, I should have begun as follows: 'Once upon a time there was a boy who was born in September 1886 at a house in Kent. He had two brothers who were born in 1884 and 1887, but we all behaved as if we were the same age. After 1891 we did not see our father very often. Our mother was unhappy because he had gone away to live in London and would not speak to her any more. Our nurse, whose name was Mrs Mitchell, did not tell us why this had happened.'

1895 In the middle of March, Pappy died. I wondered how long I ought to go on crying about him, for I felt as if I should never stop. Mrs Mitchell took my brothers to the funeral, which was at the Jewish cemetery in London. I was much too upset to go. It was no consolation to assume that he had gone straight to Heaven, like Grandmama (Thornycroft)—entering by a different gate owing to his being buried in Hebrew instead of English.

1896 I now vaguely believed that I was going to be a poet, and had taken to reading Longfellow, Shelley and Tennyson. I was rather secretive about it, feeling that poetry was a thing I wanted to keep to myself. I had opened Shelley at random and the first few lines of *Queen Mab* had made me eager to read some more.

> How wonderful is Death,
> Death and his brother Sleep!

I had a tendency to expect all the best poetry to be gloomy, or at any rate solemn. Eternity and the Tomb were among my favourite themes and from the accessories of Death I drew my liveliest inspirations. Apart from Posterity, the audience I addressed was my mother, and I didn't want to disappoint her by being insipid and unimaginative.

S.S. to F.C. 25 June 1965

On 18 June a man came to pump me—writing a book about the Sassoon family*—an ex-barrister, very jolly and unlegal, with a nice reticent wife. I had to give out a lot of details, but he has done some expert research and told me things unknown to me of interest—for instance, that my great-grandpa's family had lived in Baghdad for centuries and had influential connections with Jewish communities all over the East, and were known as 'Princes of Israel'. He had been to see my old brother, who showed him round Weirleigh. The main interest, of course, is the story of old David's starting the enormous merchant business. A book about the Thornycrofts would be much more worthwhile. I sometimes surmise that my eastern ancestry is stronger in me than the Thornycrofts, and how I bless the Thornycroft sanity which I inherited from my mother. Introspective though I have been, I could stand aside and look at myself—and laugh. You have got it *right* about my Jewish blood. My artistic talent derives from the Thornycroft side. But what made me different from the gracious serenity of Uncle Hamo's work† was the mixture of west and east. The daemon in me is Jewish. And as a poetic spirit I have always felt myself—or wanted to be—a kind of minor prophet. I suppose most poets aim at being prophetic communicators. But the idea has always been very strong in my mind. And found utterance in the war poems, of course. Sassoon. . . . It is just a rather absurd susurration in the silence of Eternity. But it is the name I 'go by'. To Oblivion with it!

I think the September St Sigfrid is the one for me. My mother named me because of her admiration for Wagner's Ring—a lucky choice for me—as it has always made me want to be a hero, though I don't think Wagner's S. was a specially admirable person

---

* Stanley Jackson *The Sassoons* William Heinemann Ltd 1968

† Sir Hamo Thornycroft, R.A. cf. G. M. Hopkins to R. W. Dixon, 30 June 1886: 'I saw the Academy. There was one thing, not a picture, which I much preferred to everything else there—Hamo Thornycroft's statue of the *Sower*, a truly noble work and to me a new light.' From *The Correspondence of Gerard Manley Hopkins and Richard Watson Dixon*, edited by Claude Colleer Abbott, O.U.P., 1935.

to imitate! Yes; in a way I suppose I *was* my mother's favourite. She always said I was her 'second self'. I have a copy of Coleridge's Lectures on Shakespeare inscribed by her to me on my third birthday. Very odd, as she was a very practical person, not the least 'high falutin'. Whatever made her do it? You ask me about genius and talent. I suppose some people only have rare flashes of genius—I may be one of them! But surely powerful genius always comes out top and is unmistakeable—a kind of divine madness in many cases. ('Was Coalridge mād—or was it his intellect that was mād?' I once heard Willie Yeats oracularize.) Talent is like having a beautifully made *body*. Genius is akin to the supernatural?

I got out my 1897 poems—given to my mother on her birthday, 28 March—here are two of them, *The Sea of Life* and *The Passing*. Really, really! Why that at 10½? I think I pinched the last line of *The Passing* from somewhere. Like Edith Sitwell and T. S. Eliot, I did quite a lot of paraphrasing. Anyhow I was before my time—free verse!

The Sea of Life

The shadows settled round the trees
Like mystic phantoms of the night.
Then a night wind moaned, like some soul
Who could not rest, but paced the shore
Of the great sea of life:
Which rose and fell.
It could not enter in that sea again.
Once it had passed without,
It rose from Death
Who clutched it in his hand:
It fell
Into the still calm lake of Sleep.
Once in it, man did rest.
But rose, no more.

The Passing

O haggard, weary, life-worn soul
Pass on.

Through death hast past, through life hast struggled on.
Pass, into darkness, or the land above.
Methinks the grave must feel a colder bed.

To the Wild Rose.
In glory grows the sweet wild rose
In every place
Of sweet repose.
In queenly grace
It hangs its petals down
As though it wore a crown.

(*Ibid.*)

He must have been an attractive, possibly a trifle morbid, certainly a precocious little fellow. Like most juvenilia, his 1897 poems provoke a smile, yet despite an occasional flop, the technique and sentiments of these youthful indiscretions are amazingly assured. He shows a true poetic feeling for storm and sea and sunset and birdsong and—more strangely—for death. However touched his mother may have been by the triumph of filial affection evident in the delicately illustrated poems, written out with such conscientious care in a red leather exercise book, she can hardly have shared her ten year old son's sense of achievement as his haggard, weary, life-worn soul fled from his body's shade. His memoried mind was to be death-haunted all his life. Dead soldiers would people his dreams, would 'wake and walk and live like men', strew his path as he walked down Piccadilly in broad daylight, revisit him as friends in solitude; and in the strangely prophetic poem which closes this book, he would once more watch the marching of his soldiers as he fell asleep, and count their faces, faces, sunlit faces—lit at last with the radiance of eternity. The child was father of the man.

From the manuscript *More Poems* by S. L. Sassoon, with illustrations, inscribed 'For Mamsy from Siegfried, October 20th–December 25th, 1897'

In the Churchyard

The chapel-walls were moulded and decayed
Within great men had been for ever laid.
Each with his head on pillowy stone, reposed.
With his hands uplifted and his eyelids closed.
  Let me not enter in the dark night hour.
  Lest they should wake and walk and live like men.

The Old Century

I was beginning to discover that solitude could quicken my awareness of aspects within and around me. My pneumonia had revealed that I had a mind with which I liked to be alone. Ellen Batty had got it into her head that there was some connexion between Mrs Mitchell and my pneumonia. I supported the idea that I had caught sight of Mrs Mitchell doing something to my sheets with a sponge. After my first gratification at having caused such a stir I began to feel guilty and remorseful. I knew that every good little boy had a conscience, which was a contrivance attached to him by the Almighty, like the lamp of a safety bicycle, to be used in the dark. Mine had now become both active and uneasy, not so much because I had maligned Mrs Mitchell as for fear of being punished for it by God. The more I worried about it the surer I was that hell-fire was waiting for me. Our Saviour was no use to me now; for I had put myself beyond his power to save me, and Satan would be there waiting for me as soon as I was dead. Miserably I resigned myself to everlasting perdition; all I could do was to put it off as long as possible by living to be about a hundred.

From *More Poems*, 1897

An old and weather beaten beech
Hanging its boughs across a rippling stream.
And towering far above, from mankind's reach
And mid grey mists; looking, like in a dream.

When man doth feel at rest, and heareth not
The mocking voice that ever haunts his life.
Ah, 'tis the Evil one, who forms a blot
On his mortal time; who ever holds a strife
With Man; the victory only but to gain
And form bad things upon his sinful brain.

The Old Century

Toward the end of 1897 my mother took me to London to see the Watts Exhibition. What I admired about Watts was his loftiness and grandeur. He painted the things I wanted to write poems about. Vaguely impressive and symbolical, his figures had their existence mostly in spiritual surroundings. They made me feel lofty-minded and ambitious. That I can still find poetry in these paintings does not seem to me strange. What does strike me as strange is the memory of myself, a dreamy and impressionable child, gazing ecstatically at *The Court of Death* and *Time, Death, and Judgement*—gazing at them with unquestioning delight and going home to try and write poems about them.

From *More Poems*, 1897

The Court of Death

There lay the lake of sleep: eternal sleep
   That looked so still.
And far beyond, the palace of King Death
   Who hidden lay:

. . .

The nobleman came up with bowèd head
The loyal knight came there to lay his sword
There at the foot of death, who robed in black
Looked on the people who came up to him
To throw themselfs, into the sea of gloom.

. . .

>   And he spake thus: 'I hold the lives of men
>   From the beginning to the end.'
>   And, yea, behind him angels stood
>   Guarding the things unknown, beyond the Tomb.

❦ The dramatic monologue was S.S.'s favourite medium of expression; he wanted subjective utterance rather than impersonal narrative, and this not only in verse but also in prose. *Something About Myself*, the earliest prose example written at the age of eleven, might appear in verse as *Joan of Arc*, the *Daffodil Murderer*, *The Old Huntsman*, the 'I' that opens some sixty poems or more, and then reappear in prose as the *Memoirs of George Sherston* or the Siegfried Sassoon of the three volumes of straight autobiography. The high-spirited cat autobiography presented to Mamsy at Christmas 1897 is a piece of sheer Sassoonerie, yet its imagination, irony, understatement, and cunning preparation of climax and anti-climax are all pointers to the subtle and accomplished writing of its mature counterpart, *The Old Century*, forty years later. ❦

The Old Century

If I could return to Weirleigh on some ordinary-looking morning in August 1897, I should find the place rather pauseful and absent-minded. Peter, our plebeian old tabby cat, would be crouching intently under an Irish yew near the pigeon's bath while the white fantails pecked up maize.

From *More Poems*, 1897

Something About Myself

Of course it isn't of any consequence but it might be of some use to tell you about myself, and how I came to be what I am. I might have told you before that I'm very well bred for one thing: and very beautiful for another, though perhaps I can't exactly say my mother was, and a greater part of her relations are most decidedly common, if not vulgar; and as her great-grandfather abided among the lowly chimney-pots of London, I can't exactly call my decent illustrious, in spite of my great beauty. Some cats say that I am cocky, but I can't see any harm in righteous pride!

My two brothers (both of whom disapeared in wicker-baskets) weren't exactly ugly, though, as my mother says I'm of rather a critical disposition. I expect if they had been my cousins, I should have considered them decidedly plain, but as it is, I should think they were rather pretty, though of course, not so perfectly exquisite as myself.

Well myself and my mother lived in a little hollow in a huge wall, covered with moss and lichen and nearly overgrown with ivy, and if I looked out, I could see all the people on the lawn walking about on their hind legs, purring in loud voices much louder than I ever purr, though my mother does say that my purr is really remarkable for its loudness. I've heard that my mother's swearing is exceptionally loud, and my Uncle Tim, who is the biggest poacher in these parts, says that my swearing is very good for a kitten of my age, which I consider a highly flavoured compliment. I might also tell you that my uncle is a proffessor in the noble art of snarling, and he practises for an hour daily on two young kittens kept for the purpose, and he says he's going to teach me some day.

You see that in the picture my uncle is holding up one of his hind-legs as if to scratch himself, but you may have noticed that just behind him there is another cat, and if he were very angry with that cat, he would turn round, lift up one leg, spin round again on the other, and give forth a most effectual exhibition of snarling. I only hope he'll include the figure in my lessons.

Well on the day when I begin my story my mother announced to me the awful news that three great vulgar cats had come into the garden with the intention of sweeping both me and my mother clean off the face of the earth, though I never did know that it had got one. 'Phist, quack, fizz, grrrrn!!!!' These were the sounds that came upon my ears. Plucking up courage I clawed a big ivy leaf aside and looked out. The moon was full and lit up the whole lawn brilliantly. But I hadn't time to take the scene in, for there in the middle of the lawn were three enormous cats. Tim and my mother were facing them, and the five of them were indulging in snarls and cusses of a base key. I hesitated, but only for a moment, and spitting with all my might, I sprang out and bounded across the lawn. In a moment I found there was a large tabby cat sitting on my chest and glaring at me. 'Ya'a'a,' was all I could say, for in another moment another cat came rushing along and began pommeling me. 'Oh my ears and whiskers! pssha sssh!' I exclaimed, and after a desperate struggle I unseated my opponent and dashed into the bushes, climbed a laurel bush and remained there. After a while, one by one, those vulgar cats dissapeared, and at last I was alone.

So I commenced singing a song in a minor key. Suddenly I heard someone coming and it was my uncle. 'Hullo' he ejaculated. 'Frrrrol, ffreela, freeli, froolerum, froleree,' I sang. 'Come down from there, or I'll fetch you down,' he said sternly. So I decended. He led me away under a tree, and there lay my mother; as dead as a door-nail.

'That finishes the ole gal,' I remarked gaily, for I never did like her piticularly. But here I must end my Story, for my uncle is going to give me a snarling lesson. Though, I might tell you, I am a kitchen cat now, and catch lots of mice.

The End

The Old Century

1897   No one will want to read those two 1897 manuscript books. But there is one thing about them which seems worth pointing out. The handwriting of the earlier volume has a sort of innocent refinement, and the little decorations are really rather charming. In the later volume the calligraphy is large and untidy and the drawings have become crude and insensitive. The poems themselves, with a few exceptions, are similarly different. There is a transition from the serene simplicity of childhood to something uncontrolled, self-conscious, and wilfully lugubrious. The poetic impulse in me had become more impetuous, while the artistic sense was about to leave me to my own devices until such time as I was old enough to call it back.

1905 'In three months I shall be twenty, and I don't seem to have done anything at Cambridge except buy books in vellum bindings,' I thought. The Lent term reduced me to blank despondency. Dodging about in Thatcher and Schwill's *General History of Europe* I found little, except dates and names, which I could reproduce verbally to my history coach; he complained of my preoccupation with the career of Joan of Arc, about whom I was privately meditating a long poem in blank verse. 'You really must put in some solid work on the struggle between the Empire and the Papacy,' he remarked. To which I dutifully agreed, and spent most of the next day reading *The Earthly Paradise* in a punt. Meanwhile I was consoled by having my first volume of poems in active preparation. No one knew about it, not even my mother, for whom it was to be a splendid surprise. When I say 'no one', I mean no one except me and the Athenaeum Press. The book numbered thirty-six pages and was bound in thick white cartridge paper. My book was anonymous.

S.S. to F.C. 30 May 1962
Feast of St Joan of Arc. 10.15 p.m. I wonder what you will think of my juvenile effusion about her in the 1906 poems which I enclose for your further information re my remote self. I wrote *Joan of Arc* in a state of rapt afflatus—a sort of 'first-love' affair with blank verse. I really was bursting with poetic feeling that year, though so immature. Something went wrong afterwards, and I lost the urgency and directness, and became rather Ninetyish and artificial. Something likewise went wrong with my religious innocence (and I had to wait fifty years to recover it!). I hope you will have a good laugh at some of the poetizings, their naive moralizing, verbal imprecision, and auto-intoxication with word-sounds. Swinburne was the main influence of that time. I loved Tennyson but was incapable of imitating his distinctness. Dante Rossetti also, and I'd imbibed quite a lot of Browning, *Saul* being my prime favourite. Anyhow, there I was, doing it all on my own

steam, with no one to tell me how to do it professionally. (Gosse didn't see this volume.) And I'm thankful that I was not a sophisticated youth, and really experienced those aspirations and vague upliftments. Wasn't it better to be like that than to write the stuff most of the young do now—all cleverness and dissatisfaction and uncertainty? (Poor lambs, it is the age they exist in, alas!) Have been listening to Cortot playing Schumann's Kreisleriana, mingled with meditations on my melodious immaturity and idyllic ignorance. How much has that creature learnt in fifty-six years? Nothing through success and periods of prosperity. Only through things endured and overcome, and through errors admitted and understood. With that stupendous platitude, I will close down.

From *Joan of Arc* 1906

The sunset fades about the mountain-tops,
And the last light has gleamed along the vales
Till all the land is shadow: lit by stars
Comes quiet Evening with her sister Sleep,
And stills the clamour of the wearied earth:
Now the long pageant of the day has passed
With the dying brightness, and the hills grow blue—
Deep blue, and vague with dreams of heights unclimbed,
And tranquil waters of unvoyaged seas.

I shall not seek the pathless summits more
When roses strew the road of rising day;
I shall not from the silence of the hills
Look down upon the basking vale below
In the haze of summer noontide; never more
Young hope shall yearn to scale the western clouds,
Nor in the dreaming depths of youthful eyes
Glimmer the light of many dawns to be,
And many fires of energy unquenched.

With darkness to the valleys we descend,
And in shadows find our shelter; be it so:

I have walked the steeps of Life, and at the last
Whither may I pass but into dark once more
By the path that all must tread, or soon or late?

VII

The sunset fades about the mountain-tops,
And the last light has gleamed along the vales;
Yea, and the last sweet bird-song dies away,
As one by one the stars come out.
      O God,
Ever have I beheld Thee in Thy stars,—
Turned ever toward Thee when the night drew on,
And through long hours of darkness felt Thee nigh:
Now, in the twilight of transition I turn
Mine eyes unto Thine infinite heavens and Thee;
Comfort Thou me, my Comforter, and lead
My soul into Thy presence without fear,—
Found worthy of Thy trust, and to the last
Raising aloft the sword and cross of Faith.

S.S. to D. Hildelith Cumming **14** September 1962
I begin this to the strains of the Freischutz Overture—what a *happy* composer Weber was! The National Book League label was sent me when they returned the 1906 *Poems* (in which, by the way, the first line of the first poem is 'Doubt not the light of Heaven upon the soul'—not a bad start!). It will be fun to make a list of my favourite piano works, but must restrict my choice to shortish ones—the range runs from Bach & Handel & Gluck to Grieg & Debussy & Franck. . . . I have played the piano a little since I came back, lingering over my two favourite Elizabethan songs—'Fain would I change that note' & 'When to her lute Corinna sings'—but how lovely Dowland and all of them are. In music, as in poetry, some things are *final*—affirmation (a supreme example is the theme of Bach's Violin Chaconne). But I could talk to you about music for ever.

Doubt 1906

Doubt not the light of Heaven upon the soul;
Doubt not the lyric passion, giving all
Desire and Hope and Wonder to its thrall;
    Doubt not the goal:

Doubt not the rapture of the smitten lyre,
The fearless hours, magnificent with might;
Creation from a Chaos of delight,
    Doubt not the fire.

Cast off all bonds and turn unto the fray
Unshackled from such fears as only bind
Beyond an hour the weakling, beauty-blind,
    Cast them away!

Heed not the night of Failure; none may rise
Save with much stumbling to those peaks that shine
Above all Dawn or Darkness, for a sign
    To lifted eyes.

. . .

Yet all our journey follows but a gleam
Elusive, and our steps forever bend
After the fleeting glimmer of a dream,
Who knows unto what end?

🙢 1906 Sassoon was twenty years of age and a decade had passed since the presentation of his childish poems to his mother. Yet he was still haunted with thoughts of the conflict between human passions and aspirations, with the transience of all things earthly, and the finality of death and judgement. Perhaps it was mere portentous poetizing but if, as he afterwards maintained, he never said a formal prayer, his poetry indicates that at least he was well practised in what spiritual writers call 'meditation'. 🙢

Sic Transit 1906

Leave him alone as he lies in his perfect repose,
Neither disturb ye the house whence his spirit hath flown;
None hath been here save the merciful Healer of Woes;
Yea—whom the sovran of Shadows all shadows hath shown,—
                    Leave him alone.

Glory of earth is a garment man wears for awhile;
Life is a season that brings him or harvest or dearth;
Time at the last must take all; and the dead with a smile
Unto the deed acquiesce; thus God weighs at its worth
                    Glory of earth.

Passion and Pride that have warred for the flesh, must take flight
When the day dawns: and lo, Time who is watchman, hath cried,
'Hear ye the end of all vigil; that after the night,
Death and his brother Attainment rise up and divide
                    Passion and Pride!'

This is the end of all striving,—for man being here
But a wayfarer, his journey accomplish'd—must wend
Homeward; and lo, he goes back to his judge without fear,—
Nothing would alter at parting, and nothing would mend,
                    This is the end.

The Weald of Youth

1908 Early in the spring I had put forth my second privately-printed volume. This was a typically juvenile performance, though a shade more sophisticated than the naive 1906 *Poems*. Entitled *Orpheus in Diloeryum*, it was in the form of an unactable one-act play which had never quite made up its mind whether to be satirical or serious. ... Orpheus himself, by what I considered an effective dramatic device, made but one brief appearance, at the end, to admonish and stampede a clique of pseudo-artistic persons who had failed to recognize that he was the real thing, though disguised in a shepherd's cloak. Mr Edmund Gosse responded with a letter of lively encouragement. 'Your delicate and accomplished little masque,' he called it. (He) ended his letter by saying that he had observed, with great satisfaction, my richness of fancy and command of melodious verse, and hoped that I should make a prolonged study of the art of poetry and advance in it from height to height.

From *Orpheus in Diloeryum*

[Enter ORPHEUS, carrying a lyre twined with roses.]
ORPHEUS. Who called so loud on Orpheus?
DISCORDIA. What art thou,
Disturber of this lyric hour's delight?
ORPHEUS. All lyric hours are mine.
DISCORDIA. All lyric hours? Then are you rich indeed.
ORPHEUS. My wealth is not for hoard.
DISCORDIA. You moralise,
But there is something drunken in your logic.
MAECENAS. Go hence; we'll have no witless rustics here.
DORGRELIAN. Nay, make him sing to us before he go:
He shall be lashed with strings if he be flat,
And garlanded with nettles.
DISCORDIA. Come, lout, if you would save your feet from thorns,
Sing up; and then methinks you will no more
Go masquerade as Orpheus in the woods.
   They laugh, lifting their flagons to him in derision.
ORPHEUS. Hush! for the dawn grows red beyond the hills;
The earth is awed with prayer.
         And now the trees
Loom dark and clear against the flushing sky.
Silence, and holy pureness in the air,
While the sweet land steals out of dusk to day.
Now do I strike one chord upon this lyre;
And all the woodland answers, giving praise
For darkness ended and triumphant light.

A bird chirps faintly from the trees below: then another joins, and another, until the woods are filled with a tumult of song. The feasters hang back, half-awed for a moment, their faces looking pallid in the first glow of dawn.

ORPHEUS stands apart, touching his lyre lightly, and his music lost in the universal melody of the birds.

DISCORDIA (starting forward). Fool, canst control the woods, or hinder day?
Up, servitors, and whip this madman hence!

They make towards ORPHEUS, who lifts both his hands, whereat they fall back for a second. In a dead pause, a startled blackbird goes scolding away among the trees. A band of satyrs enter, driving the feasters off in terror and confusion: loud clamour and crashing sounds of pursuit, dying away little by little into stillness and peace.

TIME goes wearily past, carrying a scythe. As the scene closes ORPHEUS is left standing alone gazing sadly towards the rising sun.

The Weald of Youth

1909   The sonnet was the form in which I felt most comfortable, though I used it somewhat loosely, seldom adhering to the strict Italian model and often indulging in irregular schemes of rhyming. Investigation reveals that the two things about which I wrote with most fullness of feeling were music and the early morning. For me, music was the handmaid of the muse, and all roads led toward sunrise. Searching the sonnets for evidences of mental autobiography, I interpret—from an occasional line or two—something written with seeming unawareness of its significance. And I am left to make the only comment which occurs to me—a tag from some forgotten popular song which comes into my head uncalled for—' 'E dunno where 'e are'.

🙠 The verses published privately this year, largely a derivative mass of experiments, can be dismissed for the most part as being musical, grandiloquent and mindless. Yet among them there is one, *Before Day*, a sonnet of exquisite perfection which, down to its least part, bears the individualizing touch of pure Sassoon. 'Written with seeming unawareness of its significance,' all the poet's youth is in it. The song sings of his loves: sunrise, early morning mist across the valley, the cherry orchards and the Weald and himself standing with arms outstretched as so often in childhood, calling out to, listening for, a voice heard only in silence.

Before Day 1909

Come in this hour to set my spirit free
When earth is no more mine though night goes out,
And stretching forth these arms I cannot be
Lord of winged sunrise and dim Arcady:
When fieldward boys far off with clack and shout
From orchards scare the birds in sudden rout,
Come, ere my heart grows cold and full of doubt,
In the still summer dawns that waken me.

When the first lark goes up to look for day
And morning glimmers out of dreams, come then
Out of the songless valleys, over grey
Wide misty lands to bring me on my way:
For I am lone, a dweller among men
Hungered for what my heart shall never say.

The Weald of Youth

I had conferred a copy (of *Sonnets and Verses*) on our old friend Helen Wirgman. She uttered nothing to suggest that my latest poems had disappointed her: but she did somehow imply that I should beyond all doubt do better next time. When she was staying at Weirleigh in the summer of 1910, I showed her a few of my latest productions in verse, and once again she hinted that I was moving in a wrong direction. Wouldn't it be better if I were to put some solid thought into my poems and go in for more honest everyday words? Somehow she felt that I ought to be writing in a more *physical* way. And what had happened to my admiration of George Meredith? I see now that she could hardly have said anything more significant.

1912   In the middle of December 1912 there was a spell of tempestuously wet weather. About three months before, I had written a grandiose *Ode for Music*. It was a hundred lines in length and I had composed it in a condition of ecstatic afflatus. I had in fact felt like an enthusiastic cathedral organist with all his swellest stops pulled out. Not wholly uninfluenced by *The Hound of Heaven*, I had climbed, taken wing, triumphed, and rejoiced in 'storms of jubilation' and 'psalmodies of splendour'. I had overheard 'symphonies of flame' and 'raptures of resistless lyring', and towards the end I claimed to have shared 'celestial commotion'! Here, at last, I thought, was my liberation from anaemic madrigals about moonlit gardens, thrummed by the lutes of ill-starred lovers.

S.S. to F.C. 1 June 1962

I am submitting my 50 year old *Ode for Music* for your scrutiny. It was the first time I reverted to my 1906 religiousness and tried to let myself go. I suppose it is rather bosh—rhapsodic bombilating in the void. My comments on it in *The Weald of Youth* seem right. Yet Crosland, who was a good judge of verse, found merit in it. One thing that *can* be said of my pilgrimage as a poet is, that it was like no one else's. For one thing, until I met R. Graves in 1915, I knew no writer of my own age, or anywhere near it. My progressions were entirely private and personal. Hunting, cricket and golf occupied the remainder of my existence, and very few of those associates knew that I wrote at all.

T. W. H. Crosland to S.S.
Dear Sir,
   I have read with pleasure your *Ode for Music*. You may take it from me that it is a good piece of work, and as fine, and nobly intended, as anything we have had in this way for a long time. But it suffers from what we may call 'youngness' and want of

mellowness and beating out. If you like, I will print the Ode in the next issue of my paper *The Antidote*. I can't pay you for it, because I have no money; but I can make a song about it, and you will be in good company and in the only paper which doesn't take advertisements.

      Yours truly,
       T. W. H. Crosland.

P.S. I shall be rather heart-broken if you don't let me have this Ode. So that unless there are insuperable difficulties please say the word.

From *An Ode for Music*

Angels of God and multitudes of Heaven,
 And every servant of the soul's aspiring,
Be with me now, while to your influence bending
I strive to gain the summits of desiring;
 Grant me in music's name
 Your symphonies of flame;
Come, and with rapture of resistless lyring,
 Where sense with spirit has striven,
 Through stellar spaces riven,
Bring vastness to my human comprehending:
 That I may know you near,
 Let me awake and hear
The rumour of your earthward wings descending.
 The rhythmic, mighty sound
 Of heavenly hosts unbound,
And the tumultuous glory there attending!

III

My spirit from its wonted place withdrawn,
Yields, overmastered by transfiguring light,
Lifted through deepening terraces of dawn,
And pinnacled above the vanquished night;
 Where I was sunken low,
Now in this hour I know
The dream which was a dream, a state unreal;

For the primordial message floated down
Reveals the perfect city and the crown,
The power, the jewel and the height ideal;
   I spread toward God at last
   Wings that may span the vast
   Spaces that lie between
   The seen and the unseen;
And in a bright and passionate revelation,
I am part of all endeavour that has been,
Music eternal and yet transitory,
Which in the universal celebration
Surges from life to life through gates of glory!

The Weald of Youth

Edward Marsh to S.S.

I think it certain that you have a lovely instrument to play upon and no end of beautiful tunes in your head, but that sometimes you write them down without getting enough meaning into them to satisfy the mind. Sometimes the poems are like pearls, with enough grit in the middle to make the nucleus of a durable work, but too often they are merely beautiful soap-bubbles which burst as soon as one has had time to admire the colours. It seems a necessity now to write either with one's eye on an object or with one's mind at grips with a more or less definite idea. Quite a slight one will suffice.

🖝 Marsh's astringent advice and creative criticism, of which this is the earliest sample, did much to transform Sassoon from poetaster into poet, so preparing him for the task of the war years. It was Edmund Gosse who brought them together in 1913. In both *The Weald of Youth* and *Siegfried's Journey*, S.S. expresses his appreciation of the drilling Marsh gave him in the literary and social graces, to say nothing of generous introductions into the society of the fashionable intelligentsia. Yet the two seem never to have touched any deeper level and when, upon Sir Edward

Marsh's death, Christopher Hassall published his Memoir, *Ambrosia and Small Beer*, Sassoon had merely this to say of his former patron:

S.S. to F.C. 28 July 1965

Hester had *Ambrosia and Small Beer* and read a few bits aloud to me. But I couldn't get myself to look at it. As you say, dear old Eddie was hollow inside—a prime example of what Belloc wrote in *Portrait of a Child* about people who discard sacredness. He did many good services to the arts; but was inwardly frivolous, and ended in despair—all his social world having collapsed. 'Non-conductive' was the word Max applied to him. He never seemed to be quite *real*.

The Weald of Youth

December 1912   I was in the silent studio. And there—on one of the shelves along which my eyes indolently wandered, was Masefield's *Everlasting Mercy*. I had raced through the poem about twelve months before, and had been wildly excited by the impetus and naturalness which had made it so famous. Why not amuse myself by scribbling a few pages of parody? Having rapidly resolved to impersonate a Sussex farm-hand awaiting a trial for accidental homicide of the barman of the village ale-house, I began his story in crudest imitation of Masefield's manner. After the first fifty lines or so, I dropped the pretence that I was improvising an exuberant skit. While continuing to burlesque Masefield for all I was worth, I was really feeling what I wrote—and doing it not only with abundant delight but a sense of descriptive energy quite unlike anything I had experienced before. Never before had I been able to imbue commonplace details with warmth of poetic emotion. Wholly derivative from *The Mercy* though it remained, my narrative did at any rate express that rural Sussex which I had absorbed through following the Southdown hounds and associating with the supporters of the hunt. In other words I was at last doing what had been suggested by Wirgie in 1911—writing physically.

From *The Daffodil Murderer*

I was christened Albert Meddle;
My father used to trudge and peddle
From house to house with tracts and hymnals,
And books that godly folk and criminals
Could read and take a sober lesson from,
And hope to gain God's holy blessin' from.

Dad never loafed in public-houses,
But bought his whisky by the dozen;
Bottles, bottles, how he loved 'em;
Along the cupboard-shelf he shoved 'em,
One by one he'd count their number:
His children were like useless lumber.

Nine young children had he got,
Live or die, it matter'd not:
Mother went without her dinner,
And watched us grow, not tall but thinner:
Mother loved when first she mated him;
When she died, cripes, how she hated him!

Now the stars come out and gleam
Over flood and field, and stream;
Rooks and daws have gone home winging;
Cows are in, and church-bells ringing:
Train goes by and stops at station;
Foxes bark in Firle plantation,
Out there I labour'd from a lad,
And lived and found it none so bad.
Here like a rat in a cage I wait
For the hangman and his mate.

*   *   *

O seasons passing by
Like clouds across the sky,

There's sunset mortal strange
In storm and shine and change;
I see it now so clear,
The waking of the year,
When Easter wind is keen
And woods are growing green;
O dusty summer days
When cattle drink and graze
Till harvest builds the rick,
And ground's as hard as brick,
O autumn falling slow,
When maids and children go
For blackberries, and fill
Their baskets on the hill.

O golden autumn weather,
And apples ripe to gather,
And white rime-frost at morn,
When huntsman blows his horn;
O all things I remember,
Who've seen my last September.
O all pure things I've known,
Let now my feet be shown
The way that leads aright
My spirit through the night;
And when my breath shall cease,
Grant me to sleep in peace.

S.S. to F.C. 14 February 1961

About *The Daffodil Murderer*—when Sydney Cockerell gave it to Wilfrid Blunt he replied on a p.c. 'It is better than Masefield, in the same way that Swinburne's parody was better than Browning.' I don't agree with that! As you say, it is good stuff where it is serious. But its main significance is that it was the first sign of my being capable of writing as I did during the war, and the first time I used real experience. It also revealed my gift for parody, which is considerable. I have stopped to hail your perceptiveness about Frances Cornford's poems. She succeeds through keeping on her own ground of feeling and experience. She *did* feel and suffer deeply. But it is all overlaid by Cambridge intellectualism and refinement (one might say the same of Virginia Woolf?). It is a cultured humanistic mind speaking, with perfectionist verse-craft. The power and the glory of spiritual aspiration are absent. Thoughts and emotions beautifully, sometimes poignantly, articulated. But never 'the roll, the rise, the carol, the creation'. Much as I admired her, I did feel that she was too intense, analytic and cultured for me. That vibrant voice of hers had a quality of academic aloofness in it. One couldn't imagine her outside of Cambridge. You have put your finger on what she lacked—spiritual warmth and breadth of vision. So sensitive and precise in personal responses, so artistically uplifted by Blake and Donne and all that, but—always a Darwin. Since dinner I have evolved you a rather naughty parody:

Farm Philosophers*

With what unconscious charity these cows
Moo me 'Good-morning' where they breathe and browse!
And what rebuke to reason is revealed
By a few turnips frost-bound in a field.
And with what geometric give and take
The turnips for the cows will munchment make.
   Also, how quietly the untravelled trees
   Forgo all academic-gowned degrees!

I have a fiendish knack for parody—can imitate anyone if I try—but F.C. wouldn't use as much alliteration as I do.

You ask about 'Wirgie' (a hard G). She was an old friend of all my mother's family. Her brother, Theodore Blake Wirgman,

---

* Cf. Frances Cornford's *Weekend Stroll*
       Step to the garden from the cool-roomed house:
       What sun-hot grass; what Canterbury Bells:
       How rich along the lane the rustic smells
       Of flowering elder and of hidden cows;
       What buzzing happy silence where they browse;
       What wealth of caverned shade among the boughs,
       What breadth of light on the receiving corn!
       July is born.

was a fairly good portrait painter. I have his portrait of Uncle Hamo, painted in 1887. He also painted Gosse. He lived to be 88, poor, proud, and rather solitary. She never had any profession, but was a naturally gifted pianist. I never knew much about her early life. She was just 'Wirgie', who was much the most exciting person I knew from the time I was ten years old. She was a sort of genius, I think, imaginative and impulsive. All young people loved her, & she understood them. Oddly enough, I knew nothing of her religious life, and can't remember her ever going to church when she stayed with us. But there she is, in my two books, & everyone said it is 'her to the life'. I saw her seldom after 1914, and now wish I had done more about it. But after 1918 my existence was so distracted and experimental and confused, and a lot of the old connections were jettisoned. And she was difficult and easily offended. But when I began writing about her I realized how much she had meant to me, and how kindred to my temperament.

Memory 1919

When I was young my heart and head were light,
And I was gay and feckless as a colt
Out in the fields, with morning in the may,
Wind on the grass, wings in the orchard bloom.
 O thrilling sweet, my joy, when life was free
 And all the paths led on from hawthorn-time
 Across the carolling meadows into June.

But now my heart is heavy-laden. I sit
Burning my dreams away beside the fire:
For death has made me wise and bitter and strong;
And I am rich in all that I have lost.
 O starshine on the fields of long-ago,
 Bring me the darkness and the nightingale;
 Dim wealds of vanished summer, peace of home,
 And silence; and the faces of my friends.

The Weald of Youth

1914 An article in *The Times* had informed me that we should have to go to war in aid of France. Germany, France, and Russia were all rumoured to be mobilizing. I had rushed to the conclusion that war was a certainty, so what else could I do but try to have a gun in my hands when the Germans arrived, even if I didn't know how to fire it properly? The landscape wore no look of imminent doom: no thunderclouds were above the skyline; the weather was perfect, and devoid of all atmosphere of fatefulness. But the aspect of things was within me, imbuing what I beheld with significances of impending disaster. The years of my youth were going down for ever in the weltering western gold, and the future would take me far from that sunset-embered horizon. Beyond the night was my new beginning. The Weald had been the world of my youngness, and while I gazed across it now I felt prepared to do what I could to defend it. And after all, dying for one's native land was believed to be the most glorious thing one could possibly do!

PART II

1914–1934

They were not true, those dreams, those story books of youth;
I left them all at home; went out to find the truth;
Slammed the green garden gate on my young years, and started
Along the road to search for freedom, empty-hearted.
                                                    Vigils 1934

👂 The battlefront brought Sassoon's protracted adolescence to an abrupt close. 'Passion with poisonous blossoms in her hair' gave way almost overnight to brown rats, sludge, machine-gun fire and riddled corpses. This time he was undeniably writing physically with his eye on the object. Realistic as it was, his war poetry was not all rough and bitter. As will be evident, some of it was strangely Christian in tone, some of it (*The Hawthorn Tree, The Dug-Out, Reconciliation*) tempered with deep compassion. Possibly the many wayside shrines dotted throughout Flanders, then as now, brought home to him as he watched youth martyred in that flaming furnace, the significance and symbolism of the crucifix. Had *The Redeemer* been written in 1917 instead of 1915, one might have suspected Wilfred Owen's influence. As it is, in 1917 Wilfred could write of it in a big-brotherly way to his sister: ' "*The Redeemer*," I have been wishing to write every week for the last three years. Well, it has been done and I have shaken the greater hand that did it. "*The Death-Bed*," my dear sister, should be read seven times, and after that, not again, but thought of only.' The curious dialogue in *Christ and The Soldier* leaves the speaker listening to the Divine silence—a typical touch. 👂

Memoirs of an Infantry Officer

It was now midnight. The five parties had vanished into the darkness on all fours. It was raining quietly and persistently. Five, ten, fifteen minutes passed in ominous silence. An occasional flare revealed the streaming rain, blanched the tangles of wire that wound away into the gloom, and came to nothing, bringing down the night. . . . Two killed and ten wounded was the only result of the raid. Nothing now remained for me to do except to see Kinjack on my way back. He was sitting on his plank bed, wearing a brown woollen cap with a tuft on the top. His blond face was haggard. This was a Kinjack I'd never met before.

The Redeemer 1915

Darkness: the rain sluiced down; the mire was deep;
It was past twelve on a mid-winter night,
When peaceful folk in beds lay snug asleep;
There, with much work to do before the light,
We lugged our clay-sucked boots as best we might
Along the trench; sometimes a bullet sang,
And droning shells burst with a hollow bang;
We were soaked, chilled and wretched, every one;
Darkness; the distant wink of a huge gun.

I turned in the black ditch, loathing the storm;
A rocket fizzed and burned with blanching flare,
And lit the face of what had been a form
Floundering in mirk. He stood before me there;
I say that He was Christ; stiff in the glare,
And leaning forward from His burdening task,
Both arms supporting it; His eyes on mine
Stared from the woeful head that seemed a mask
Of mortal pain in Hell's unholy shrine.

No thorny crown, only a woollen cap
He wore—an English soldier, white and strong,
Who loved his time like any simple chap,
Good days of work and sport and homely song;
Now he had learned that nights are very long,
And dawn a watching of the windowed sky.
But to the end, unjudging, he'll endure
Horror and pain, not uncontent to die
That Lancaster on Lune may stand secure.

He faced me, reeling in his weariness,
Shouldering his load of planks, so hard to bear.
I say that He was Christ, who wrought to bless
All groping things with freedom bright as air,
And with His mercy washed and made them fair.

Then the flame sank, and all grew black as pitch,
While we began to struggle along the ditch;
And someone flung his burden in the muck,
Mumbling: 'O Christ Almighty, now I'm stuck!'

S.S. to F.C. 28 July 1965
Here's a curiosity—from my 1915-16 war note-book, dated 18 December 1915 (about the same time as I wrote *The Redeemer*). Headed

A Child's Faith

God is my father in the clouds, and he
Gave me this earth for heaven; God is good;
He is the sunlight and the garden bee,
And water flowing down the windless wood.

Sometimes my boat is lost upon the deep,
And I'm alone in endless hours of night.
But God is with me when I fall asleep,
And he awakes me in the morning light.

These vague references to God can't have meant much, as there was no informed thought behind them. Sort of pantheism, I suppose. At that time I was the happy warrior—in pleasant surroundings where we remained until 30 January. And on 10 February, I wrote *In the Pink*, my first admonitory war poem.

The Old Century

We had all gone to the Norfolk coast for a change of air, and for the time being our address was Edingthorpe Rectory, which my mother had taken for two months.... My mother, in that old purple cloak of hers, is packing herself in with the picnic-basket and bathing gear. My brother Michael is on his bicycle, with one foot on the ground, while my younger brother Hamo and I are mounting our donkeys. I have just remembered that I have forgotten my sand-shoes, so I dash back into the house while my mother begs Hamo not to allow the donkeys to eat the laurels and poison themselves. . . .

Sed miles, sed pro patria. In the shadow of that gate, in that moment of my mind, the words were beautiful and unbitter. For it was in the autumn of 1915 that my brother Hamo had been buried at sea after being mortally wounded on the Gallipoli Peninsula—he whom I had idly remembered as a little boy on a donkey. 'Don't let the donkeys eat the laurels!' my mother had said to him. Laurels and donkeys. The donkeys who made the Great War were generous enough with their laurels, I thought.

To My Brother 1915

Give me your hand, my brother, search my face;
Look in these eyes lest I should think of shame;
For we have made an end of all things base,
We are returning by the road we came.

Your lot is with the ghosts of soldiers dead,
And I am in the field where men must fight,
But in the gloom I see your laurell'd head
And through your victory I shall win the light.

Memoirs of a Fox-hunting Man

I can see myself sitting in the sun in a nook among the sandbags and chalky debris behind the support line. I am scraping the caked mud off my wire-torn puttees with a rusty entrenching tool. A little weasel runs past my outstretched feet, glancing at me with tiny bright eyes, apparently unafraid. Against the clear morning sky a cloud of dark smoke expands and drifts away. Slowly its dingy wrestling vapours take the form of a hooded giant with clumsy expostulating arms. Then, with a gradual gesture of acquiescence, it lolls sideways, falling over into the attitude of a swimmer on his side. Somewhere on the slope behind me a partridge makes its unmilitary noise—down there where Dick was buried a few weeks ago. He had been hit in the throat by a rifle bullet while out with the wiring-party, and had died at the dressing station a few hours afterwards. Later on, when it was dark, we stood on the bare slope while the Brigade chaplain went through his words; a flag covered all that we were there for; only the white stripes on the flag made any impression on the dimness of the night.... A sack was lowered into a hole in the ground. The sack was Dick. I knew Death then.

S.S. to F.C. 25 September 1964
You ask about *The Last Meeting*. It was all experienced and written at Flixécourt—an elegy on my dear David Thomas,* whom I called Dick Tiltwood. I *lived* it with intense emotion and afflatus. I don't think it was poetizing—it was so real. No one has ever commented on it except the nice Methodist parson, Leslie Hayes, who came here a few times and used to include it in the readings he gave. *No. Don't* include *Good Friday Morning*. In the context of the war it was a wholesome shocker, but it is best forgotten now.

From *The Last Meeting* May 1916
III

I know that he is lost among the stars,
And may return no more but in their light.
Though his hushed voice may call me in the stir
Of whispering trees, I shall not understand.
Men may not speak with stillness; and the joy
Of brooks that leap and tumble down green hills
Is faster than their feet; and all their thoughts
Can win no meaning from the talk of birds.
My heart is fooled with fancies, being wise;
For fancy is the gleaming of wet flowers
When the hid sun looks forth with golden stare.
Thus, when I find new loveliness to praise,
And things long-known shine out in sudden grace,
Then will I think: 'He moves before me now.'
So he will never come but in delight,
And, as it was in life, his name shall be

---

* cf. Robert Graves *Goodbye to All That*, chapter 18

Wonder awaking in a summer dawn,
And youth, that dying, touched my lips to song.

From *The Death-Bed* 1916

He drowsed and was aware of silence heaped
Round him, unshaken as the steadfast walls;
Aqueous like floating rays of amber light,
Soaring and quivering in the wings of sleep.
Silence and safety; and his mortal shore
Lipped by the inward, moonless waves of death.

. . .

Light many lamps and gather round his bed.
Lend him your eyes, warm blood, and will to live.
Speak to him; rouse him; you may save him yet.
He's young; he hated War; how should he die
When cruel old campaigners win safe through?

But death replied: 'I choose him.' So he went,
And there was silence in the summer night;
Silence and safety; and the veils of sleep.
Then, far away, the thudding of the guns.

S.S. to F.C. 28 June 1962
Christ and the Soldier will probably make you say, like Alice, 'Curiouser and curiouser'. Proof, anyhow, that I wasn't pagan-minded in 1916. But how write that and go through the whole war without saying a prayer? My only religion was my vocation as a poet, and my resolve to do my duty bravely. I don't think I quite knew what I was trying to say. I suppose that behind it was the persistent anti-parson mentality—and it *was* difficult to swallow their patriotic pietism, which seemed unreal to many of us front-liners. But apparently a little of the reality came through to me in that tentative poem. (I made a few minor alterations when I rediscovered it in one of my war note-books, but nothing which affects its significance.)

Christ and the Soldier unpublished

1.

The straggled soldier halted—stared at Him—
Then clumsily dumped down upon his knees,
Gasping, 'O blessed crucifix, I'm beat!'
And Christ, still sentried by the seraphim,
Near the front-line, between two splintered trees,
Spoke him: 'My son, behold these hands and feet'.

The soldier eyed Him upward, limb by limb,
Paused at the Face; then muttered, 'Wounds like these
Would shift a bloke to Blighty just a treat!'
Christ, gazing downward, grieving and ungrim,
Whispered, 'I made for you the mysteries,
Beyond all battles moves the Paracelete.'

2.

The soldier chucked his rifle in the dust,
And slipped his pack, and wiped his neck, and said—
'O Christ Almighty, stop this bleeding fight!'
Above that hill the sky was stained like rust
With smoke. In sullen daybreak flaring red
The guns were thundering bombardment's blight.

The soldier cried, 'I was born full of lust,
With hunger, thirst, and wishfulness to wed.
Who cares today if I done wrong or right?'
Christ asked all pitying, 'Can you put no trust
In my known word that shrives each faithful head?
Am I not resurrection, life and light?'

3.

Machine-guns rattled from below the hill;
High bullets flicked and whistled through the leaves;
And smoke came drifting from exploding shells.
Christ said, 'Believe; and I can cleanse your ill.

I have not died in vain between two thieves;
Nor made a fruitless gift of miracles.'

The soldier answered, 'Heal me if you will,
Maybe there's comfort when a soul believes
In mercy, and we need it in these hells.
But be you for both sides? I'm paid to kill;
And if I shoot a man his mother grieves.
Does that come into what your teaching tells?'

4.

A bird lit on the Christ and twittered gay;
Then a breeze passed and shook the ripening corn.
A Red Cross waggon bumped along the track.
Forsaken Jesus dreamed in the desolate day—
Uplifted Jesus, Prince of Peace forsworn—
An observation post for the attack.

'Lord Jesus, ain't you go no more to say?'
Bowed hung that head below the crown of thorns.
The soldier shifted, and picked up his pack,
And slung his gun, and stumbled on his way.
'O God,' he groaned, 'why ever was I born?' ...
The battle boomed, and no reply came back.
   (Written at Somerville College, Oxford,
         August 1916)

The Hawthorn Tree 1917
 Not much to me is yonder lane
  Where I go every day;
 But when there's been a shower of rain
  And hedge-birds whistle gay,
 I know my lad that's out in France
  With fearsome things to see
 Would give his eyes for just one glance
  At our white hawthorn tree.

. . .

Not much to me is yonder lane
  Where *he* so longs to tread:
But when there's been a shower of rain
I think I'll never weep again
  Until I've heard he's dead.

Siegfried's Journey

1917 My next January entry commemorates a concert in Liverpool at which I heard Elgar's Violin Concerto for the first time, an emotional experience which my afterthoughts impelled me to report in terms that had, it now seems, little relation to the music.

'In all the noblest passages of this glorious work I shut my eyes, seeing on the darkness a shape always the same—the suffering mortal figure on a cross. And around it a host of shadowy forms with upraised arms—the souls of men, agonized and aspiring, hungry for what they seek as God in vastness and confoundment.' This is followed by a poem which I now find just worth rescuing from the page where it has remained hidden since I scribbled it in a fine—and perhaps foolish—frenzy.

I have seen Christ when music wove
Majestic vision. Storms of prayer
Deep-voiced within me marched and strove.
The sorrows of the world were there.

A god for beauty shamed and wronged,
A sign where faith and ruin meet
In glooms of vanquished glory thronged
By spirits blinded with defeat,
His head for ever bowed in pain,
I feel his presence plead above
The violin that speaks in vain
The crowned humility of love.

O music undeterred by death
And darkness closing on your flame,
Christ whispers in your dying breath
And haunts you with his tragic name.

S.S. to F.C. 29 April 1964

Thinking about you reading *Sherston's Memoirs*, and wondering how you'd react to my disrespectful comments on Rouen Cathedral. I wondered also what special day it was in Lent and got out the diary. It seems to have been 26 February, a Sunday. Easter was 8 April that year, and the battle of Arras began on the 9th, after three days of terrific bombardment. I then came upon the lines I enclose, which I'd forgotten about—with a careful drawing of the wonderful window. That diary at the Base is an extraordinary mixture of inconsistent moods—bitter resentment and disillusion about the war, boredom and disgust with my surroundings in the comfortless camp, alternating with periods of serenity when I was alone and away from it. In Sherston I had to eliminate most of my excitability & intolerance, as it had to be a fair-minded account of war experience. I was quite sure I should be killed (and only by a hair's breadth wasn't) and all my diatribes against the war ended in being recommended for a D.S.O.! The whole thing now seems incredible and mad, but it still has me in its grip. One odd thing—somehow I always thought of R.C. as part of foreign life—didn't connect it with English Catholicism. But St Ouen completely got me—I liked it far better than the Cathedral, which didn't make me feel holy at all.

A bonny boy at the BBC (Overseas Talks and Features) writes requesting an interview. 'I want to try and analyse the differences and similarities between the consequences expected and calculated by those influencing events at the time, and the real consequences, in so far as we can judge them, 50 years on.' He is referring to the 1914–18 war. He wishes to record my views. One word suffices. *Rats.*

> *In the Church of St Ouen* 4 March 1917 unpublished
> Time makes me be a soldier. But I know
> That had I lived six hundred years ago
> I might have tried to build within my heart
> A church like this, where I could dwell apart
> With chanting peace. My spirit longs for prayer;
> And, lost to God, I seek him everywhere.

Here, where the windows burn and bloom like flowers,
And sunlight falls and fades with tranquil hours,
I could be half a saint, for like a rose
In heart-shaped stone the glory of Heaven glows.
But where I stand, desiring yet to stay,
Hearing rich music at the close of day,
The Spring Offensive (Easter is its date)
Calls me. And that's the music I await.

A Mystic as Soldier 1917

I lived my days apart,
Dreaming fair songs for God;
By the glory in my heart
Covered and crowned and shod.

Now God is in the strife,
And I must seek Him there,
Where death outnumbers life,
And fury smites the air.

I walk the secret way
With anger in my brain.
O music through my clay,
When will you sound again?

S.S. to F.C. 17 May 1965

The world sends me almost nothing except prose cuttings about war poetry and requests for war poems in anthologies—4 this month; Longmans asked for 10 of the most provocative, and even Francis Meynell only asked for *Blighters* and *Base Details*. A man from Leeds University called without warning one Sunday afternoon—writing a book on war poets for Chatto & Windus—had been to see Blunden. Why can't they realize that the war poems were improvised by an impulsive, intolerant, immature young creature, under extreme stress of experience? I've been asked to lend manuscripts to two '14 War Exhibitions—one at Cheltenham

Festival and one in London—the latter has borrowed my portrait from the Fitzwilliam. I have lent them the *Infantry Officer* MS.—final version in minute writing. The BBC have issued a booklet, *Poems & Plays*, for use in all govt. schools. I am represented by *They* and *The Hero*! I was shown it by Mrs Humphries, who comes in several days a week and does all the housework. And yet another war poet anthology has appeared with 12 of mine in it—mostly ones I'd have omitted, and the *Sunday Times* says I'm 'a good second to Wilfred Owen', though less compassionate, which I deny, since I was bursting with it, wasn't I, when I made my famous and futile protest, which many now consider reasonable? O dear, there's my ego cropping up, though my 1917 self seems like someone else, and too impulsive to be taken seriously.

Siegfried's Journey

1917   It was now the middle of June, and the short statement of my reasons for protesting against the prolongation of the war had been put on paper. There, under the green-shaded lamp, were the words I had just transcribed.

'I believe that this war, upon which I entered as a war of defence and liberation, has now become a war of aggression and conquest.'

Somehow the workings of my mind brought me a comprehensive memory of war experience in its intense and essential humanity. It seemed that my companions of the Somme and Arras battles were around me; helmeted faces returned and receded in vision; joking voices were overheard in fragments of dug-out and billet talk. These were the dead, to whom life had been desirable, and whose sacrifice must be justified, unless the war were to go down in history as yet another Moloch of murdered youth. Perhaps the dead were backing me up, I thought; for I was a believer in the power of spiritual presences. By the time I went to bed I had written a slangy, telephonic poem of forty lines. I called it *To Any Dead Officer*.

From *To Any Dead Officer*

Well, how are things in Heaven? I wish you'd say,
Because I'd like to know that you're all right.

Tell me, have you found everlasting day,
  Or been sucked in by everlasting night?
For when I shut my eyes your face shows plain;
  I hear you make some cheery old remark—
I can rebuild you in my brain,
  Though you've gone out patrolling in the dark.

. . .

Good-bye, old lad! Remember me to God,
  And tell Him that our Politicians swear
They won't give in till Prussian Rule's been trod
  Under the Heel of England . . . Are you there? . . .
Yes . . . and the War won't end for at least two years;
But we've got stacks of men . . . I'm blind with tears,
  Staring into the dark. Cheero!
I wish they'd killed you in a decent show.

Diary

7 February 1954   Had a strange dream last night about Wilfred Owen. He had returned to life (à la '*Mary Rose*'). I was my young self, but was explaining to him all that had happened about his becoming so famous. It was a pleasant dream, with Weirleigh background. Wilfred looked more like his brother Harold—had fair hair. It may have been induced by my thinking about my poems before falling asleep, and wishing I could get advice about them from Parnassian departed friends. But W. said nothing about my work, and I was merely happy at his return and taking charge of him. At the end of the dream we were leaving Weirleigh and going off abroad together. I have never dreamt of him being with me before, though he has been so often in my mind in the last thirty-five years. 'O Wilfred, how wonderful, that you are back again alive!' I exclaimed to him. During this dream I half-awoke more than once, but the dream continued.

☙ *Invocation*, a companion-piece to *Before Day* 1909, was written, not from the paradise of the Weald, but from the hell of the

Somme. Yet the poet could still gaze unafraid upon the face of the angel of Death, could still invoke him as friend and soul's delivery, the personification of bliss, the recovery of all that life had denied or destroyed. There was nothing morbid or macabre in his musings. Death was filled with gladness and a life more intense than even poetry could express.

Invocation 1917

Come down from heaven to meet me when my breath
Chokes, and through drumming shafts of stifling death
I stumble toward escape, to find the door
Opening on morn where I may breathe once more
Clear cock-crow airs across some valley dim
With whispering trees. While dawn along the rim
Of night's horizon flows in lakes of fire,
Come down from Heaven's bright hill, my song's desire.

Belov'd and faithful, teach my soul to wake
In glades deep-ranked with flowers that gleam and shake
And flock your paths with wonder. In your gaze
Show me the vanquished vigil of my days.
Mute in that golden silence hung with green,
Come down from heaven and bring me in your eyes
Remembrance of all beauty that has been,
And stillness from the pools of Paradise.

Sherston's Progress

1918   Away from the shell-hole there was another dug-out—larger, but not very deep—where we slept and had our food. Everything seems to be going on quite well, I thought, groping my way in, to sit there, tired and wakeful, and soaked and muddy from my patrol, while one candle made unsteady brown shadows in the gloom, and young Howitt lay dead beat and asleep in an ungainly attitude, with that queer half-sullen look on his face.

The Dug-Out July 1918

Why do you lie with your legs ungainly huddled,
And one arm bent across your sullen, cold,
Exhausted face? It hurts my heart to watch you,
Deep-shadow'd from the candle's guttering gold;
And you wonder why I shake you by the shoulder;
Drowsy, you mumble and sigh and turn your head...
You are too young to fall asleep for ever;
And when you sleep you remind me of the dead.

Siegfried's Journey

1918   That inveterate memoirizer George Sherston has already narrated a sequence of infantry experiences—from the end of 1917—which were terminated, on 13 July, by a bullet wound in the head. Looking through my war diary I have found some lines, written at the beginning of that year after a conversation with a bemedalled and congenial brother officer who took a gloomy view of his prospects of coming through alive.

> Saved by unnumbered miracles of chance,
> You'll stand, with war's unholiness behind;
> Those years, like gutted villages in France,
> Done with; their shell-bursts drifting out of mind.
> Then will you look upon your time to be,
> Like someone staring over a foreign town
> Who hears church bells and knows himself set free,
> And to the twinkling lights goes gladly down.

I hadn't much fancied my own chances of survival, yet here I was at the end of my journey, apparently none the worse for it, and refusing to bother about the immediate future.

Reconciliation 1918

When you are standing at your hero's grave
Or near some homeless village where he died,

Remember, through your heart's rekindling pride,
The German soldiers who were loyal and brave.

Men fought like brutes; and hideous things were done;
And you have nourished hatred, harsh and blind.
But in that Golgotha perhaps you'll find
The mothers of the men who killed your son.

Siegfried's Journey

4 October 1918   It was about half-past-ten when I went on to Half Moon Street for the very special purpose of saying goodbye to Robbie [Ross], who was about to leave England for several months in order to give the Melbourne Art Gallery the benefit of his expert advice. I found him sitting at his table reading a little red-bound Bible. He explained that he wasn't getting ready to meet his Maker. The next evening while resting before dinner, he died of heart failure. He emerges in the mind-portrait of memory, his face—tired and old before its time—masking the sadness of wounding experience with a mood of witty reminiscence and word-play. There he would stand, in his loose grey alpaca jacket, wearing a black silk skull-cap and smoking his perpetual cigarette in its jade-green holder, emphasizing his lively pronouncements with controlled gestures of the left hand, on the third finger of which was a fair-sized scarab ring. He more than once warned me that my own hands were somewhat over-illustrative, urging me to be less precipitate and inaudible; he added that this union of gesticulation and indistinctness was probably inherited from the paternal branch of my family.

Elegy 5 October 1918
To Robert Ross

Your dextrous wit will haunt us long
Wounding our grief with yesterday.
Your laughter is a broken song;
And death has found you kind and gay.

We may forget those transient things
That made your charm and our delight:
But loyal love has deathless wings
That rise and triumph out of night.

So, in the days to come, your name
Shall be as music that ascends
When honour turns a heart from shame . . .
O heart of hearts! . . . O friend of friends!

S.S to F.C. 4 August 1961
At the Garrick Club dinner I sat between R. Hart-Davis, very nice, and Harold Nicolson, very agreeable—we talked about Tennyson & Swinburne, & Gosse, Matthew Arnold—and Robbie Ross, whom he loved. By the way, I have got R.R.'s Bible—he told me that he often read the *Old Testament* 'because there were such good stories in it'. I wish he'd read the New one oftener. I never knew that Robbie was a Catholic until the volume of letters to him came out.* And I can't remember him ever commenting on religion. (Had he done so, I wouldn't have been able to contribute much!) I never talked to him about Oscar Wilde. Now and again he would refer to him indirectly, but the whole subject was so painful, owing to his persecution by Alfred Douglas. O dear, it is all dreadfully painful to think of, even now. And he *was* so chivalrous and good to others.

Siegfried's Journey

1919   One evening in the middle of April I had an experience which seems worth describing for those who are interested in

---

* *Robert Ross: Friend of Friends* (1869–1918) Jonathan Cape 1952. As Oscar Wilde's executor, Ross rehabilitated both his financial affairs and his literary reputation. At his own request, Ross's ashes were burned in the cemetery of Père-Lachaise in Paris, being placed in Oscar Wilde's tomb designed by Jacob Epstein. In his painstaking study of Siegfried Sassoon's work, Mr Michael Thorpe's summary treatment of the loaded last line of Sassoon's *Elegy* on Robert Ross suggests complete ignorance of all that underlies it.

methods of poetic production. It was a sultry spring night. I was feeling dull-minded and depressed, for no assignable reason. After sitting lethargically for about three hours after dinner, I came to the conclusion that there was nothing for it but to take my useless brain to bed. On the way from the arm-chair to the door I stood by the writing-table. A few words had floated into my head as though from nowhere. I picked up a pencil and wrote the words on a sheet of notepaper. Without sitting down, I added a second line. It was as if I were remembering rather than thinking. In this mindless, recollecting manner I wrote down my poem in a few minutes. I then went heavily upstairs and fell asleep without thinking about it again. *Everyone Sang* was composed without emotion, and needed no alteration afterwards. I wasn't aware of any technical contriving. Yet it was essentially an expression of release, and signified a thankfulness for liberation from the war years which came to the surface with the advent of spring.

Everyone Sang 1919

Everyone suddenly burst out singing;
And I was filled with such delight
As prisoned birds must find in freedom,
Winging wildly across the white
Orchards and dark green fields; on—on—and out of sight.

Everyone's voice was suddenly lifted;
And beauty came like the setting sun:
My heart was shaken with tears; and horror
Drifted away ... O, but Everyone
Was a bird; and the song was wordless; the singing will never be done.

❧ On 14 August 1963, the copyright department of William Heinemann Ltd wrote to S.S. asking his permission to quote *Everyone Sang* in a forthcoming book entitled *Traditional Virtues Reassessed*, edited by Alec Vidler. S.S. forwarded the letter to Stanbrook, with this comment:

> When Canon Vidler's team has rearranged,
> Embellished, modernized and reassessed
> The Christian virtues, might it not be best
> To leave faith, hope, and charity unchanged?

1918 to 1920 were years of extraordinary poetic output. Sophisticated and sardonic as Sassoon might appear at the time to Harold Owen, he was writing lyrics almost unbearable in their depth of imaginative perception. Some of them escape classification and make selection difficult. *Ancient History*, with its unexpected twist—a sharp counterblast to Henry Vaughan's *Abel's Blood*—and the terrifying exposure of *Devotion to Duty*, show a biblical preoccupation with the sameness of man's sorrow and sin from generation to generation. As for *To a Childless Woman* one is tempted to exclaim, 'How *could* he? What business had he to realize it, to write it? It is almost too sacred, too intimate!' And among the love poems in the language, is there another like *The Imperfect Lover*?

Ancient History 1918

> Adam, a brown old vulture in the rain,
> Shivered below his wind-whipped olive-trees;
> Huddling sharp chin on scarred and scraggy knees,
> He moaned and mumbled to his darkening brain;
> '*He was the grandest of them all—was Cain!*
> 'A lion laired in the hills, that none could tire;
> 'Swift as a stag; a stallion of the plain,
> 'Hungry and fierce with deeds of huge desire.'
>
> Grimly he thought of Abel, soft and fair—
> A lover with disaster in his face,
> And scarlet blossom twisted in bright hair.
> 'Afraid to fight; was murder more disgrace? ...
> '*God always hated Cain*' ... He bowed his head—
> The gaunt wild man whose lovely sons were dead.

Devotion to Duty Spring 1919

I was near the King that day. I saw him snatch
And briskly scan the G.H.Q. dispatch.
Thick-voiced, he read it out. (His face was grave.)
'This officer advanced with the first wave,
'And when our first objective had been gained,
'(Though wounded twice), reorganized the line:
'The spirit of the troops was by his fine
'Example most effectively sustained.'

He gripped his beard; then closed his eyes and said,
'Bathsheba must be warned that he is dead.
'Send for her. I will be the first to tell
'This wife how her heroic husband fell.'

S.S. to F.C. 16 February 1962

I should say myself that the essential quality (of my poems) is that I have been true to what I experienced. All the best ones are truly experienced and therefore authentic in expression. I could prove this by annotation, particularly from *The Heart's Journey* onwards, when my inward life took shape and ceased to be poetizing —which some of the earlier non-war poems were. I have just re-read *To a Childless Woman*. As you say, I don't know how I dared to write it—but out it came early in 1919, when I was in a ferment of post-war emotional release. 'The enhaloed calm of everlasting Motherhood'—I rub my eyes when I read that line, so unknowingly prophetic, so ignorantly applied to the poem, I who had never so much as bowed to our Blessed Lady! But there you are—the whole Journey now seems to have been a sort of bemusement until I woke up and wrote *Deliverance*.

To a Childless Woman 1919

You think I cannot understand. Ah, but I do...
I have been wrung with anger and compassion for you.
I wonder if you'd loathe my pity, if you knew.

But you *shall* know. I've carried in my heart too long
This secret burden. Has not silence wrought *your* wrong—
Brought you to dumb and wintry middle-age, with grey
Unfruitful withering?—Ah, the pitiless things I say . . .

What do you ask your God for, at the end of day,
Kneeling beside your bed with bowed and hopeless head?
What mercy can He give you?—Dreams of the unborn
Children that haunt your soul like loving words unsaid—
Dreams, as a song half-heard through sleep in early morn?

I see you in the chapel, where you bend before
The enhaloed calm of everlasting Motherhood
That wounds your life; I see you humbled to adore
The painted miracle you've never understood.

Tender, and bitter-sweet, and shy, I've watched you holding
Another's child. O childless woman, was it then
That, with an instant's cry, your heart, made young again,
Was crucified for ever—those poor arms enfolding
The life, the consummation that had been denied you?
I too have longed for children. Ah, but you must not weep.
Something I have to whisper as I kneel beside you . . .
And you must pray for me before you fall asleep.

S.S. to F.C. 12 November 1961

Before dinner I was relaxing my mind melodically in the library. You would laugh if you could hear some of my sumptuous selections. ('Siggy plays with such feeling,' as my mother used to say.) And today 'None but the weary heart' was rendered with rich resonance, and Fauré's Après une Rêve. Sentimental melodies are very much a part of me. And what would life be without an infusion of sentiment? The emotionless music that is prevalent now seems a contradiction of what is natural. How people find it satisfying defeats me. Blake said that 'a tear is an intellectual thing', but I can't agree with him. Mine aren't, anyhow. And as for my intellect, I regard it with deep distrust, as my mother remarked to Mr Arnold about his 1895 motor car. Looking through this evening a MS. volume of the poems I wrote in the 1930s, it seemed that my intuitions were of more value than my thoughts and philosophizings. (By the way, on the title-page of *Vigils* I wrote 'My heart and my flesh cry out for the living God' —but I had to wait 25 years to find Him!) Surely what God looks to in us is our humanity & the responses He can awake in its imperfection. What can He do for our 'lordly intellect' when it claims authority over life? I suppose *supreme* intellects, like St Thomas Aquinas or Newton, are part of His purpose. And Newton said that the 'great ocean of truth lay all undiscovered before him'. Those cold altitudes are not for me. Give *me* the homely pastures of the valley. But this is an extensive subject, & *I* am no Plotinus, nor Aristotle either. Merely a believer in the religion of the heart.

Lovers 1919

You were glad tonight: and now you've gone away.
Flushed in the dark, you put your dreams to bed;
But as you fall asleep I hear you say
Those tired sweet drowsy words we left unsaid.
Sleep well: for I can follow you, to bless
And lull your distant beauty where you roam;
And with wild songs of hoarded loveliness
Recall you to these arms that were your home.

From *The Imperfect Lover* 1919

I never asked you to be perfect—did I?—
Though often I've called you sweet, in the invasion
Of mastering love. I never prayed that you
Might stand, unsoiled, angelic and inhuman,
Pointing the way toward Sainthood like a sign-post.

But I've grown thoughtful now. And you have lost
Your early-morning freshness of surprise

S.S. and his son George

Malaga, March 1934: "The Prince of Israel?"

At being so utterly mine: you've learned to fear
The gloomy, stricken places in my soul.
And the occasional ghosts that haunt my gaze.

You dream long liturgies of our devotion.
Yet, in my heart, I dread our love's destruction.
But, should you grow to hate me, I would ask
No mercy of your mood: I'd have you stand
And look me in the eyes, and laugh, and smite me.

Then I should know, at least, that truth endured,
Though love had died of wounds. And you could leave me
Unvanquished in my atmosphere of devils.

At the invitation of a Lecture Agency, Siegfried Sassoon spent the greater part of 1920 on a tour of the United States, where he read selections from his war poetry before packed audiences.

Siegfried's Journey

Sydney Cockerell had given me an introduction to Miss Belle Greene, of the Pierpont Morgan Library. I can remember sitting there one afternoon with my eyes on a folio page of faded brown writing.

> This light and darkness in our chaos join'd
> What shall divide?—the God within the mind.

An odd rhyme-ending, I thought; and then remembered that, in those days, joined was pronounced *jined*. For a moment, time dissolved; the millionaire museum was transmuted to immateriality. For I was staring at the original manuscript of Pope's *Essay on Man*. Whispering the words, I found them applicable to my own temporarily disordered existence, in which the God within the mind was being obliterated. I had been looking at an album of Keats' relics. In the presence of such things my heart cried out for the living word. The living word. . . . What had it felt like to be my true poetic self? I had left that inmost self in England.

No interviewers awaited 'England's Young Soldier-Poet' when he arrived at Southampton. That object of public interest had ceased to exist. In a moment of clairvoyance he realized that he had come to the end of the journey on which he had set out when he enlisted in the army six years before. And though he wasn't clearly conscious of it, time has since proved that there was nothing for him to do but begin all over again.

A Prayer to Time 1921

▶ S.S.'s note: Written in 1921, & revised in 1947—de la Mare said it is one of my best. The first two lines an echo from Sir Thomas Browne—'Time, who antiquates antiquities'. ◀

> Time, that anticipates eternities
> And has an art to resurrect the rose;
> Time, whose lost siren song at evening blows
> With sun-flushed cloud shoreward on toppling seas;
> Time, arched by planets lonely in the vast
> Sadness that darkens with the fall of day;
> Time, unexplored elysium; and the grey
> Death-shadow'd pyramid that we name the past—
>   Magnanimous Time, patient with man's vain glory;
>   Ambition's road; Lethe's awaited guest;
>   Time, hearkener to the stumbling passionate story
>   Of human failure humanly confessed;
> Time, on whose stair we dream our hopes of heaven,
>   Help us to judge ourselves, and so be shriven.

S.S. to F.C. 27 April 1963

At 3.15 today I was listening to the Gold Cup at Sandown (£8000 steeplechase—3½m.) with tense anxiety, as my friend the Marlburian Ian Balding was riding the favourite, trained by his brother—32 starters. Ian riding a waiting race & all seemed well, but he fell half way round—'Freedom shrieked when Koshyoosky fell'—& so did I when Caduval did so. Ian and his fiancée are coming to tea tomorrow. Such lovely young people—her brother was Cambridge cricket captain last year, and she is a fine musician.

Played some Liszt fluently last time they came, & we had a glorious music talk, I reminiscing about Pianists of the Past. She is doing a setting of *A Prayer to Time*. I explained its Sir Thomas Browneishness which, she said, encouraged her to be romantic. Difficult to set, I'd say, being such an incantation.

Siegfried's Journey

I had said my say: the stimulus of experience and emotion had ceased. I had it in mind to attempt realistic poems about everyday life. For, although my existence since the war had been undirected and adrift, my literary instinct was sufficiently wide-awake to warn me against allowing the vehemence of my war writings to become a mannerism. In the *London Mercury* I demonstrated my transition to the new style of versifying which I proposed to cultivate. It was the pattern for a series of descriptive pieces in which I assumed a laconic, legato tone of voice.

From *On Some Portraits by Sargent*
April 1921 *London Mercury*

The Royal Academy has been much maligned
By modern aesthetes . . . For myself, I find
More motives to applaud than to condemn
An edifice so apposite . . . ahem! . . .
Climbing the stairway in a cloud of chatter,
I am pledged to practise cogitant concision
And to reject all parenthetic matter
While ambulating round the exhibition

. . .

If Sargent could have called his soul his own
And had not been the hireling of the Rich,
There'd not be many portraits now re-shown
Of ladies lovelified to ball-room pitch;
Nor would these multiplied admirers crush
To crane their necks at sempiternal hostesses
Whom by the brilliant boredom of his brush

He silenced into fashion-dated ghostesses . . .
   Nor would my soul feel quite so mocked and chilly
   When I rejoin plebeian Piccadilly.

S.S. to F.C. 25 October 1965
Looking up a date, I found this scribbled in pencil in a 1921 diary. What do you make of it? Just silliness, I suppose! My mind was quite chaotic in the first years after 1918.

August 1921

It is rumoured of God Almighty that He has made us
'In His own image.'
Pessimists complain, 'Our Creator has betrayed us.'
'And Life,' they say, 'is a self-defensive scrimmage.'
I prefer to think that each potential corpse
From its own life must fashion
God, an encompassing dream. With crowns and harps
Men fill their future unperturbed by passion.
Such Heaven is but a gilded make-believe
Where God's imperial palace is 'To Let'.
God! Everyman has got Him up his sleeve.
He haunts them like a tradesman's unpaid debt.

God is spontaneous. Springs from God knows where.
And when I meet Him he resembles—what?
Nothing on earth except myself. I stare
At Him, and say, 'O God, I've such a lot
To tell you.' And He replies,
'I know your thoughts. I know your heart's whole story.'
And I am lifted up into His glory.

August 1921

From *Sheldonian Soliloquy* 1923

My music-loving Self this afternoon
(Clothed in the gilded surname of Sassoon)

Squats in the packed Sheldonian and observes
An intellectual beehive perched and seated
In achromatic and expectant curves
Of buzzing, sunbeam-flecked, and overheated
Accommodation. Skins perspire ... But hark! ...
Begins the great B Minor Mass of Bach.

Hosanna in excelsis chants the choir
In pious contrapuntal jubilee.
Hosanna shrill the birds in sunset fire.
And Benedictus sings my heart to Me.

Sheldonian Revisited 1965

S.S. to F.C. 11 March 1965

I will now inform you that a fortnight ago I received a missive from the Registrar at Oxford offering me an Hon. D.Litt. I was then still feeling so run down that my first reaction was a sinking sensation in the midriff. I pictured the Encoenia and all its horrific publicity, doubting whether I could face it. In fact I became extremely Scholar Gipsy minded. But I subsequently discovered that my date—5 June—is a secondary degree giving, so comparatively unalarming. To cap it, Geoffrey Keynes wrote to tell me that *he* is getting one the same day! Ten or fifteen years ago it would have bucked me up quite a lot. Now I can only see it as giving pleasure to my friends. I've got such a bee in my bonnet about worldly distinctions. But the bonnet must be assumed, and they have already asked for my size in hats. I just say, O well, I suppose I'll get through it pleasantly, staying at All Souls with John Sparrow; but my *Sheldonian Soliloquy* will be about Ronald's Romanes Lecture* and not about being an applauded aged author who would prefer to be walking in Heytesbury Wood. Anyhow Let Dames Delight, and that *will* give me pleasure. Tell D. Scholastica that although a Cavalier, if I'd met her at Marston Moor I wouldn't have hurt a hair of her.

* On 11 June 1957 Ronald Knox, then in a dying condition, delivered his Romanes lecture *On English Translation* in the Sheldonian, with all his characteristic brilliance. Knox's friendship and his spiritual writings were to remain an abiding inspiration to S.S. during the closing decade of his life.

S.S. to F.C. Whitsunday 1965

I got through the 24 hours remarkably untired (arrived at All Souls 5 o'clock on Friday & left 5 o'clock yesterday—fetched on Friday and brought back by Colin Fenton—the Warden's friend who edited Ralph Hodgson's poems—a very untiring person to be with because kind and considerate).

The Sheldonian was packed, as B.A.'s were also being bestowed after us Doctors.* The main object of interest was the famous Russian poetess—a most impressive and noble woman—sat opposite me at the Vice-Chancellor's lunch party, so I could study her face—most serene and lovely in expression. She speaks no English. She was degreed first, the Italian professor 2nd, G.K. 3rd, *me* 4th. Colin says that my ovation exceeded even the poetess's, but I was in a sort of dream—it all seemed so extraordinary. Anyhow I was clothed in something besides 'the gilded surname of Sassoon'. (My hat was much too big, so I never put it on!) As for the 'citation', you will see that it was fully gracious and comprehensive. (David Cecil said he gave them advice.) You will probably feel that the word 'spiritual' might have been included, but I suppose 'the world' was being on the safe side, as usual. Religion isn't mentioned in academic conversation. Colin is driving me to Mells this afternoon to tell darling Katharine† all about it. Daphne Acton is staying there. On Tuesday I am venturing up to the Old Stables for Garrick Club, and Tommy‡ L. is threatening to take me to a

---

* On Saturday, 5 June 1965, Dr Wheare, Vice-Chancellor of Oxford University, conferred the honorary degree of D.Litt. on the Russian poetess Anna Akhmatova, Professor Gianfranco Contini, Sir Geoffrey Keynes, and Siegfried Sassoon.

† Katharine (Mrs Raymond) Asquith in her beautiful home, The Manor House, Mells, provided not only Ronald Knox but also Siegfried Sassoon with that gracious hospitality and 'civilized' conversation so dear to both. S.S. lies buried in the village churchyard at Mells, a few yards away from his beloved Ronald.

‡ *S.S. to F.C.* 3 May 1960: 'Yesterday I was visited by Sir Alan Lascelles, brought here by a young friend, and new to me, though he was at Marlborough with me (like the Archbishop of Canterbury). Sir A. was private secretary to the last three kings, so an outstanding contrast to *this* avoider of what is known as "the great world". A charming and cultivated man—drew me out about

cocktail-party at the old Duchess of Kent's. 'Good heavens!' exclaimed the Archdeacon.

Alone 1924

'*When I'm alone*'—the words tripped off his tongue
As though to be alone were nothing strange.
'*When I was young,*' he said; 'when I was young ...'

I thought of age, and loneliness, and change.
I thought how strange we grow when we're alone,
And how unlike the selves that meet, and talk,
And blow the candles out, and say good-night.
Alone.... The word is life endured and known.
It is the stillness where our spirits walk
And all but inmost faith is overthrown.

S.S. to D. Hildelith Cumming 27 February 1964

Alone has been one of my most successful poems. I value it, because it was the first of my post-war poems in which I discovered my mature mode of utterance (what I call 'my cello voice'). Last night I heard Saen-Saen's variations on a Beethoven theme, which I like very much—it seems akin to Schumann, though Beecham called S.-S. 'the best second-rate composer in the world', which is quite true.

S.S. to F.C. 29 November 1960

Someone is playing a Brahms Intermezzo in B flat minor, which I love. What depth of sadness there is in some of those late piano pieces of his. Henry Vaughan? Claimed for himself the epithet Silurist because his family had always lived in that part of Breconshire which was the home of the ancient Silures. Also called himself Olov Iscanus—the Swan of Usk. Like Herbert, who was his

Hardy & Max Beerbohm—and was at Oxford with Ronald, and knew Katharine's brother Edward Horner and her husband well—so all went easily.' Sir Alan (Tommy) Lascelles was to become a valued friend of S.S.'s closing years.

master & protoype, he seldom wrote a perfected poem, but in his finest lines he excels them all with a kind of radiant naturalness—'I saw Eternity the other night'—'I see them walking in an air of glory Whose light doth trample on my days'. He had visionary genius. Could find in flower & stone & tree their celestial 'pedigree' (sweet quaintness). 'Each Bush and Oak doth know I AM.' But there is a lot of moralizing which one could do without. (Can anyone moralize poetically well? Wordsworth, I suppose. I prefer the aphorists.)

On Poetry

Donne was a 'black and white man'. And he never took light and darkness for granted in the natural way. My suggestion is that when his genius was active he instinctively exploited his visual darkness, as being an inherent element of his intensely personal poetic idiom.

As a contrast to Donne I have chosen another metaphysical poet, Henry Vaughan, who, though a much less professional writer than his mighty predecessor, was a heaven-born visualizer. Their affinity, I think, was a personal directness of expression: deliberately startling—and often disconcerting—in Donne; loveable and unassuming in Vaughan. Donne is frequently defiant and argumentative in his beginnings. Vaughan is invariably persuasive, reassuringly acquiescent, or charitably inquiring.

From George Herbert he had learned the potency of the sudden homely image or epithet, equally potent in Donne, with whom he shared that intense awareness of darkness and light.

But how differently he saw that darkness. In Donne's midnights you cannot see your hand before your face until he calls for a candle. Vaughan was a visionary. For him the night shone with 'white celestial thoughts'. Let me read you four of his best-known stanzas, as an example of mental imagery inwardly illuminated, 'felt, seen, and heard of the spirit within the sense'.

> They are all gone into the world of light!
> And I alone sit lingering here;
> Their very memory is fair and bright,
> And my sad thoughts doth clear.

It glows and glitters in my cloudy breast
Like stars upon some gloomy grove,
Or those faint beams in which this hill is drest,
After the Sun's remove.

I see them walking in an air of glory,
Whose light doth trample on my days:
My days which are at best but dull and hoary,
Mere glimmerings and decays.

. . .

And yet, as Angels in some brighter dreams
Call to the soul, when man doth sleep:
So some strange thoughts transcend our wonted themes,
And into glory peep.
>	(From the Arthur Skemp Memorial Lecture
>	University of Bristol, 16 March 1939)

At the Grave of Henry Vaughan 1924
Above the voiceful windings of a river
An old green slab of simply graven stone
Shuns notice, overshadowed by a yew.
Here Vaughan lies dead, whose name flows on for ever
Through pastures of the spirit washed with dew
And starlit with eternities unknown.
Here sleeps the Silurist; the loved physician;
The face that left no portraiture behind;
The skull that housed white angels and had vision
Of daybreak through the gateways of the mind.
   Here faith and mercy, wisdom and humility
   (Whose influence shall prevail for evermore)
   Shine. And this lowly grave tells Heaven's tranquillity.
   And here stand I, a suppliant at the door.

Sassoon the Socialist in sandy-coloured tweeds, yellow waistcoat, and pink shirt was, to quote Wirgie, coming on quite terrifically, as he more and more frequented the company of 'titled blokes and blokesses' rather than that of workers on the march waving the red flag. While the social satires that poured as a result from his too-facile pen betrayed a spiritual malaise visible in *A Breach of Decorum* (founded on an incident at the house of Lady Cunard), his true self rejected the conscious pose and burst into Vaughan-like lyrics of white-hot intensity such as *Nativity* and *The Power and the Glory*. At the same time, as one having deep affinities with the Metaphysical poets, he never ceased to stand apart, look upon life, and wait for the closing of the door.

From *A Breach of Decorum* 1925

I have seen a man at Lady Lucre's table
Who stuck to serious subjects; spoke of Art
As if he were in earnest and unable
To ascertain its function in the smart
World where it shares a recreational part
With Bridge, best-selling Fiction, and the Stable.

I have seen her fail, with petulant replies,
To localize him in his social senses:
I have observed her evening-party eyes
Evicted from their savoir-faire defences.
And while his intellectual gloom encroached
Upon the scintillance of champagne chatter,
In impotent embarrassment she broached
Golf, Goodwood Races, and the Cowes Regatta.

The luncheon over, Lady Lucre's set
Lolled on her lawn and lacked an epithet
Sufficiently severe for such a creature ...
'Such dreadful taste!' 'A positive blasphemer!'
'He actually referred to our Redeemer
As the world's greatest Socialistic teacher!'

Forty Years On
Plus ça change, plus c'est la même chose.

S.S. to F.C. 25 June 1965

You ask, at the end of your newsful letter, whether I went to that party. I did. You figure me, at 6.30 on 9 June, treading numbly to Kensington Palace portals—a bow-shot from the Lascelles' bower eaves. Entering, one heard a sound as of a disturbed beehive on a large scale—caused by about sixty people in their best clothes all talking at the top of their voices. Princess Marina wrung my hand—her equerry beamed upon me—and A.L. inveigled me to the outside edge of the horde, whereat was a large sofa, which I resolved to occupy as soon as possible. A.L. then introduced me to the Lady-in-Waiting, Lady Rachel Pepys, a daughter of the [old] Dook of Norfolk. I could think of nothing to say except that Ian Balding is a friend of mine—he having told me that he trained a horse of her sister's. This didn't get us far, and she slipped betimes away. (A.L. told me afterwards that she hadn't even registered my name, owing to the noise.) After a couple more dames had been presented without much result, he luckily hit on Lady Hambleden, sister of the present Lord Pembroke, who knew Edith Olivier well & had met me long ago with her. Safely established on the sofa I had quite a comfortable chat with her, helped by the fact that her late husband's sister married Hester's cousin, John Morrison, and that she is a very sweet lady, who laughed at my improvised anecdotes—barely audible in the uproar. White-jacketed servitors proffered Champagne and other stimulants to conversation, but I only sipped orangeade. Marina herself then arrived, hovering over me with exuberant adulation, and I continued the process of being a lively rattle. After a few minutes of this, A.L. removed me discreetly, but not before Marina had kissed me! She really was very attractive, and playing her part to perfection. Thus ended my one and only experience of royal hospitality. I suppose parties can only be performed in that way, but how they survive it I can't think. No place for contemplative poets, as I learnt long years ago. Yet one old dowager did tell me that she had been reading *The Old Century*. Perhaps Marina will!

Now to complete the allegory, let me put the clock back to 4.15. You figure me, yet again, now relaxed in an arm chair in the parlour at 23 Kensington Square.* Absolute peace pervaded me, and all the sustenance in the world. Could any contrast more exemplify the reality and unreality of my experiencings? It took me a week to recover from the sense of fatigue and wishfulness that the world would ignore my existence, and forget that I wrote war poems.

The Power and the Glory 1925

Let there be life, said God. And what He wrought
Went past in myriad marching lives, and brought
This hour, this quiet room, and my small thought
Holding invisible vastness in its hands.

Let there be God, say I. And what I've done
Goes onward like the splendour of the sun
And rises up in rapture and is one
With the white power of conscience that commands.

Let life be God . . . What wail of fiend or wraith
Dare mock my glorious angel where he stands
To fill my dark with fire, my heart with faith?

Nativity 1925

S.S.'s annotation: 'I love this one dearly. "And my unsealèd sight" anticipates Deliverance. In the second stanza line two should read "What powers unknown your seed have sown."† I found that it sounded better when reading it aloud.'

A flower has opened in my heart . . .
What flower is this, what flower of spring,
What simple, secret thing?
It is the peace that shines apart,
The peace of daybreak skies that bring
Clear song and wild swift wing.

* The Convent of the Assumption
† In *Collected Poems* this line runs: 'What powers unknown have sown your seed.'

Heart's miracle of inward light,
What powers unknown your seed have sown
And your perfection freed? . . .
O flower within me wondrous white,
I know you only as my need
And my unsealèd sight.

Siegfried's Journey

Our host (Mr Frank Schuster) was in ordinary evening clothes, over which he afterwards donned a hooded evening cloak. The ball was coming to an end and the John Peel Gallop was being danced with exuberant gaiety. Looking up, I observed the grey-cloaked figure of Frankie Schuster, who was watching from the musician's gallery. For the moment I saw him with the mask of social sprightliness discarded, and as though he were comparing this latest evocation of festivity with those many others which had gone their way of impermanence with the caravan that starts for the Dawn of Nothing when the door is closed behind the last departing guest. It was a face world-weary and saddened by the pursuit of pleasure, yet still in love with life, still demanding stimulation from the spectacle of youth in action. In after years I often saw him thus, and I used to wonder whether the words *vanitas vanitatum* were in his mind. On that first occasion, however, the cloak and hood made me perceive him as a sort of party-giving Prospero. Were he to clap his hands, I thought, the whole rout of merry-makers might suddenly vanish, and he be left alone with his beautiful empty house and the solitude of his Epicurean philosophy.

One Who Watches 1927

S.S.'s note: 'Written on 28 October 1927 after spending the evening at 17 H.T.'*

We are all near to death. But in my friends
I am forewarned too closely of that nearness.

* Sir Edmund Gosse, who lived at 17 Hanover Terrace, died a few months later.

Death haunts their days that are; in him descends
The darkness that shall change their living dearness
   To something different, made within my mind
   By memories and recordings and convenings
   Of voices heard through veils and faces blind
   To the kind light of my autumnal gleanings.

Not so much for myself I feel that fear
As for all those in whom my loves must die;
Thus, like some hooded death, I stand apart
And in their happiest moments I can hear
Silence unending, when those lives must lie
Hoarded like happy summers in my heart.

S.S. to F.C. 15 October 1961

On 18 December 1931, I was made an Hon.D.Litt. at Liverpool University (and exactly two years later received the degree of matrimony). Time gets more and more peculiar. 'A long time ago'—and yet, somehow telescoped. I was still quite 'unorientated' except for my resolve to be a poet. By the way, I only got the D.Litt. because A. E. Housman refused the invitation.

Thoughts in 1932

Alive—and forty-five—I jogged my way
Across a dull green day,
Listening to larks and plovers, well content
With the pre-Roman pack-road where I went.

Pastoral and pleasant was the end of May.
But readers of the times had cause to say
That skies were brighter for the late Victorians;
And 'The Black Thirties' seemed a sobriquet
Likely to head the chapters of historians.

Above Stonehenge a drone of engines drew
My gaze; there seven and twenty war-planes flew

Manœuvring in formation; and the drone
Of that neat-patterned hornet-gang was thrown
Across the golden downland like a blight.

Cities, I thought, will wait them in the night
When airmen, with high-minded motives, fight
To save Futurity. In years to come
Poor panic-stricken hordes will hear that hum
And Fear will be synonymous with Flight.

The Merciful Knight 1932

🙠 S.S.'s note: ' "Between the stirrup and the ground, Mercy I sought & mercy found" suggested it.' 🙠

Swift, in a moment's thought, our lastingness is wrought
From life, the transient wing.
Swift, in a moment's light, he mercy found, that knight
Who rode alone in spring . . .
The knight who sleeps in stone with ivy overgrown
Knew this miraculous thing.
In a moment of the years the sun, like love through tears,
Shone where the rain went by.
In a world where armoured men made swords their strength
  and then
Rode darkly out to die,
One heart was there estranged; one heart, one heart was
  changed
While the cloud crossed the sun . . .
Mercy from long ago, be mine that I may know
Life's lastingness begun.

S.S. to F.C. 16 February 1961
I should like to hear you telling Ian Davie's opposite number Donald what you think of him. He wrote recently to the *Sunday Times* belauding Ezra Pound (from Caius College, Cambridge). The odd thing is that these clever chaps exalt Yeats, Pound and

Eliot as the greatest poets of the century, and have now made Robert Graves the most important poet now active. Meanwhile R.G. has the poorest opinion of all three of them, and has often said so in print. What a tiresome mix-up the literary world is! Since about 1927 I have differed from Robert Graves about almost everything, and he from me. He was the first to label me 'Edwardian', and when I sent him *The Merciful Knight* his response was, 'I can't see much point in mercy long ago'. R.G.'s modernism was derived from America. In 1925 he discovered a poet called John Crowe Ransom and began writing in that way (and for fifteen years was inseparable from Laura Riding, who thought she knew more than God and wrote unreadable free verse under the influence of Gertrude Stein—'a lily is a lily is a lily is a lollipop' and that sort of thing). Mendelssohn's Octet has burst into song and my pen dries up. O how I love that first movement—direct utterance and rhapsodic concord. One evening by accident I turned on Paris and got Bartok's Sextet. It was most strange stuff, terribly clever, but like evil whisperings and creakings and knockings, poltergeist music—what can it mean? Frustrate feeling? Or merely experimenting in noises? But all the arts have gone the same way—dry bones and caricature and discontent and distortion and ungracious ingenuity. But it's no good grumbling. The real stuff is still there.

Here, for a relief, is de la Mare defining the qualities of a fine book: 'Lucidity, order, arrangement, balance, coherence, proportion, progression; an evident pattern and design; significance, invention, originality; the pervasive presence of light, an apt accordancy between sound and sense; style and simplicity; humour, wit, irony, perhaps; fancy, even vision; always profound if hidden feeling, a sentient heart, and at best magnanimity'. I copied this on the first page of a notebook (Meredith notes and poems—'46–50). Looking through it, I find 3 pages of notes on 3 visits to de la Mare in '48–49. Here is an extract: 'I asked him if he'd heard or read Sherrington's talk on the Physical Basis of Mind. He hadn't. I explained that it was about the changed attitude of Man towards Nature etc. which made him speak urgently about Science, "the modern Tyrant". "A whole life could be spent looking at a flower. . . . Nature, as we call it, is limitless, inexhaustible. We are all part of IT", he said, meaning Creation. Where do we come from—where do we go? . . . We've had too much *Memento Mori*. What we need is to know whether death is a good or an evil. What does Science know? Can it explain Vaughan and Traherne's sense of heavenliness in childhood? . . . He said he is on quite good terms with himself up to the age of 12. After that, he doesn't know what he was like.'

Siegfried's Journey

The fireside autobiographer wonders what his obsolete self would say if some prophetic presence came and warned him that he would one day commemorate twenty-five years with a quotation from Ecclesiastes: *The heart of the sons of men is full of evil, and madness is in their hearts while they live, and after that they go to the dead.* If I could make my obsolete self listen to me, I would tell him to stick to his trust that somehow good will be the final goal of ill. For despair is death, and belief in life is the essence of it.

A Premonition 1933

A gas-proof ghost, I climbed the stair
To find how priceless paintings fare
When corpses, chemically killed,
Lie hunched and twisted in the stilled
Disaster of Trafalgar Square.

To time's eternities I came;
And found the Virgin of the Rocks
Dreaming with downward eyes the same
Apocalypse of peace . . . The claim
Of Art was disallowed. Past locks
And walls crass war had groped, and gas
Was tarnishing each gilded frame.

Litany of the Lost 1933

In breaking of belief in human good;
In slavedom of mankind to the machine;

In havoc of hideous tyranny withstood,
And terror of atomic doom foreseen;
Deliver us from ourselves.

Chained to the wheel of progress uncontrolled;
World masterers with a foolish frightened face;
Loud speakers, leaderless and sceptic-souled;
Aeroplane angels, crashed from glory and grace;
Deliver us from ourselves.

In blood and bone contentiousness of nations,
And commerce's competitive re-start,
Armed with our marvellous monkey innovations,
And unregenerate still in head and heart;
Deliver us from ourselves.

Sherston's Progress

My definite approach to mental maturity began with my contact with the mind of Rivers.* My talks with him had increased my awareness of the limitations of my pre-war life. He had set me on the right road and made me feel that I should be starting on a new life's journey in which point-to-point races and cricket matches would no longer be supremely important. A spontaneous remembrance would reveal him alert and earnest in the momentum of some discussion. When walking he moved very fast, talking hard, and often seeming forgetful that he was being carried along by his own legs. I would give a good deal for a few gramophone records of my 'interchanges of ideas' with Rivers. He has been dead nearly fourteen years now and he exists only in vigilant and undiminished memories, continuously surviving in what he taught me. It is that intense survival of his human integrity which has made me pause perplexed. Can I hope to pass the test of that invisible presence, that mind which was devoted to the service of exact and organized research? He would have said of himself that he was merely a plain scientist, and he would have added that it

* Dr W. H. R. Rivers 1864–1922, Fellow of St John's College, Cambridge, author of *Instinct and the Unconscious* Cambridge University Press 1922

pained him deeply to feel that he was 'at war' with German scientists. At that time I did not know that he had studied at Heidelberg.

Revisitation 1934
Dr W. H. R. Rivers

What voice revisits me this night? What face
To my heart's room returns?
From that perpetual silence where the grace
Of human sainthood burns
Hastes he once more to harmonize and heal?
I know not. Only I feel
His influence undiminished.
And his life's work, in me and many, unfinished.

O fathering friend and scientist of good,
Who in solitude, one bygone summer's day,
And in throes of bodily anguish, passed away
From dream and conflict and research-lit lands
Of ethnologic learning,—even as you stood
Selfless and ardent, resolute and gay,
So in this hour, in strange survival stands
Your ghost, whom I am powerless to repay.

Diary 1952

I should like to meet Rivers in 'the next world'. It is difficult to believe that such a man as he could be extinguished. People like to think of death as liberation, the gateway to understanding, and so on. I used to think of it as a state where one would be able to see into the minds of the living as though their heads had glass foreheads. But why should one be able to understand people any better because one is dead? Can the dead listen to one's thoughts if they are 'liberated'? And is what I call my soul an instrument which counts for much in comparison with the extremely carnal element which functions through my brain? The soul always seems to be only just keeping its head above the waters of animal experience. My 'spiritual life' is an idea which I cling to (and only in my later years have I separated it from my emotional life). But the spirit, and its aspirations, must continually contend with uncontrollable human *behaviour*. It is being shouted down all the time by a crowd of adolescent instincts and attitudes. Are not these very words I scribble an exhibition of muddle-headedness and unknowingness?

Again the Dead 1935

Again the dead, the dead again demanding
To be, O now to be remembered strongly—
The dead, reminding mindsight of their darkness—
The dead who overhear us, listening longly.

Musician, now reverberant in our playing;
Poet, the presence haunting urgent words;
Dead youth, in love with life, now June-awakened
To hear through dream the dawn-delighted birds;
How can you be believed in, how made certain,
How sought beyond the silences of learning?
And how, revisitants by life envisioned,
Can what we are empower your quiet returning?

At this crucial point in the reconstruction of his life, S. S. challenges his editor F. C. with this self-revealing passage from his *Meredith*:

Meredith

In imagination I am confronted by [his] protesting presence as he was in his prime. He reminds me that though I have been thinking about him for many months with concentrated industry while exploring a mass of printed material concerning his career, I am still far from justified in generalizing about what he was like. He asks me to consider the impossibility of unshrouding an author who preferred his personality to be private. He goes on to say, in most kindly and forbearing tones, that a man cannot be re-created from a few printed letters which happened to be preserved, and were never intended to be used for the purpose of propping him up like a ventriloquist's dummy.

What I was in my forties (he concludes) can never be known to you or anyone else. You can see *through* me, but you will never see *into* me. The best of me is in my books, such as they are. Make what you can of them, particularly the poems, but beware of suppositions about my everyday life. The evidence is inadequate. Meanwhile I extend cordial condolences to you in your contest with the posthumous opacity which I have phantasmally interrupted.

Bowing with a sort of elaborate courtesy, he vanishes. His career, however, remains. My bookshelves are crowded with it, and portfolios of press-cuttings are piled intimidatingly on a table. Squaring my elbows, I return to my task.

PART III

1934–1957

Change of Garments unpublished
The man I was, went differently dressed:
A mantle of emotion once his wear,
Fine feelings covered ignorance unconfessed
Against inclement air.

The man I am, for conflict against cold
Deliberately travels thinly clad:
He, though the climate's bleak for one grown old,
Goes gauntly glad.
MS. Sequences

PART III

ARRAY

From *What Hope for Poetry?*

Everyday life has a knack of making poetry seem superfluous. Have poets always felt like that, I wonder—as they do now when losing confidence—that they aren't really needed?

People write poetry in a blind belief that they are communicating something valuable. The acceptance of poetry by 'ordinary people' is an act of faith. And it is for 'ordinary people' that the finest poetry ought to be written, because to experience it seems to be one of their few chances of becoming—for the time being—extraordinary. There will always be a small 'cultured' public for original poetry, but one wants to believe that the whole world expects poets to be doing their duty. And it needs a lot of nerve to believe that. Contemporary poets are trying to bring poetry up to date by ingenious experiments in versification and imagery. Will they succeed?

'The effects of poetry are to reproduce a state of mind, or to cause interest and pleasure, or both,' writes Mr Day Lewis. Personally, I divide poetry into (a) that which stirs my deep emotions about human life—as *music* does; (b) that which stimulates my mind, i.e. verse in which *ideas* seem to be forbidding any 'show of feeling'—that is to say, words without music (not the same thing as unmusical words). Complete satisfaction comes when poetry combines transmuted intellect with controlled emotion in simple and direct utterance. At the risk of being considered a hopeless Philistine, I announce my utter inability to obtain poetic pleasure from:

> And God the Father (Boja d'un Dio!)
> Having made all things he cd
> Think of, felt yet
> That something was lacking, and thought
> Still more, and reflected that
> The Romagnolo was lacking, and
> Stamped with his foot in the mud and

>   Up comes the Romagnolo:
>   'Gard, yeh bloudy 'angman! It's me.'

Which is the opening of Ezra Pound's 28th Canto, fortuitously selected from about 150 closely packed pages. If that 'elegant extract' is to be my only possibility of being caused interest or pleasure, or both, then give me the dentist's chair every time! But if it does really reproduce Mr Pound's 'state of mind', that is his own affair and need not concern anyone else.

Literary criticism has its *Rue de la Paix*. In poetry, as in other human concerns, there must always be a 'latest fashion'. The names which evoke the most solemn and profuse jargon are Yeats, D. H. Lawrence, and Eliot. I have long admired all three for variant reasons and in varying degrees of enthusiasm, but I have never regarded them as being, beyond argument, the master spirits of the age in poetry. I say this because so much critical nonsense has been conferred on them. As a final warning to such critics I offer the following quotations, which deserve careful consideration:

> (i) The sage, and the beetle at his feet,
>   hath each a ministration to perform:
>   The briar and the palm have the wages
>   of life, rendering secret service.
>   Neither is it thus alone with the de-
>   finite existence of matter—
>   But motion and sound, circumstance
>   and quality, yea, all things have
>   their office.
>
> (ii) There is the organic connection, like
>   leaves that belong to a tree.
>   And there is the mechanical connection,
>   like leaves that are cast to the earth.
>   Winds of heaven fan the leaves of the tree
>   like flames and tunes,
>   But winds of heaven are mills of God
>   to the fallen leaves

> Grinding them small to humus, on
> earth's nether mill-stone.

Are these passages similar? Might they, just possibly, be by the same writer? I merely ask. The second passage is by D. H. Lawrence. The first one was taken, almost at random, from *Proverbial Philosophy*, by Martin Tupper.

S.S. to F.C. 25 October 1961
I knew you'd chuckle over a *Hope for Poetry*. The article was a talk I gave to the Bank of England Literary Society—the only time I've ever been in that edifice. Wasn't I a bright boy in 1935? As far as I remember the Tupper quote was chanced on at once. *Proverbial Philosophy* is all like that. And even faintly reminded me of parts of Eliot's *Quartets*, dare I say it?

☙ The entrance of mankind upon an atomic age with its horrific possibilities forced Sassoon to intensify his search for order amid potential chaos. Man, he concluded, standing midway between the solar system and the ape, confronted now with bodily annihilation, must endure no matter how rough the road, and by an affirmation of faith recover the clear vision of childhood. ☙

Vigils 1934

> Lone heart, learning
> By one light burning,
> Slow discerning of worldhood's worth;
> Soul, awaking
> By night and taking
> Roads forsaking enchanted earth:
> Man, unguided
> And self-divided,
> Clocked by silence which tells decay;
> You that keep
> In a land asleep
> One light burning till break of day:

You whose vigil
Is deed and sigil,
Bond and service of lives afar,—
Seek, in seeing
Your own blind being,
Peace, remote in the morning star.

Sherston's Progress

A ruminator really needs two lives; one for experiencing and another for thinking it over. Knowing that I *need* two lives and am only allowed one, I do my best to *lead* two lives; with the inevitable consequence that I am told by the world's busybodies that I am 'turning my back on the contemporary situation'. Such people are usually so busy trying to crowd the whole of life into their daily existence that they get very little of it permanently inside their craniums. My own idea is that it is better to carry the best part of one's life about in one's head for future reference.

Past and Present 1934

My past has gone to bed. Upstairs in clockless rooms
My past is fast asleep. But midnight reillumines
Here in my ruminant head the days where dust lies deep.

Sleep-walkers empty-eyed come strangely down the stairs.
These are my selves,—once proud, once passionate with
   young prayers,

Once vehement with vows. I know not when they died,
Those ignorant selves . . . Meanwhile my self sits brooding here
In the house where I was born. Dwindling they disappear.
Me they did not foresee. But in their looks I find
Simplicities unlearned long since and left behind.

Siegfried's Journey

Quietude is essential to human happiness. This fact needs to be comprehensively rediscovered. 'The solitary and contemplative man sits as safe in his retirement as one of Homer's heroes in a cloud, and has this only trouble from the follies and extravagances of men, that he pities them. I think it advisable for every man that has sense and thoughts enough, to be his own companion (for certainly there is more required to qualify a man for his own company than for other men's), to be as frequent in his retirements as he can, and to communicate as little with the world as is consistent with the duty of doing good, and the discharge of the common offices of humanity.' Written by Norris of Bemerton, a seventeenth-century Platonist, these words are worth bearing in mind.

Elected Silence 1934

Where voices vanish into dream,
    I have discovered from the pride
Of temporal trophydoms, this theme,
    That silence is the ultimate guide.

Allow me now much musing-space
    To shape my secrecies alone:
Allow me life apart, whose heart
    Translates instinctive tragi-tones.

How solitude can hear! O see
    How stillness unreluctant stands
Enharmonized with cloud and tree...
    O earth and heaven not made with hands!

Meeting and Parting 1936

My self reborn, I look into your eyes;
While you, unknowing, look your first time on me.
Thus will *you* stand when life within me dies,
And you, full knowing, my parting presence see.*

Alone I stand before my new-born son;
Alone he lies before me, doomed to live.
Beloved, when I am dying and all is done,
Look on my face and say that you forgive.

* When Siegfried Sassoon died, his son George was present at his passing.

S.S. to F.C. 18 February 1960
Tim White called *Meeting and Parting* an apocalypse—it seems to be one of those things that no one else had said before. T. H. White I regard as a good man with bad patches in him. Ralph Hodgson spotted it when he met him here; and after taking to him at first, suddenly shut up like an oyster. T.H.W. is over-emotionalized, I think. Some exuberant demon takes control of him and plays havoc with his spiritual stability. And there is something about his talent which goes with this—almost widely facile & inventive—alcoholic humour too. A strange being, unadjusted, I suppose, but full of stimulating aliveness, and can write like an angel at his best—something of Goldsmith in him, but he doesn't talk like poor Poll. Puck's* letters brought an inward radiance to this room. She understands Tim, and what she says confirms what I've felt about him, and why I gave up attempting to cope with him, much though I admire his talent, and delightful though I found him. But the drink has been his curse—though it seems as if these unbalanced, emotional & creative people are doomed to it, to relax their 'tensions' in some cases. I wish I could do something for Puck.

The Child at the Window 1939

Remember this, when childhood's far away;
The sunlight of a showery first spring day;
You from your house-top window laughing down,
And I, returned with whip-cracks from a ride,
On the great lawn below you, playing the clown.
Time blots our gladness out. Let this with love abide . . .

The brave March day; and you, not four years old,
Up in your nursery world—all heaven for me.
Remember this—the happiness I hold—

---

* For 'Puck', Miss Florence Collier, the deaf-blind friend of T. H. White, see *T. H. White* by Sylvia Townsend-Warner, London Cape & Chatto 1967. S.S. never in fact met Puck, but he compassionately made financial provision towards her maintenance, a kindness continued by Mrs Sassoon after his death.

In far off springs I shall not live to see;
The world one map of wastening war unrolled,
And you, unconscious of it, setting my spirit free.

For you must learn, beyond bewildering years,
How little things beloved and held are best.
The windows of the world are blurred with tears,
And troubles come like cloud-banks from the west.
Remember this, some afternoon in spring,
When your own child looks down and makes your sad
  heart sing.

Heart and Soul 1939

Growing older, the heart's not colder;
Losing youngness, the eye sees clearer.
  (Inward eye, while our sight grows blurred.)
Living longer, the soul grows stronger.
Looked on, the darkening weald grows dearer.
  (Weald of youth, a remembered word.)

Soul undaunted and heart death-haunted
Dwell together, estranged yet one.
  (Starlight lonely and firelight room.)
Heart, be brave as you go to your grave;
Soul, be girt for the race unrun.
  (Holpen both by ghosts from the gloom.)

S.S. to Sydney C. Cockerell 12 August 1939

I am glad you like that poem *Heart and Soul*. I think the last 2 lines of the first stanza have some quiet magic in them. In several of the poems I seem to have achieved intensity by an unconsciously artful alliteration, & by a texture of vowels and consonants which somehow suggests control. One can't say how it is done—except that most of the short ones were written without any apparent effort. Poetry *is* a mysterious thing, isn't it?

I think economy of one's significant material is part of the secret—at my age. One has to wait—and pretend not to be trying.

The line 'Weald of youth, a remembered word', for instance, epitomises a great deal of *The Old Century* & the intense feeling I have about the view from Weirleigh gardens. . . . I am more & more drawn toward the idea of simple & unambitious writing. It is the equivalent of 'cultivating one's garden' which seems to be the only sensible thing to do in these times. Mentally we live in such a hullaballoo of ideas & inventions & non-reticences that the perennial undertones of decent humanity are having a very bad time.

❧ The years 1928 to 48 saw the publication of all Siegfried Sassoon's major prose works. Faced with 'the Black Thirties' and the horrors unleashed by the Second World War, his poetic output noticeably lessened. In a talk given in 1951 *To some boys at Oundle* where his son George was at school, he set forth the qualities he valued in English prose. As nothing could better summarize his own practice, the following extract from his faintly-pencilled notes is included at this point as being the considered opinions of an acknowledged master of English prose style. ❧

From S.S.'s talk *To some boys at Oundle*

What I want to talk about is aliveness and durability in literature, & the qualities through which these can be sought for and tested. I am not an eclectic reader—my likings include most of the acknowledged masterpieces. These masterpieces retain their hold on us thro' certain moving and memorable elements. If those elements were absent, aliveness would also be lacking. Whence are those elements derived? One answer is the well-known saying that memory is the mother of the Muses. Yes; memory of experience absorbed during the impressionable years —say from 18 to 25. The second quality in aliveness is Ripeness— usually at over 40 when early experience has been transmuted into creative richness. Now I have investigated my theory in most of my favourite authors, and I seemed to discover that their writing had this special quality of aliveness and ripeness when they were drawing on early experience. My theme is—not the *recording* of

Sic sedebat—1952 (see Introduction, p. 35), probably taken by his son George Sassoon

March 1959: See letter 26.10.59, p. 174 ('resting in Mother Church, as it were')

Unveiling a tablet to Walter de la Mare in St Paul's Cathedral 1961

past experience but the transmutation of it into literature which has survival power—durability and aliveness. Why is it that so many books, admired and found interesting by contemporary taste, lose their vitality and become neglected by posterity?

One reason is that ideas, philosophies, social commentaries and criticism become obsolete and outmoded. Such literature remains readable through literary art. But the art must be *humanized*—posterity rejects literary *artifice*. Why are certain books timeless in their reflection of the period which produced them? How did they acquire that companionable quality, that unfading distinctness, and immediate appeal to one's mind? My reply to that is one word—Ripeness.

This brings me to one of my stock notions—that all my favourite authors are at their best when drawing on early experience for their matured performances. It really seems that the impressionable period of youth provided them with their most effective & moving material. Such passages in their works have a special quality of aliveness, impetus and creative richness. When one meets with such passages one exclaims that *this* is the sort of thing which he or she alone can do. They are safe in their unique province of experience, observation and human feeling—the magic of memory is alive in them, and something has emerged which is unmistakable. These are the great moments in masterpieces (and almost all masterpieces are unequal in achieved composition). And the writers who produce them do so with a delighted awareness that they are expressing something which belongs to their whole being, something which has probably been incubating for half a lifetime, for these things do not arrive by accident. They are the outcome of intensely absorbed experience, recreated or evolved by some mysterious fusion of craftsmanship and emotion. If asked to generalize about my most memorable enjoyments in English prose literature, I would say that my strong preference is for homeliness and under-emphasized humour. I like to be moved and transported by the little things of life—by the humour which has a note of pathos in it, for humour is often closely allied to pathos—*sunt lachrymae rerum*.

And this essential homeliness is worth considering—it is apparent in so many of our best authors. And in this homeliness they are acknowledging their nearness to everyday humanity & demonstrating their fundamental good sense.

🙰 The poems written between 1948 and 1956 were published in the latter year by Faber as *Sequences*. The title is a technical one, a reminder that in his day Sassoon had contributed music criticism to various newspapers and periodicals. A musical sequence, the repetition of a definite group of notes in different positions of the scale, is a vital element in musical form, and powerfully suggestive of how Sassoon manipulated his ideas. In an extraordinarily compact space, rarely exceeding twelve lines, he has expressed each thought—an emphatic assertion, an equally emphatic denial, a tentative query, an equally tentative reply, never an exact repetition, transitions and modulations, changes of emphasis, dissonance finally resolved into harmony. S.S. annotated F.C.'s copy as reproduced. 🙰

An Asking 1948

Primordial Cause, your creature questions why
Law has empowered him with this central I;
Asks how to carnal consciousness you brought
Spirit, the unexplained of sovereign thought;
And whence your influent essence quickened first
In hungry heart, and brain's unscienced thirst.
My heritage I ponder. Who was he,
In geologic gloomed pre-history,
That glimpsed beyond his death-environed cave
The soul—a star—a gift he yet might save?

Resurrection March 1949

🙰 S.S.'s note: 'This was the first "spiritual" poem of those in this book (viz. *Sequences*)—by which I mean the first which "cried out for the Living God" *in me.*' 🙰

Suppose, some quiet afternoon in spring,
The hour of judgement came
For me and my mistakes when journeying
Along with that defence for nullity, my name.

Suppose, while sauntering in the primrosed wood,
To body and soul's dispute a voice cried *halt*,
And I that instant stood
Absolved of unfulfilment and essential fault.

Suppose this resurrection, this release,
This self-surrender wrought;
And the word heard within, *Depart in peace*;
Take to the everlasting all that time has taught ...
What, for the spiritual service some foresee
Beyond probational breath,
Would then emerge from marred and mystic me
To stand with those white presences delivered through death?

In sending S.S. a proof copy of *Resurrection* for inclusion in *The Path to Peace*, the Stanbrook printer had inadvertently omitted an r in the title. S.S. inserted the missing letter with this comment:

> Some say, my dear Dame Hildelith,
> 'This substantive is but a myth'—
> But you and all the faithful know
> That no 'mythprint' can make it so.
> (To D. Hildelith Cumming,
> 19 September 1960)

Diary

Why all these enquiries about the Creator? Wouldn't it be more profitable—and entertaining to public readers—to write something nearer everyday reality? There is always satire, of course, which I can do with gusto when stirred up. But I have outlived all impulse to wax indignant with the world—the state of it has gone beyond satire. My existence consists in facing the circumstance of growing old and teaching myself to submit to it philosophically and learn what I can from the process. This results in eliminating most human activities as no longer worth taking seriously. One watches with some interest; but wonders how they manage to go on believing in the urgent occupations. *And very few themes seem worth writing about. Only one, really . . .* the situation of a thoughtful human being against the background of nature and the universe. And the achievement of faith in spiritual guidance from beyond the apparitional existence of the flesh. Yet, most of the time, I don't feel any confidence in myself as a spiritual person. All I can do is to want to be spiritual minded. Solitude compels one to discover what one's mental resources amount to. Mine appear to be very limited. I have made all my discoveries in poetry, and gone through all my admirations. My old favourites remain, and I return to them at intervals—mainly the Victorians. But I am an indolent and intermittent reader.

Praise Persistent 1948

Alone with life, I heard massed choirs declare
For humankind conjunction with the unseen
Essence which rules redemption. On the air
Hosanna in excelsis swelled serene
As through cathedral'd centuries that have been.

This was the moment's affirmation. And then
On gloom-girt winds of time I heard it blown
With dwindling resonance, from mouths of men
Forever claiming kinship with the unknown—
Forever their one hope on earth pursuing
In perishable pilgrimage, in doomed defeat,
Fooled by phantasms that wreak their dire undoing,
Yet mindful of the Maker they would meet.

Thus, praise persistent, year beyond wrought year,
Those paeans rise and fade and disappear—
Held to what infinite heart—heard by what immanent ear?

Diary

26 December 1949 Thinking about T[homas] H[ardy]'s conception of the Immanent Will or Prime Cause has made me ask myself, 'What *do* I really believe in?' T.H. found this idea

more *possible* than the all-wise Creator with a plan for the world, in whom his reason forbade him to believe. All I know at this moment is, that if the world is run on *Dynast*'s lines, life can't be anything more than a booby trap for those born into it. But I am wondering what difference it would make if I ceased to have any hope of the existence of God (by which I mean Spiritual Power, active in human affairs, and perpetually in conflict with powers of darkness). I suppose I should just go on living out my life, trying to behave decently, and grow old with philosophic dignity. I have long since habituated my mind to the idea of there being no personal survival for me. Nor do I feel that I *want* my consciousness to survive. But that is due to being tired and longing for peace and oblivion. The young want *not* to die; they want 'the glory of going on', and their idealisms make them see themselves in a higher existence of service. I used to feel like that, and thought of myself as an elected spirit with a spiritual vocation. *Now* I feel that life is only a matter of making what one can of it. I used to say, 'If *I* fail, life has failed. Life is a responsibility which I must live up to.' Now I say, 'If I fail, what earthly difference will it make to anyone?' (apart from trying to make a success of human relationships). But if the Almighty exists, what does He do for me—what help does He give me on my journey to the grave? Has He made it any easier for me to get through the trials and tribulations of the last years? In my troubles and heart-searchings I have turned for help—not to Him—but to those dead friends who have sustained me in the past, and have found comfort from my half-belief in their spiritual survival, and their awareness of— and nearness to—my distracted mind. Lying awake, I have carried on imaginary conversations with them. But they only told me things which my own mind had invented. It is all so *personal*— now I come to think of it, I *do* want to be a spiritual survivor. ... I suppose unquestioning faith is the only solution. 'Just as I am, I come to Thee' and so on. But life—as it is now—in the tormented and disillusioned world—what reassurance does it offer me? B. Russell said that 'unyielding despair' is the only basis we can live on now. His attitude is understandable. (... The interesting thing is that next night I wrote *The Unproven* and on 29 December *Redemption*.)

The Unproven

Looking at Life, some unbelieved-in angels
    Asked one another when
Science would overhear them and encourage
    Their ministries to men.

Listening outside Eternity for Knowledge
    And divination of Death
Stood Science. Hushed was Heaven; and all those angels
    Still hopeful, held their breath.

Redemption

I thought; These multitudes we hold in mind—
This host of souls redeemed—
Out of the abysm of the ages came—
Out of the spirit of man—devised or dreamed.

I thought; To the Invisible I am blind;
No angels tread my nights with feet of flame;
No mystery is mine—
No whisper from that world beyond my sense.

I think: If through some chink in me could shine
But once—O but one ray
From that all-hallowing and eternal day.
Asking no more of Heaven I would go hence.

S.S. to F.C. 16 February 1961

Two days of sun and 'February fair-maid'. Grubbing up ivy and making a beech leaf bonfire this afternoon. Could have gone out after tea. 'The latening twilights of advancing spring'—how I love them. But one's responses to nature *do* diminish. Belloc said 'One of the bores of growing old is that you lose your pleasure in landscape'.

Euphrasy 1949

The large untidy February skies—
Some cheerful starlings screeling on a tree—
West wind and low-shot sunlight in my eyes—
   Is this decline for me?

The feel of winter finishing once more—
Sense of the present as a tale half told—
The land of life to look at and explore—
   Is this, then, to grow old?

S.S. to F.C. 12 November 1961

Two visits in the past fortnight, one a young man who had written that the *Sherston Memoirs* is the best book he's ever read—*barring none*—and could he see me? Transpired to be a C.I.D. detective from Scotland Yard! A splendid chap—modest and unaffected, self-educated, was at a national school. He had been to Kent, detecting the background of Sherston, and got to know my old brother, who showed him round. He had even visited 'Watercress Well'. He was here for four hours, & I enjoyed it all. He sent me a pound of Earl Grey tea. The other one was a little woman of about forty. On her way home to Sunbury-on-Thames (not far from Walton, where my Sassoon grandpa had a big house in a park—a house once owned by Cardinal Wolsey, if you please —now pulled down and built over) from a short holiday on Exmoor, some impulse made her telephone asking if I could see her. I knew at once that she was good stuff—intelligent and unpretentious—had worked in a public library, but now looks after an aged mother, and does other whole time unselfish duties. A great poetry reader—one of those touching, lonely-minded unmarried people. And she *was* so nice. Had walked 20 miles a day on Exmoor and 'the only person I met was a caterpillar crossing the road'. Goes about repeating memorized poems. Said that on Exmoor she was watching a tit in a tree, and repeated my poem about the cole-tit and found complete peace.

An Example 1950
I stood below a beech
And said to stillness, teach
Tranquillity. I told
Dumb patient earth to hold
My unquiet mind from speech.

A cole tit in the tree
Pecked, flitted, marked by me
Around whom nothing stirred
But this food-finding bird.

The moments passed; and I
No self-concernment knew
But one small purposed thing
Which from my presence flew
On deft unstartled wing . . .
And I was tranquil too.

S.S. to F.C. 15 September 1964

Reading an article in *Country Life* about Henry Vaughan, with a photograph of his gravestone, I looked in my diary of August 1924 for details of visiting it and writing the sonnet. And chanced on this, in an account of a visit to the Hardys. 'Florence told me this morning that T.H. has been writing a lot of poems, and has 30 or 40—nearly enough for a new book. "Mr Cockerell is afraid of his writing too much, like Wordsworth, and has warned him about it." ' What a subject for Max! S.C.C. gazing sternly down at T.H. sitting at his desk. 'Now, Hardy, I really must forbid you to write any more poems until you are 90.' Poor T.H. looking rather rueful, murmuring, 'I suppose Cockerell is right. But I thought that last one was rather good, I must confess.' 'At tea we discussed cathedrals. T.H. said, "There were six large abbeys in Dorset. If they'd been preserved Dorset would be quite a *show county*!" '

That somehow reveals his naturalness, doesn't it? It was that simplicity which made me love him. I was thinking yesterday that there are three writers I have known well who meant, and mean, more to me than any others—Hardy, de la Mare, and Max [Beerbohm]. (To them I would add modest E.B. [Edmund Blunden] of course.) Max so different from the other two (who were kindred spirits), and *gave* me something quite different. T.H.'s philosophy of life depressed me, & is now utterly unacceptable, needless to say. His humanity remains with me, and is there in the poems I love best. 'Well, well, well . . . God, God forgive us all!' as the doctor rightly remarked in Macbeth.

At Max Gate 1950

Old Mr Hardy, upright in his chair
Courteous to visiting acquaintance chatted
With unaloof alertness while he patted
The sheep dog whose society he preferred.
He wore an air of never having heard
That there was much that needed putting right.
Hardy, the Wessex wizard, wasn't there.
Good care was taken to keep him out of sight.

Head propped on hand, he sat with me alone,
Silent, the log fire flickering on his face.
Here was the seer whose words the world had known.
Someone had taken Mr Hardy's place.

Siegfried's Journey

What I was offered at Max Gate was homeliness. On that basis we discussed Shakespeare and Shelley, Keats and Browning, with uncritical gratitude for their glories. When I asked him why *Ah, did you once see Shelley plain?* is such a memorable poem, he replied, 'Because Browning wrote from his heart'. But I have watched him when he was in shadow and repose, and have held my breath in contemplation of what seemed the wisdom of the ages in human form. For that time-trenched face in the flicker of firelight was genius made visible, superhuman in its mystery and magnificence. This was the face of the life-seer who had transmuted the Wessex country into a cosmogony of his imagination, who had humanized it and revealed its unrecorded meanings and showings with patient power and mastery of half-tones and subdued colours, who had learned the secret of underemphasized radiance and the rich significance of shadows, overhearing the semitones of sounds in Nature, and observing the qualities and characteristics of his native country until he had made them all one with the English heritage of recreated life. Here was the real Hardy, unmeasurable by intellectual standards, who will haunt the civilized consciousness of our race when the age he lived in has become remote as the Roman occupation of Britain.

Befriending Star 1950

Befriending star, hung low above the mountain gloom,
Empower my human frailty to conceive you kind:
Be only what these earth-homed eyes behold, for whom
Aeonian-rapt remoteness overwhelms the mind.

Withdraw, while watched by me, your magnitude—your dire
Unmeaningness for man. Heart-simplified, appear
Not in ferocity of elemental fire
But, for my lowly faith, a sign by which to steer.

S.S. to F.C. 17 February 1960

5.45 p.m. and still some daylight. On Sunday I saw what I call 'my star' for the first time—the one Meredith describes in *The Thrush in February*—'a little south of southern colour'—and the one *I* put in my *Alcuin* poem—'watching, at spring's approach, that beckoning star'. Moving day by day from south-east to west, it always accompanies me out of the weary winter and, as G.M. wrote, 'homelier makes the far'—observed year after year from my tall bedroom window. Such little things go to make up one's meditative existence—I could almost compile a calendar of them—and all the little associative memories of my son George's childhood, innocent genii loci.

Awareness of Alcuin 1950

At peace in my tall-windowed Wiltshire room,
(Birds overheard from chill March twilight's close)
I read, translated,* Alcuin's verse, in whom
A springtide of resurgent learning rose.

Homely and human, numb in feet and fingers,
Alcuin believed in angels; asked their aid;
And still the essence of that aching lingers
In the aureoled invocation which he made
For Charlemagne, his scholar. Alcuin, old,
Loved listening to the nest-near nightingale,
Forgetful of renown that must enfold
His world-known name; remembering pomps that fail.

Alcuin, from temporalities at rest,
Sought grace within him, given from afar;
Noting how sunsets worked around to west;
Watching, at spring's approach, that beckoning star;
And hearing, while one thrush sang through the rain,
Youth, which his soul in Paradise might regain.

S.S. to F.C. 16 April 1962

The visit of Robin Lindsay, Helen Waddell's nephew, coincided with Ian Davie here for a night. What he made known to me about Helen was this. For several years she has been completely extinguished in all mental capacity. All memory and thought gone. I had feared that she was existing in a state of invalid half-aliveness, deprived of all mental activity and resources, & too weak to enjoy seeing her friends—as she was beginning to be in 1955—so this is a relief to me. I can now think of her great soul at rest, awaiting release and reward. The afternoon provided an amazing experience. Ian had told me about a broadcast she gave, from Ireland, where her eldest sister lives, in 1955. He said it was

* See the five poems from Alcuin contained in *Mediaeval Latin Lyrics* Constable 1929, translated by Helen Waddell. Her novel, *Peter Abelard*, to which the following letter refers, was first published in 1933.

quite wonderful & had haunted him ever since. She described how, when about 35, while doing intense research in Paris about Abelard, she was taken ill, and in a convent hospital lapsed into a prolonged coma in which she *became* Eloise as an old Abbess—lecturing to her nuns and remembering Abelard, and fearing she might be infusing heresies (impossible to epitomise it). And afterwards re-reading Peter the Venerable's letter to her about Abelard's death, & fingering the great Seal of Cluny. Imagine my feelings when R. Lindsay produced a disc recording of this, and put it on my gramophone! For more than eight years I had longed to hear that beloved voice. And now it was with me in the library—incomparable in wording & expression. It quite overwhelmed me, & I staggered out of the room & sat on the stairs shaken with sobs; and small wonder! For, as I have told you, Helen's disappearance was a catastrophe for me, & the thought of her has been suppressed misery ever since.

Acceptance 1951

Man, who by youth beguiled has trusted time and thriven—
Man, from whose tortured lips the lie to life was given—
Man, dumbly reconciled to suffer where he had striven—
Simpleton, accuser, and acceptor, each in turn
Mortality's enigma must enact and learn,
Till, in the presence of his one deliverer, death,
'Take not Thy holy Spirit from us, Lord,' Man saith.

Diary

29 March 1951 I muddle along, still trying to evolve my spiritual faith, still striving to write the sort of poem which Emily Brontë achieved triumphantly in her *Last Lines*—direct utterance of dramatized emotion and spiritual awareness. These poems of mine, though I felt as if I were saying something good during the process of writing, may be of no value at all, either as poetry or as 'thought'. They are, as usual with me, deficient of imagery and full of abstractions. The only thing I can claim for them is that they belong to my spiritual autobiography. They are part of my human cry for salvation and my reaction against the modern

denials of religious faith. I now have a sequence of about a dozen of this category, mostly written since *Resurrection* (February 1949). 'Take not Thy holy Spirit from us' is all they amount to. But it is something that I should have been brought to a realization of this as the only hope—the only thing that matters. I said it before, in an emotional way, in some of my 1925 & 1935 poems. But I have said it now from a darkened world, from the darkness of my own spirit, and an increased awareness of what one's faith in life must contend with. And I have thought about God much more intensely than ever before. And the process was different. No rhapsodic excitement now, no delighted sense of finding expression. Just a concentration of the mind with no preliminary conceptions of what I'm trying to say. The *process* appears to be authentic.

The Messenger 1951

S.S.'s note: Vide The Humbled Heart.

    Mind, busy in the body's life-lit room;
    Seldom in strength, unpiloted at best;
    How ignorant you admit from outer gloom
    The soul, in all God's world, most welcome guest.

    These two, it seems, are separate. The soul
    On incorporeal errands comes and goes
    With rumours and reportings from the Whole
    For mind, which only brain experience knows.

    Poor mortal mind, when you, in me, decay—
    When once delighting faculties grow dim—
    Cry on the parting soul for power to say,
    With passion, 'I befriended was by Him'.

Diary 1951

In the endless quest for spiritual illumination and my elementary little expressings of it, I see myself as no nearer to essential understanding of human existence than my remote ancestors in the East (probably moon-worshippers, T. E. Lawrence once said). I claim to be freed from superstition, which ruled their minds and behaviour. I have picked up a smattering of knowledge, by reading about knowledge in a casual way. But take away that smattering, of which my mind retains so little, and what remains? An intelligent animal staring at the night sky and knowing nothing—a physical apparatus attempting to convince itself that it has aspirations towards heavenly-mindedness. It is only my environment which prevents me from being a moon-worshipper and slave of superstition. The created Me knows nothing of its significance or insignificance in Creation. Its mind merely plays about with what it has overheard. So it would seem that the 'content' of my poems amounts to nothing except an exhibition of echoings from other minds. I have made no discoveries, evolved no ideas. Meanwhile the world is a hubbub of discussings and speculations and assertions and investigations by homo sapiens trying to find out who he is and where he is going. The Tower of Babel is continually being rebuilt. Where shall wisdom be found? Only in simplicities, one prefers to believe. O, what a power has white simplicity (said Tennyson). And in my childish way I have tried to find my own self-realization in simplicities.

World Without End 1951

First-found beliefs remain. I cannot free
My thought from looking on Eternity
As highway for the unresting soul of Man.
For though there be no everlasting life in me,
No end I see to what the idea of God began.

Innocent conceptions change. No more I find
Notioned Eternity in telescopes
Exploring timeless time. Yet, in my mind,
It dwells as when for childhood fatherly designed
To be enduring home for heart-envisioned hopes.

I see myself, one body on that invisible road;
Brief bird on air, blind burrowing mole, dumb
    fish in stream.
I trust Eternity as being's elect abode,
Where the idea of God pervades our daunted dream.

Diary 1951

I continue to ponder over my MS. of poems, trying to criticize and reconsider their effect and significance. I suppose people will see them as a curious withdrawal from sensory existence—a concentration of mind on unphysical reality and refutation of aliveness. A man alone with a self which asks awareness of God, but only gets as far, in his mysticism, as saying that He *must* be there. He claims to have received intimations and sustainments, and is on the side of the angels. But what intimations has he really had? How much spirituality was there in him when he wasn't writing these meditations? His dreams are all quite unspiritual and seldom even serious in their echoings of past experience and their improvisings on trivial promptings and frustrations. Reading a few of Gosse's letters this evening (when looking up his references to Ibsen) I was reminded that human relationships and associations are one's nutriment and one's responsibility to the business of being alive. I could have known so many people so much better than I have. And now it is too late. The curtain has descended on most of them. And it doesn't rise on any new ones. I am left alone with my efforts to make friends with God, who doesn't appear to be a forthcoming conversationalist. Too busy with that Universe of His, I suppose. I did *feel* spiritual when I was younger. But I know now that it was only emotional behaviour and self-deception, more like being moved by music. Perhaps I am in the dark night of the soul, and may yet come through to my reward. But when I ask what my 'consciousness' is, I am utterly unable to define it or analyse its mechanism. The more I learn about life, the less I know.

The Need 1951

Nobody knows
Whither our delirium of invention goes.
Who turn toward time to come
Alone with heart-beats, marching to that muffled drum.
Nobody hears
Bells from beyond the silence of the years
That wait for those unborn.
O God within me, speak from your mysterious morn.

Speak, through the few,
Your light of life to nourish us anew.
Speak, for our world possessed
By demon influences of evil and unrest.
Act, as of old,
That we some dawnlit destiny may behold
From this doom-darkened place.
O move in mercy among us. Grant accepted grace.

S.S. to Sydney C. Cockerell 26 August 1952
George is doing extremely well at Oundle. His Physics master reports him as brilliant, & they intend him to try for a scholarship, at King's, Cambridge, & regard him as a certainty. He evidently takes after H.'s brother Oliver Gatty, but they say 'his mind works in flashes', which is what used to be said of my uncle, old Sir John Thornycroft.

8 September 1953   A very nice thing has just happened. Young Wavell is on a course at Warminster, and wrote asking to come and see me. He came yesterday and I had four hours' splendid talk with him. What an admirable fellow he is. And I noticed at dinner the way he was looking at George (who was giving us some lively comments on modernist poetry)—it was the great Wavell over again.... I rejoiced that you were vigorous enough to send in to *The Times* that admirable tribute to the wonderful Abbess of Stanbrook.

On Scratchbury Camp 1951

Along the grave green downs, this idle afternoon,
Shadows of loitering silver clouds, becalmed in blue,
Bring, like unfoldment of a flower, the best of June.

Shadows outspread in spacious movement, always you
Have dappled the downs and valleys at this time of year,
While larks, ascending shrill, praised freedom as they flew.

Now, through that song, a fighter-squadron's drone I hear
From Scratchbury Camp, whose turfed and cowslip'd
   rampart seems
More hill than history, ageless and oblivion-blurred.

I walk the fosse, once manned by bronze and flint-head spear:
On war's imperious wing the shafter sun-ray gleams:
One with the warm sweet air of summer stoops the bird.

Cloud shadows, drifting slow like heedless daylight dreams
Dwell and dissolve; uncircumstanced they pause and pass.
I watch them go. My horse, contented, crops the grass.

Diary

16 November 1952   Bob Gathorne-Hardy writes: 'I don't feel at all that your poems suffer from a restricted vocabulary: you have a beautiful carefully-cultivated garden, which improves from year to year. After my reading, I thought this: "The occasion, the causes of your poems, are almost always moments of feeling." This doesn't require vivid images—sense impressions—sight and sound. You don't use such effects very much, except in some of your satirical poems. The reader doesn't miss anything: your approach is what I believe is called, in no derogatory way, cerebral.'

17 November 1952   'Swinny' [Frank Swinnerton] in a letter today: 'I am glad you are finding it possible to write poetry. It is very hard to assess the value of meditational verse; some might find it tame, but to me, as I have said (of *C.C.* and *E. of E.*), a true poetic emotion is conveyed which is quite beyond the power of the 'difficult' versifiers, who really are in the same position as yourself, of feeling the cruse a little empty, or at any rate rare, and who make the mistake of trying to startle or impress. Nature finds them out, for it says, "Why, they've got nothing to say!" So it will be proved in time that while they have been doing handsprings, you have been quietly producing something that will last for its intrinsic quality. I have no fear about what you are doing: merely for the sake of immediate prestige, I should like

you to do something imposing; but if you said, "I will do something imposing," you would become what is impossible to you, a charlatan like the rest.'

30 December 1952
>From inexperience I was wont to claim
That one seraphic utterance could prevail
Against the force of tyrants in their pride.
Now, though my surest belief remains the same,
I must admit that where the oppressors fail
Is difficult to discern or to decide.
Victory for the intangible has been
To those who watch appropriately unseen.

H.M.T[omlinson] assures me that these little pieces are all right—'stellar thoughts' he calls them, and urges me 'never to doubt one twinkle of a star'. But my confidence in 'spiritual versifying' is continually assailed by awareness of the dire reality of life as shown in the present state of the world. And I ask what my poor little dream of a life-redeeming God amounts to—poor indeed in the eyes of the ruthless rationalists and despairing intellectuals.

Apologia 31 December 1952 unpublished
My words—that non-surprising choice—
My thoughts—not found evocative—
My untransparent tone of voice—
   Forgive.

Word, thought, and voice but testify
What time has urged me to believe:
This, in a world gone much awry,
   Receive.

From one whose solitudes would share
Such good as mind and heart can make
With others. Homespun it is there
   To take.

Diary

2 July 1953 Finished *Food of Gods*—a wild fantasy, with all H.G.'s* weak and strong points in it, humour, prejudice, vivid imagination, obsession about changing the world by short cuts, journalistic utopianism, and so forth. He was a world-scale dreamer of things that might be, a breeder of big loose ideas and ideals. Vastly stimulating as he went along. But alas! how he did get things wrong! And how he loved violent action. An impatient idealist and innovator rather than a constructive thinker. Life a huge lark. Mankind in the Making . . . and he lived to see it unmaking itself in the big things, while his social reform plannings became a *fait accompli*. Thirty years ago and after, even I dreamed my dreams of a quickly improved world—dreams backed by almost complete ignorance of human history and conditions and the terrible forces of Nature. What does one *believe* in now? Only in the human decency and goodness which one has met with in one's own tiny experience and environment. One's awareness of Evil has been much increased. One's sense of significance as a single human being has shrivelled almost to nothing. I see myself as a fly buzzing against the window pane of 'reality' beyond which there is the world of the spiritual and the supernatural, the Universe and all the rest of it! No use attempting to understand what it is all about.

9 August 1953 Have just listened to a discussion on the reading and speaking of poetry between J. Kirkup and J. Reeves, which made me wonder what my own efforts in verse have to do with these expert discussings. It all sounded extremely dreary and professional and specialized, and made me long to be hearing de la Mare and Hodgson talking about poetry in a non-intelligentsia style. Why *must* modern poets be so self-conscious about it? Yet, when J.K. came here four years ago he talked quite simply and sensibly, though my conversations with him consisted mainly of my telling him what poets he hadn't read—and the gaps in his knowledge were numerous!

*H. G. Wells (1866–1946)

Credo 1933

The heaven for which I wait has neither guard nor gate.
The God in whom I trust shall raise me not from dust.
I shall not see that heaven for which my days have striven,
Nor kneel before the God toward whom my feet have trod.

But when from this half-human evolvement man and woman
Emerge, through brutish Me made strong and fair and free,
The dumb forgotten dead will be the ground they tread,
And in their eyes will shine my deathless hope divine.

Diary

26 October 1953   About 20 years ago I wrote a rather naïve poem called *Credo* in which I announced that my 'future life' would be only in a higher evolution of the human race. If asked now about the survival of the spirit I would say, 'We do not know'. If one's earthly consciousness is to survive, the obvious question must be 'Which consciousness?' My consciousness of life, my mental make-up—these are not what they were even 20 years ago. I have matured. And my human interests have narrowed—or condensed through elimination of activity and enterprise. An elderly man's consciousness is like someone living in one room. The younger mind is an adventurer of experience. If I were to die tonight my only earthly interest would be in George's future. I don't think I should care whether my literary works were remembered or forgotten. More than ever it seems that creative human existence as a whole is what matters to the future. (How obvious!) That the spirit of God (or good) should pervade and prevail. My own existence seems so insignificant. And my ageing body craves eternal rest—as it craves each night for dreamless sleep (which it never gets).

20 November 1953   Went to Warminster for X-ray of tooth, and did my shopping which was typical of my needs. I purchased $\frac{1}{2}$ lb of bulls' eyes, some pipe cleaners, some lighter fuel, a notepaper pad and envelopes, some iodized throat lozenges, and changed a cheque for £5 at the grocer's. Since dinner have dipped

about in V. Woolf's diaries, which I approached without eagerness, but became interested. She was a good diarist, as might be expected, catching the immediate moment, and observing with novelist's eye. But what I've read makes me understand why it was that I avoided the Woolfs.

The Tasking

To find rewards of mind with inward ear
Through silent hours of seeking;
To put world sounds behind the hope to hear
Instructed spirit speaking.

Sometimes to catch a clue from selfhood's essence
And ever that revealment to be asking;
This—and through darkness to divine God's presence—
I take to be my tasking.

Diary

6 December 1953   *The Tasking*. This seems quite authentic (written on 20 December 1952) as a foreword to the sequence I have accumulated. Such verse as I've written in the last five years or more really has been a dedication of the spirit to its task. The lines describe the process by which I now produce my best verse —the complete absence of emotional excitement or preliminary mental chemistry, just listening for the message to come through, unstimulated by any other mental experience.

Retreat from Eternity

Just now I stared out on a star-strange sight
With man's habitual wonder at the sight,
And the old lonely question—stellar space
Coincident wherefore with one human face?

Then, while the firelight flickered, musing here,
I saw, in mimic constellation shown,
Reflected sparkles on the chandelier,
And was no more benumbed by the unknown.

The Visitant

Someone else I know of—neither young nor old—
Seated late at night in my accustomed chair,
Willed to an intended thing which must be told,
Catches intimations brought from otherwhere.

Someone else invades me for an hour or two.
Clocked occluded self wrote never lines like his.
Me he has no need of. And I know not who
Or from what irrational inwardness he is.

Diary

13 December 1953   'Occluded self' of course, next morning, accuses this of being 'all my eye'. All the more reason, then, to regard that 'known of' self as worth believing in. For he does seem someone separate from the creature who winds the clocks and worries about trivial concerns. 'How did I do it?' I ask, when contemplating one of my lucky performances in verse. It wasn't my ordinary self who sat there in a state of intense mental concentration, and who overheard something which he couldn't have achieved by conscious thinking.

Anyhow, that seeker for intimations from outside the limbo of everyday affairs and animal activity is a phenomenon worth investigating—even though his verses may be mere furniture-making, as works of literary art. 'Rational mindedness' however isn't much help. Under that official scrutiny the whole poetry business goes to pot. Life must be handled in prose, one is told. Poetry is only 'playing about'. For example, I've been reading Dylan T.'s poems (which I'd never given a chance before). D.T.'s poetic cosmos is a good instance of splendid irrationality, a defiance indeed of 'rational thinking'. Many of them are written in a private language of his own from which I fail to interpret the meaning. Rhapsodies, controlled by a tight technique of verse-craft. They make my own poverty of language painfully apparent. But I believe that D.T. would have agreed with my suggestion that the poetic impulse is a visitant from elsewhere. He too must have had moments when he wondered what his symbolic effusions amounted to—though in his case, the word-magic is indisputable. The question remains—would he have been wildly rhapsodizing if he'd lived to my advanced age? Or would he have arrived at plainsong and essential expression?

15 December 1953   I had not realized that D.T.'s verse patterns were so strictly controlled and contrived. One can't help suspecting a bit of hocus-pocus in some of his earlier pieces, but his best poems are superb and the general effect is of rediscovering language. As E.B. said to me, he is 'a local bard'. But his localizations make the other modern poets look extremely uninspired. Often his drift is beyond my understanding, but I assume that his private symbolism was authentic to *him*. Of the exciting quality of his word idiom there can be no doubt. *Absolute* poetry, they call it. Thirty years ago and more *I* tried in vain to produce absolute poetry. But it seemed like faking. And I didn't know how to do it. D.T. did. And was working through to a less elaborate and hit-or-miss utterance.

17 December 1953   Today is a damp drizzle of mist and I'm thankful to be in bed with my still throaty cold, and my continued attempts to decipher the cryptic utterances of D.T. and discover how much he really had to say, apart from his celebration of the sexual organs and his admirable revisionings of his Welsh seascapes and coasts and valleys. *Words*, I feel, were too much his masters—marvellously though he manipulated and overheard their overtones and meanings. For in the very few poems where he is clearly comprehensible, he is such a true and beautiful singer. If one didn't trust his integrity, the cabalistic mannerisms of his—to me—almost impenetrable pieces would be suspect of pseudo-prophetic pretentiousness. A sort of modern Marlowe, he seems, strongly influenced by Hopkins (and Wilfred O. and Edith S.).

20 December 1953   A gracious day of sunshine yesterday, an absolute legacy of light. Cloudier today, but quite good. Bronchial cold still on me; but being in bed has been a blessing to my mind, which has been mainly employed on a long letter to de la Mare, from whom arrived yesterday morning his new poems and a nice letter, which caused me to feel copiously communicative as usual

when I hear from him—and why not? since his mind is one of my most precious possessions.

23 December 1953   Have remained recumbent, enjoying de la M.'s *Come Hither*—the best of all anthologies, being *his*, and again delighting in his Preface and Appendix. Last thing on 21st, I produced a poem. As usual, it arrived as it were from nowhere—quite unpremeditated.

The Making

This making is a mystery. Me He made
And left to build my being as best I could:
A child afraid who for protection prayed,
Worsted by wrong, but wanting to grow good,
A man betrayed yet blessed by circumstance,
Seeking self-knowledge, learning through mistake,
To shaped experience half compelled by chance.
What work was His, where mind its self must make?

It is He that hath made us, and not we
Ourselves. One moment's aftercome I live,
Flawed with inherited humanity,
And fooled by imperfections wrought through race.
This He first fashioned; this He can forgive
When granting His unapprehended grace.

The Best of It

Spring, surgent in the sense-delighted blood;
In daybreak being all the burst of bud.
This, beyond argument, was well begun.

Prosperities of summer that pervade
Ongoing while headstrong hope and vision are made
Aware and eager. Nothing there to shun.

Autumnal toned attainment, trouble-taught
To mastery of emotion-hindered thought.
Passion outlived. Regret there need be none.

Star-sown eternity for mindsight old.
Winter endured. Time past a tale retold.
Wisdom and wonder, faithful to enfold
Life, that by no disaster is undone.

The Worst of It

Here's Man, with all that knowledge to his name,
All that magnificent music in his mind,
And long achieved reliance on the soul.

Here's Man, empowered by armaments of flame,
Unfuturing his future; self-assigned
To suicide, through the secrets which he stole.

Here's Me; who neither ask nor aim to be
More than the mote in heaven's revealéd ray.
Here's Life, that might move fortunate and free,
Condemned by circumstance to doom's dismay.

Diary

25 December 1953 *The Worst of It*. This is what I call one of my 'loud-speaker poems', and this declamatory way of doing it seems to suit me best. My obviously effective poems have always been rather like strongly drawn cartoons. But aren't they a bit too obvious? The indirect approach is what I should like to achieve—instead of bawling out these generalizations as though addressing the Albert Hall. My other type of poem usually seems to be a soliloquy, in which I am merely talking to myself (as in the sonnet *The Making*). The loud ones always end with a fortissimo line; and over-emphasis is a thing I should prefer to avoid. But there again, it is all direct utterance, no felicities of suggestive expression. Reading these poems I bemoan the absence of visual evocation. They make me *see* nothing except the words. They are only a *voice*, modulating the word-sounds skilfully. Bob G-H [Robert Gathorne-Hardy] described this as cerebral verse, and said that the absence of sensory effects doesn't matter. But I can't

help feeling that a poem like *Another Spring* is a more satisfying performance because more alive. The odd thing is that my mind works pictorially much more than in ideas. Yet I can't introduce visual imagery. I suppose that in my old age I am trying to be one of the 'mages who ply the midnight quill' (as T.H. said), and my addiction to alliteration is almost ludicrous, but I brought myself up on Swinburne, and his music can still enchant me.

Another Spring

Aged self, disposed to lose his hold on life,
Looks down, at winter's ending, and perceives
Continuance in some crinkled primrose leaves.

A noise of nesting rooks in tangled trees.
Stillness—inbreathed, expectant. Shadows that bring
Cloud-castled thoughts from downland distances.
Eyes, ears are old. But not the sense of spring.

Look, listen, live, some inward watcher warns.
Absorb this moment's meaning: and be wise
With hearts whom the first primrose purifies.

Diary

27 December 1953   I have been trying lately to arrange my 1952-53 pieces as a sequence, wishing that I could run the best of them into one poem, or coherent whole. But this trick won't work. They were composed as separate condensations or considerations, and the sequence, such as it is, can only be contrived by selecting such poems as express different outlooks and assumptions and commentings, and arranging them in an appropriate order. If asked what they amount to, I would say that they are merely an exhibition of the spiritual and intellectual shortcomings of a man trying to find things out for himself—*attempting to formulate his private religion* step by step, in hopes that it may be of some slight service to a period which appears to have rejected religious beliefs in favour of psychology and scientific research.

Self-Epitaph unpublished

Though much to blame for lack of enterprise
In metaphor, in metre, thought, and rhyme,
He still could claim to be for captious eyes,
'Most simple-minded poet of his time'.

The Trial

Unscientific selfhood, often drawn
To dwell with mystical imaginings,
Zealous to walk the way of Henry Vaughan
Who glimpsed divinity in speechless things,
How fare you on that faithful pilgrimage,
Environed by an unbelieving age?

Ask the night sky for intimations of God.
Moves mercy there? Astronomy replies
With numbers of light-years each twinkle has trod.
Question the tropical jungle, through what guise
He manifests therein His ministrant law,
And how he justifies fang, swamp, and claw.

Nature and knowledge daunt with dire denial
The inward witness and the innocent dream.
On such rough road must faith endure its trial,
Upheld by resolution to redeem
The soul, that world within an ignorant shape
One with the solar system and the ape.

Diary

27 December 1953   Archie Wavell's death has warned me against my too introspective attitude towards the problem of spirit and flesh. Spiritual experience and exploration should not be restricted to nocturnal meditations. This morning's sunlight, blessing my bedroom through the three high windows—is not that a 'living light' to be taken account of, when blaming the body for impeding the processes of the spirit? George Herbert and

Vaughan are there to remind me of my purblind gropings. *They* discovered God out of doors. The body must be given its due as the partaker of physical providence. 'Reason is not a shallow thing: it is the first participation from God; therefore he that observes reason, observes God' (Whichcote). Traherne said it in his famous passage—'You will never enjoy the world aright' etc. One does not find the light by trying to see in the dark. To be poetizing alone in a shuttered library late at night is not mysticism. Divination is deedful, not detached. I have been obsessed by my idea of the body as the enemy of inward redemption. The body is not responsible for one's unspiritual behaviour (apart from the conflict between frustrated sex and one's 'above the waist' self). All this merely indicates the need to be fully alive. And one can't be fully alive and receptive and sense-of-wonderish at my age. The physical faculties don't register enjoyment and observation as they used to do. So the mind retires to an anchorite's cell and sorts out its little collection of notions about Time and Eternity, the elemental and perplexing problems which confront us when assuming the omnipresence of the Deity to be benevolent and the predominant monkeydom of Man to be improvable.

31 December 1953   Dec. 31: midnight, and I've just checked down the last of my 293 line MS. of verse, so have concluded 1953 well, I hope. The whole really has an air of coherence and studied communication, though most of the pieces seem, separately, mere episodes of consideration and mood.

10 January 1954   11.30 p.m.   Have just heard with delight (Gordon) Craig's Xmas broadcast (repeat on 3rd prog.) a most subtle and delicate piece of writing, inimitably spoken. Craig fascinates me by his personality and attitude to modern life. E.'s only comment was, 'Is this about anything?' which was, from his point of view, an intelligent remark—because the talk was really only about the effect of candlelight in an old Italian theatre, the sense of the past, and so on—an elaborate, beautifully organized fantasy, meditation or soliloquy. To E.'s attentive ear it wasn't about anything. But O, the implications to mine! Civilized detachment from the hullabaloo of modern life, immense distinction of mind and mental furnishing, superb fastidiousness of selective understanding, the ripeness and richness of a lifetime

of observing and absorbing the arts. It was the voice of the arts, the authentic voice, speaking with the articulation and intonation and authority of an old master. And somehow it has made me feel the pride of the artistic vocation which makes no concessions, the untouchable integrity of unworldly service to one's art and craft. Craig is of the kingdom of heaven, the 'real right thing' (there was an element of Henry James in the style of his talk).

23 January 1954   Recd. this morning an article on Edith Sitwell in the *New Statesman*, an amusing and clever summing up of her career as a publicity personality, and her insistence on the rôle of a Literary Queen. This reminded me of the factitiousness of contrived reputation, and made me thankful that I have chosen to isolate myself from seeking to be conspicuous. E.S.'s present prestige is upheld by an insecure fabric. Had she remained quiet and unobtrusive, like Ruth Pitter and Frances Cornford (who, in their way, are as good poets as she is), she would be known and appreciated by her work as a very gifted, fantastical writer—more original than the other two—with a highly sensitive sense of word sounds and effects. But she has assumed the robes of a prophetess and oracle—much influenced by Yeats and Eliot—and her solemnities and apocalypses will, I suspect, be found to be a pretension of powers she doesn't possess. Her earlier verse was the real E.S.—lacking in design and condensation, but exquisitely fanciful and ornamental. When reviewing *Bucolic Comedies* in 1919, I said she was in the Beardsley tradition. And I still think I was somewhere near the truth. Wrote to Blunden last night.

26 January 1954   Looking at a few of Andrew Young's short poems today, I envied his objectivity and felicitous nature observation and the skill with which he finds epithets which surprise and illustrate without lapsing into the over-particularization which most modern poets indulge in. A.Y. belongs with W. H. Davies and E.B. and will hold his place. But I must admit that, much though I admire his minor mastery (minor in the best sense—there is less range in him than in W.H.D. and E.B.), I can't help seeing him as a nice clergyman botanist and field naturalist out for walks with his notebook. His poems don't excite me (and don't aim at doing so). They give me quiet pleasure, faintly tinged with boredom. (His long poem *Into Hades* did hold me interested and

impressed: I read it at a sitting.) Yet I know that his modest expert under-emphasizings are what I'd do well to imitate—incorrigible generalizer and soliloquist that I am. *Molto expressivo* can be overdone. I caress the keyboard too much when composing nocturnes.

28 January 1954   A shortish letter from de la Mare who is, I fear, becoming unable to get much done, and has taken to his bed for the present. He says, 'What I *do* want to say, is that I have again been reading and re-reading *Emblems of Experience*, and love the poems more and more. They surrender, as one reads them again, what so often was passed over before. And how magically *your* company, silence, the solitude, and all the Nature comes back.' This, from HIM, should give me confidence in what I am doing. But *E. of E.* wasn't the series of capsuled considerations which *The Tasking* seems to be. All of them, except two, are indoor poems. Not a breath of fresh air filters into them. Not one other human face appears in them. Midnight Mumblings might be taken as their title.

11 February 1954   I have tried to make the *Sequence* a kind of chart of my states of faith & unbelief in spiritual realities. Inconsistencies are, I suppose, the essence of most human strivings for spiritual guidance and assurance. I want to produce a confession of my weakness. Others *might* profit by it—you never know! But one has to admit that some of the wisest writers have been agnostics. The study of life was interest and occupation enough for them. (Yet the most eminent mystics have always been practical in approach to experience and duty to others.) Montaigne disbelieved in the survival of human personality, though a Catholic. But it has been borne in on me lately that this little sequence of poems, which has evolved itself so oddly and so tentatively, has value *for me* through its being an exposure of still embryonic understanding of spiritual problems in relation to 'the facts of life'. These poems are, mostly, almost childishly elementary and uninformed. Many of them could never have been written if I had known and read more about religion and philosophy. I feel that they may, at any rate, have some merit as a 'human document'. They have helped to teach me how little I know and how absurd were my previous presumptions to knowledge—have, indeed,

fortified my mind against the ordeal of growing old and losing hold on life. Each piece I have added to the sequence has been, in a way, a step forward, and something eliminated from the lumber of misapprehensions which I harboured. I said they had taught me; but it has been more like *being taught* by transmitted messages —the process of their composition having been so peculiar in its detachment from the 'ordinary self' which 'didn't know it was going to write anything' and then found that it had produced something unforeseen and unpremeditated. (Revision, of course, is in a different category—the dictionary does most of that.)

The Alliance

'You figure of flesh, abode of appetites,
'Duped by mean motives, frivolous in feeling,
'Go your own gait; enjoy those gross delights.
'I work elsewhere, in search of heaven-sent healing.'

Thus bragged the spirit, positive in pride,
Till from far off a wisening voice replied—
'Of body and soul there can be no division;
'Soul should embrace it, cherish and control.
'Our two great halves must share a single vision.
'Let mutual services unite them whole.'

Then spirit asked forgiveness of the brain;
And all went well. The speaker was Montaigne.

Diary

13 February 1954   I must read Montaigne again—my 1908 vol. edn. got left at Weirleigh, and wasn't returned with my books in 1948. Montaigne is astringent medicine for the mind, and his rich humanity can be helpful—his insistence on the life of the body and the realities of our corporeal condition (from which in my 1952–53 verse I have turned away in my ponderings on the imponderable). 11.30 p.m. One helpful and wholesome lesson

learnt from Montaigne today; I found a fine passage (in de la M.'s *Love* anthology) wherein he asserts the indivisibility of body and soul. I have too often assumed them to be separate agents. Have been too much disposed to regard the body as an ill-conditioned animal which impeded the activity of the spirit (though I haven't committed myself to any such opinions in my verses). But my mental attitude has been that the soul should assume superiority and 'look down' on the poor old flesh. Montaigne wisely insists that they should collaborate, our 'human condition' demanding this marriage of the two essences. I suppose one is liable to resent one's animal nature as one gets old, disliking the body for wearing out. One wants to be rid of disturbing carnality and acquire a liberated mind. But the body is one's life; the soul thrives on bodily health and energy. And only 3 nights ago I wrote some lines in which I inquired what would be left of me if I were to achieve 'survival' after death. This soul of mine has a very earthly air about it—and sometimes seems to be no more than an invented attitude of aspiration to higher things. It is permeated by humanity. Have I ever *met* it?

14 February 1954 A mild cloudy morning with blackbird whisperings foretelling spring. Looking through some poems in the penultimate section of de la M.'s *Love*, I came upon Cory's familiar lines, 'You promise heaven free from strife', and absorbed them like a fresh discovery. They epitomize what I was thinking last night—of the soul's alliance with our human condition—'Show me what angels feel'. . . . Everything one tries to express has been said better by someone else! My way isn't new—partly because I am so resolved to avoid artifice and affectation, attempting an honest 'unfeigned' style of utterance, which restricts me to an unsurprising idiom, a dangerously trite directness. The effect of so much minor poetry is made by a poetizing pose (noticeable in female verse, such as Edna Millay's, which has superficial grace and charm, but leaves one, at times, wishing she could be less literary and more natural. They just fail to convince one of their sincerity of feeling. Instinctively I demand that poetry should seem genuine).

Human Bondage

I know a night of stars within me;
Through eyes of dream I have perceived
Blest apparitions who would win me
Home to what innocence believed.

I know a universe beyond me;
Power that pervades the fluctuant soul,
Signalling my brain it would unbond me
And make heart's imperfection whole.

I, the chance-comer from creation,
Blind subject to defending day;
I, this blithe structure of sensation,
Prisoned and impassioned by my clay.

Diary

15 February 1954   Got out for an hour (pulling ivy off park wall by the lodge). Slept badly last night after working till 12 at some lines (12 as usual) instigated by the Montaigne passage about soul and body. The *Sequence* has now enlarged itself to 358 lines. In spite of my persistent unconfidence about it, I am conscious of it having become a constructed performance in me—as I used to feel about a prose book when it had got well under way. It now has the aspect of a series of considerations and abstracts for a long poem. If I weren't an epitomist, I might be writing it in blank verse. But expansion—even to the scale of G. Herbert's shorter poems, appears impossible. A first line floats into my head, and the ten or twelve lines are all I need for the expression of what I want to say. This, anyhow, saves me from pedestrian flatness and failure of impetus. The fact remains that almost all my most effective poems in the past *were* short ones.

The Contention

Then came a cry, 'No spirit—none—
'Within your deathward being dwells:
'The will of darkness must be done:
'Take this, and make the most of what your timepiece tells.'

I knew, unknowing; I heard, unhearing,
A voice beyond my bodily boding,*
'The faithful found me without fearing:
'Learn this, and look forever toward your soul's unloading.'

Diary

17 February 1954   A drizzly unpleasant day. I remained indolent, unable to do any reading till dinner time, when I perused *Apollo in Picardy*—that strange Paterian masterpiece (which fascinated me so much in my twenties). Since then, while thinking about my *Sequence*, I realize that it has a peculiar personal significance—however it fails or succeeds with others. I see now that it represents an exercise in self-discipline. Repeating them to myself, I find them helpful and stabilizing. I suppose that accounts for their homespun style of expression. One's mind was in a region beyond writing for literary effect. Meaning was what mattered, and the ordinary idiom of one's thoughts served the purpose. Surely this must constitute authenticity of a kind? Heart and head have spoken from their silences and solitudes—spoken in ultimate earnest. When I say that I knew unknowing, I heard unhearing, it is the truth. I *have* experienced that languageless communication of something 'beyond my bodily boding'. And I have subjected the sincerity of every poem to every test I could contrive, in my resolve to avoid issuing counterfeit coinage.

* S.S.'s note: A reference to the 'glimpse' recorded in *A Chord*

The Humbled Heart

🔖 S.S.'s note: This is a Platonic idea, isn't it? 🔖

    Go your seeking, soul.
    Mine the proven path of time's foretelling.
    Yours accordance with some mysteried whole.
    I am but your passion-haunted dwelling.

    Bring what news you can,
    Stranger, loved of body's humbled heart.
    Say one whispered word to mortal man
    From that peace whereof he claims you part.

    Hither-hence, my guest,
    Blood and bone befriend, where you abide
    Till withdrawn to share some timeless quest.
    I am but the brain that dreamed and died.

Diary

4 March 1954   The 12 lines I wrote on 2 March, tidied up last night, is a sort of summing-up of the sequence of self-communings about flesh and spirit. I assume 'my soul' to be a visitant from the spiritual Whole which merely frequents my physical existence. When my body dies, I announce, this guest of mine will be resumed into the whole—not as *my* consciousness. This idea, I suppose, will be condemned as a loose-minded notion. But it is my way of disclaiming any expectation of 'survival', while believing in the reality of spiritual influence on my carnal condition. I see myself as 'primitive man', on whom has been bestowed some tentative conception of spiritual immanence. But he does not even claim that 'the soul' belongs to him. It belongs elsewhere, and he has only received hints and intimations of its workings in his animal nature. A new way of saying, 'I can't call my soul my own,' anyhow! And surely it is true that most people never get beyond feeling that they *might* have a soul, if they gave it a decent chance to inhabit them? And what is *my* soul but the sustaining idea of not being wholly a fleshly being? I would like to believe

that my soul writes my best poems—that it is something separate from the person whose mind is so all too human and unspiritual. The night before last, I had no intention of trying to write anything. I seemed to have nothing in my mind at all. Then the words, 'Go your seeking, soul' came into my head, and I had a mental picture of a phosphorescent figure floating away from me. The rest of it was pencilled down, bit by bit, as though I were recovering something with difficult remembering. I suppose it is only what is called *composition*. But I simply don't know how I do it, and it *is* like something transmitted. Portentous poetizing, perhaps! But an attempt to express something from a higher plane than wondering whether income-tax will ever go back to 5/- in the pound. What worries me is the spectacle which these poems present, of someone turning away from the business of life, as though nothing else mattered except *his* soul. Humanity in general not admitted, is the notice posted on the poet's door. Mr Sassoon is too busy with his spiritual problems to receive visitors or undertake any commentaries on what is happening in the outside world. The Wiltshire minor prophet is composing his ultimate banalities about the back of beyond, his predicament in the universe, and his expectations of there being no such thing as the music of the spheres. And not even doing it with the object of being listened to by an applausive audience. No; he is doing it for his own 'self-realization'. And doing it under some inward compulsion which inhibits him from writing on secular subjects with lively inventiveness and enjoyment, as he would prefer to do. Who *wants* this stuff?

Renewals

S.S.'s note: 'Prophetic? "Be still and know that I am God"— my most often repeated words from Scripture.'

    I said to downcast eyes—
    Look up; accept surprise
    Which waits, all welcomings.
    I said to shuttered ears—
    Heed how earth music nears
    On wonder's wind-swept strings.

Unquesting heart I told
To be made manifold
Through love's resurgent will.
I said to fitful mind—
Put discontents behind;
Be silent and grow still.

Diary

6 March 1954   The spiritual situation behind these epitomizings is the conflict between 'my heart and my soul cry out for the living God' and the formidable array of discouragements which confront my natural awareness of our human condition in what seems to be a worsened world. But this 'array'—what is it? Comparing one's private and localized existence with 'facts' such as the tropical jungle, the swarming and ever increasing population of the planet, the uncivilized and brutal behaviour of the majority of humans, and all the other insoluble problems which Religion is 'up against'. One gains no more from thinking about such things than one would by reading one's poems to a rhinoceros. One cannot particularize about these immensities and inapprehensible happenings from one's armchair (unless one happens to be Shakespeare or Blake). I *did* particularize about the Western Front; but I knew something of it through experience. What I am doing now, in my verses, is to simplify myself away from past experience and be my spiritual self, such as it is—an egocentric effort to be selfless and discover 'central calm subsisting in the heart of endless agitation'. There is nothing left for me (as for all grown old) but to make my peace with life, and try to express the process. It is a private pilgrimage, authentically experienced. *The Tasking* is an accurate title for my volume. Some inward compulsion has made me do it, and has prevented me from attempting pleasanter and less anchoritic themes. An old man asking himself whether he believes in God, and unable to believe much in the spectacle of himself. 'What a pity he can't write some more about fox-hunting,' the Public will say.

A Chord

On stillness came a chord,
While I, the instrument,
Knew long-withheld reward:
Gradual the glory went;
Vibrating, on and on,
Toward harmony unheard,
Till dark where sanctus shone;
Lost, once a living word.

But in me yet abode
The given grace though gone;
The love, the lifted load,
The answered orison.

S.S. to F.C. 9 December 1959

Heart's Journey and *Vigils*—a case of undirected emotional aspiration, which ended in the spiritual desolation that preceded my conversion. *Sequences* first appeared in three privately printed volumes: 1950, 1952, 1954. I have marked the ones to read first, as being significant of my lonely seekings. About the whole of *The Tasking* is a recording of these gropings. Of course there are some things in *Sequences* which I couldn't write now, but some lines in *The Tasking* read strangely prophetic of my release. *A Chord* (the internal imagery of these lines is, striking a rich chord on the piano and then letting it vibrate on and on into silence—a trick of mine which produces a vision of a great dark church with a lit altar) expressed a momentary experience when something seemed to come through, now recognizable as grace, bestowed on the darkened pilgrim:

> 'So through the thunder comes a human voice
> Saying, "O heart I made, a heart beats here!
> Face my hands fashioned, see it in myself!"'

How often have I repeated those lines of Browning!

An Epitome

Just thinking ... Yet it may be that
My thought, which for a moment held
What seemed mind-life's epitome
From infanthood to eld,
Spoke the one word in all my time
To make endured existence known
Even as it is. *Accept your soul.*
Be evermore alone.

S.S. to F.C. 5 August 1960

As you say, *Epitome* is a classic example of getting it wrong. I have often thought of it as the antithesis to what came to me afterwards. But it was my condition when I wrote it, and surely must be for many poor souls who have no faith to sustain them? Just about the saddest poem I ever wrote, but useful to remind me of God's mercy to me thereafter. *Faith Unfaithful* was my last word, in March 1954—and then came those almost three years of what now seems to have been dark night. The worst thing in 1953 was Archie Wavell's death. His religious-mindedness seemed a life line thrown to me—as with Helen Waddell. Richard Seymour, though so holy, was too self-effacing and modest to be of any help. I was a complete ignoramus about religion. It amazes me to look back on it. I never said a prayer. Never consulted any religious book, or *thought* about doctrine. Just went blindly on, clinging to the *idea* of God, unable to believe that salvation applied to *me*, though firmly convinced of the existence of a spiritual world & a heaven above. Again & again in these past years, I have asked myself how I endured it, so unendurable it seems in retrospect. *Was* it some kind of dark night of probation? The instant release in 1957 suggests it. Reading Newman, I wonder what effect it would have made if someone had given it to me 10 years ago. Everything I needed is there, waiting for me! All clear as daylight. And as simple as falling off a log—just unconditional surrender! But I have always been queerly lacking in method in everything I have tried to do—no conscious method in verse-writing—or even in cricket and golf—or teaching myself to play the piano. Just muddling on by instinct. I can see now that I was standing at an immaterial doorway, wearing my knuckles out in vain. And M.M.* just came along and opened the door, through God's mysterious providence. It *had* to happen, didn't it? & happened in my ultimate *need*. All my life I have instinctively reacted against worldliness, only conforming to it with—as dear Robbie Ross once said—'the expression of an offended deer-hound' (observable in the Philpot portrait, which R. commissioned).

So little survives from the world I was active in, and this one bewilders and repels me in its social phenomena. It is better, I suppose, in many ways; but I long for the comparative quiet of the 1920s, when I could positively potter across from Tufton Street to The Reform Club, conversing with the pelicans in the Green Park. And everywhere those vast inhuman boxes being erected to shut out the sky, all part of the mammoth materialism of moneymaking and overcrowding. But we live in an unhomely age and I have always been rather Cranford minded—appropriately, for Knutsford, the original of Cranford, was a market town of my Thornycroft forbears. By the way, I recently found an 1872 letter from my mother to Uncle Hamo in which she divulged that Grandpapa Thornycroft had suggested to the Royal Family that he should do a statue of Queen Victoria on an elephant for India. He thought it would 'inspire the natives with affection' for her. Does that make you smile? Imagine the back view of the statue. What would an elephant by Henry Moore be like? Full of holes, I suppose, and suffering from elephantiasis. Have been stitching up the holes in my hot water bottle cover, just about my form as a public figure. Also a button on my shirt sleeve. A meditative beech leaf bonfire till dusk descended, rooks flying home overhead, & the smoke going straight up.

Faith Unfaithful March 1954

Mute, with signs I speak:
Blind, by groping seek:
Heed; yet nothing hear:
Feel; find no one near.

* Mother Margaret Mary, to whom S.S. was to dedicate *The Path to Peace* in 1960. See Introduction, p. 39 and Part IV, p. 175.

Deaf, eclipsed, and dumb,
Through this gloom I come
On the time-path trod
Toward ungranted God.

Carnal, I can claim
Only His known name.
Dying, can but be
One with Him in me.

S.S. to F.C. 22 February 1963

Clearing out a drawer in the library I found the reviews of *Sequences* I enclose. I destroyed all the others, most of them incredibly tiresome. Even these will show you how little understanding I received from the literary-minded. The *Church Times* was the best. The BBC now asks to interview me 'for their archives'. I shall stoutly refuse to be recorded. And simply *could* not listen to Dame Laurentia being impersonated with G.B.S. But somehow the conjunction of D. Laurentia and G.B.S. has never appealed to me, because *he* never did.

Meanwhile, about the anthology—you have let yourself in for it properly! But if you *were* to wade through my melancholy meanderings of 1953-54, you would realize more than ever before, the marvellous transformation since January '57. That lonely self-communer & self-deflater ceased to exist then, as by a magician's wand. Ploughing through the pages myself, I seemed to be re-experiencing a kind of purgatory. But '53 & '54 were special years of frustration & discouragement & solitude, and '55 & '56 were little better—lacking even the solace of versifying, and culminating in the ghastly reviews of *Sequences*. I have marked some passages which have significance, but they may add little to what I put in the poems. What amazes me is that I could have become so different. Could that poor man, who wrote his epitaph in *Faith Unfaithful*, have fore-read *Deliverance* and its successors! Anyhow there it all is, and no need to worry about what I was like in 1953. Everything has come right, and perhaps it did me good to endure all those desolations and discomforts. *Then*, all molehills were mountains. Now they are only wormcasts. Most of the bits I've marked are from January 1954 onwards. *Why* did I put all those weary words on paper? Because I had nowhere to turn for escape. I can only hope that in reading the rest of it, if you *can*, you will get some good laughs at the poor old pilgrim's perplexities and complaints. Every night I say, let me never forget what I was before my deliverance through Mercy. *Faith Unfaithful* has become faith unbelievable, immanent at all times, proportioning everything I experience.

PART IV

1957–1967

18 November 1955 unpublished
Last thing at night, in solitude serene,
I am unpossessed of all that I have been.
It is as though I were about to go
Some journeying far beyond what now I know:
It is as though the microcosm of Me
By mercy were made free—
Of troubling past uncluttered and washed clean.
MS. Sequences

❧ The last decade of S.S.'s life was a period of deep peace, the harvest of a quiet mind and fruit of spiritual victory. Borrowing the phrase from his friend Frances Cornford's epigram on Rupert Brooke, he spoke frequently of 'the long littleness of life', but did so with appreciation rather than complaint. Yet all the time, his childhood's longing to see beyond the visible world kept breaking through, and with eyes alight, voice full of enthusiasm, he would exclaim: 'I can hardly wait to die!' ❧

Deliverance 19 April 1957

No comfort came until I looked for light
Beyond the darkened thickets of my brain.
With nothingness I strove. And inward sight
No omen but oblivion could obtain.

He spoke. He held my spirit in His hand.
Through prayer my password from the gloom was given.
This Eastertide, absolved, in strength I stand.
Feet firm upon the ground. My heart in heaven.

26 October 1959   Heytesbury House, Warminster, Wiltshire.
Dear Dame Felicitas,

Sydney has sent me your letter, which is a comfort like everything from O.S.B.* for Downside has been so much to me since I was received there on August 14, 1957. I know Fr Hubert van Zeller well, & love him. . . .

†You say that you would like to have a photograph of me as

* Order of St Benedict and, by inference, all Benedictine monks and nuns
† Sir Sydney Cockerell had sent F.C. his copy of *Siegfried's Journey* to read. She returned it to him with a letter discussing the style and contents of the book in some detail, and asking if Sir Sydney possessed a more recent photograph than that reproduced in *The Best of Friends*. S.C.C. forwarded this letter to Siegfried Sassoon.

I am now, so I send one, taken by my son—resting in Mother Church, as it were!

I have the lovely little Stanbrook carols, and the Little Breviary has sustained me for the past 18 months, an immense help, as my Latin is very inadequate. And of course, I read *In a Great Tradition* which Sydney gave me. Dom Aelred Watkin has spoken lovingly to me of Dame Laurentia. I have not seen Sydney for a long time as I never go to London now, except passing through. The way he holds on to this life is quite astonishing, isn't it? I bless you for your help to him.

Yours in Christ,
S.S. (monogram)

Siegfried's Journey

I had known Cockerell since August 1915, when I was at Cambridge for a month's course with the Officers' Training Corps. Introduced by a letter from Mr Gosse, I had spent several evenings at his house—evenings made memorable by the wonderful books he showed me—and from which I returned to my camp bed in Pembroke College in a trance of stimulation after having handled original manuscripts of D. G. Rossetti, William Morris, and Francis Thompson. From the first he had taken a strong and kindly interest in me. On those Sunday nights in the quiet candle-lit room he seemed a sort of bearded and spectacled magician, conjuring up the medieval illuminated missals and psalters on which he was a famous expert, and bringing my mind into almost living contact with the Pre-Raphaelites whom I had worshipped since my dreaming adolescence. Brusque and uncompromising, his light blue eyes regarded me somewhat austerely as he handed me yet another of his treasures to gloat over. People were sometimes offended by his plain-spoken manner; but to be contradicted by Cockerell was an education. He shared my veneration for Hardy. He was indeed a man who had been born to become, through his practical abilities, the trusted adviser of great writers. But he will be better remembered for his directorship of the Fitzwilliam Museum, which he re-created, amplified, and enriched through thirty years of selfless service.

S.S. to F.C. 30 October 1959

Your letter has quite 'made my day'—so much in it to nourish me and make me want to talk to you. Poor old Sydney and his obdurate humanism. I have often wondered how much thought he has ever devoted to the problem of belief. All that preoccupation and expertness about Missals and Books of Hours and Bibles, and the whole thing for him merely Art & Craft & Medievalism! Yet he wrote to me two years ago, that he feels more comfortable with Catholics than almost anyone else. I had assumed that he accepted death as merciful oblivion, so did not dread it. These active, life-serving extroverts *are* a problem, aren't they? *Rationally*, they have 'got it on us' every time. Several of my best friends are like that, and I feel that it is hopeless to attempt any explanation of the gift of faith and the result of perseverance in prayer. Often I have thought 'What *has* Sydney got to sustain him in his aged inactivity?' To light a candle in his inward darkness—don't I know what *that* means!

Three years ago I was in a complete black-out: impossible to realize or comprehend now. In January '57, the Mother Superior at the Assumption Convent in Kensington Square wrote to me, after reading my volume *Sequences*, in which my spiritual predicament was apparent, & somehow I was helped to realize that deliverance had arrived. She has been the greatest benefactor of my life, and has never made a glimmer of a mistake in her guidance & influence. She is now Superior at Hengrave Hall, the School near Bury St Edmunds. All that followed was as though arranged by Our Lady. Everything fitted together. My dear friend Ronnie Knox was chaplain to her school at Aldenham during the war, as you will see in the Biography. I tell you all this because it is by far 'the most important' thing that has ever happened to me, & has completely transformed my life, & made my old age blest & endurable. 'How came it?—ask your angel—ask that vigilant voice.' (Mine talks to me quite a lot—one of my childish indulgences!) I will send you *Sequences* if you haven't seen it. No news of Fr Hubert. I must write to dear Fr Aelred or Fr Martin Salmon, who bowls to me in the nets in the summer.

Stanbrook has now joined Downside in my midnight prayers—
all Doms and Dames who have been kind to me.

S.S. to F.C. 16 January 1960

Another week got through, kept in by the weather and my congested tubes; and snowed up lately—3 men shovelling snow off the roof. In this weather much of the house is impossible to warm—you can see from the photograph what a problem it is. It was built about 1700, a red brick manor house, with garrets and a clock tower, and stone-faced and squared up in 1780; but there was a Tudor house before that, and there is a mediaeval dove-house & barn. Queen Matilda owned the manor & may have resided here—she built a chapel two miles away on the site of a pre-Norman one.* 800 years—a blink of the eye in time—will anyone think of a remembered poet in 2760? There is a huge British camp about two miles away—Scratchbury—still occupied, I suppose, when the Romans arrived, as a stronghold. The deep fosse is nearly a mile round.

Neighbours

    I pictured someone sharpening at a flint
    Near where I live, antiquities ago:
    Of me he held no neolithic hint;
    And what tomorrow meant he could not know.

    Conjecturing creatures comparable in change,
    From him to me, futurities ahead,
    I thought how prehistorically strange
    I should become, distanced among the dead.

Anyhow I am not distanced in mind from Callow End, callow Catholic though I be.

---

  * cf. *A Remembered Queen* (*Collected Poems*, p. 238)
        Like moonlight on the low mist in the park
        Is that remembered fierce twelfth-century Queen
        Who lived here once, men say.

S.S. to F.C. 21 January 1960

The sound of psalmody at Downside is echoing on in my head, as there was a wireless talk *The day of a novice* just now, which ended with a minute of recorded chanting—very consoling to the hibernating exile—it bore me back to those many Vespers I've heard on summer days, with the evening sun coming in at the west doorway, and me in my usual place by St Lawrence' Chapel, below the big crucifix on the column. Nowhere have I known more happy peace than in that glorious church. In June and July '57, I went there every Wednesday to converse with Fr Sebastian —indirect instruction—he wisely asked me no questions and just let it happen through self-expression on both sides. It seems extraordinary now, the sense of rejuvenation I experienced so intensely that summer. I had been telling myself in previous years that I had ceased to be capable of strong emotional aliveness, and supposed that that was why my poetry had dried up. And then, for most of that year, came the greatest emotional ferment of my life, in love with the supernatural, so to speak—a kind of spiritual childhood and adolescence—and have been slowly growing up ever since. I like to think that such a transformation, at nearly 71, is evidence of the agelessness of the human spirit—anyhow, the *mind* doesn't grow old, while the brain remains in sound condition. I was much inflated in my ineradicable ego by Dom Gerard Sitwell's appreciation of *Redemption*, which is one of my favourites. (I have his edition of *The Scale of Perfection*, which I love.) As you say, all the best of me is in my poetry; and that vocation has been my only directive path in my pilgrimage of learning by mistakes, the only aim I could feel sure of, until submission set me free to strive toward selfless adoration of—I leave the rest to you. I was received by Fr Francis Little with Prior Dunstan Pontifex assisting—in the Lady Chapel, Eve of the feast of the Assumption. *Received* is an understatement—my inward experience during the next few days seemed something unfathomable by the mind, & I just allowed it to happen, knowing & yet unknowing—it completely convinced me of the working of the Holy Spirit.

I wrote *Lenten Illuminations* in three days, quite easily &

unexpectedly, after having written only two short pieces in the previous four years—and have been wondering ever since how I did it (and how I had the courage to allow the Abbey to publish anything so intimate). *L.I.* epitomized the seven months of 'all things made new' before I was received.

Lenten Illuminations

I

Not properly Catholic, some might say, to like it best
When no one's in the cool white church that few frequent
These sober-skied vocational afternoons in Lent.
There's sanctity in stillness, let it be confessed,
For one addicted much to meditationment—
One who has found this church a place full of replies
Given to what, wordless in him, asked that heart be learned
A Kempis lessons; toward the invisible, new eyes
In more than meditational consciousness be turned.

This afternoon it seemed unconvert self came in,
Puzzled to perceive one at the altar rails, unminding;
Could this be he—hereafter offered him to win,
And faith revealed wheretoward he pilgrim'd without
    finding?

O unforeknowing Ego, visitant in thought,
How were you thus the captive of that banished being?
Was it ordained—the long-delayed deliverance brought—
The mercy that made plain your path? . . . O unforeseeing
Sad self, let's be together, now fortunate in freeing.

II

What were you up to—going into churches all those years
Of faith unfaithful? . . . Kneeling respectfully when others
    knelt,
But never a moment while reflective there alone.
The aids were manifest; but only for your eyes and ears,

In anthems, organ music, shaft-aspiring stone,
And jewelled windows into which your mind might melt.
The sanctuary unseen was there; but not for you; not by the
    empty altar shown;
Not in the Crucifix. (Though each Good Friday you had felt
Almost unbearable the idea of how He died.)
From your default His face seemed ever turned aside.
Not then for you the arisen Word—not then the wrought
    remedial gift of tears.

How came it (ask your Angel—ask that vigilant voice)
That you this comfort found—that thus it grew to be—
This close, child-minded calm? . . . Look; those five candles
    lit
For five who have prayed your peace. (Candles were ever
    your choice
To tranquillize the mind, since boyhood.) They are what
    they are.
Two pennies for each. But Candlemas tells purity.
And we are told their innocent radiance will remit
Our errors. Although the lights of everlastingness, as someone
    said,
Can seem, for us poor souls, to dream so faint and far,
When at our broken orisons we kneel, unblest, unbenefited.

While you were in your purgatorial time, you used to say
That though Creation's God remained so lost, such aeons
    away,
Somehow He would reveal Himself to you—some day!
For Him, the Living God, your soul and flesh could only cry
    aloud.
In watches of the night, when world event with devildom
    went dark,
You implored illumination. But never being bowed
Obedient—never conceived an aureoled instance, an assuring
    spark.

Outcast and unprotected contours of the soul,
Why in those hallowed minsters could they find no home,*
When nothing appeared more unpredictable than this—your whole
Influence, relief, resultancy received from Rome?
Look. Robed in white and blue, earth's best loved Lady stands;
Mother Immaculate; Name that shines to intercede.
Born on her birthday feast, until last year your hands
Kindled no candle, paid her heavenliness no heed.
Is it not well, that now you call yourself her child—
You and this rosary, at which—twelve months ago, you might have shrugged and smiled?

This day twelve months ago—it was Ash Wednesday—one
Mid-day between us two toward urgent hope fulfilled
Strove with submission. Arduous—forbidding—then to meet
Inflexible Authority. While the work was willed,
The riven response from others to the task undone
Daunted a mind confused with ferment, incomplete:
There seemed so much renunciant consequence involved,
When independent questioning self should yield, indubitant and absolved.

III

This, then, brought our new making. Much emotional stress—
Call it conversion; but the word can't cover such good.
It was like being in love with ambient blessedness—
In love with life transformed—life breathed afresh, though yet half understood.
There had been many byways for the frustrate brain,
All leading to illusions lost and shrines forsaken . . .
One road before us now—one guidance for our gain—
One morning light—whatever the world's weather—wherein wide-eyed to waken.

* The original line runs: 'Why, in those Anglican churches could they find no home.' F.C. raised several objections to it. S.S. agreed with her and amended the line as above in the printed edition published by Faber.

IV

This is the time of year when, even for the old,
Youngness comes knocking on the heart with undefined
Aches and announcements—blurred felicities foretold,
And (obvious utterance) wearying winter left behind.

I never felt it more than now, when out beyond these
    safening walls
Sculptured with Stations of the Cross, spring-confident,
    unburdened, bold,
The first March blackbird overheard to forward vision flutes
    and calls.

You could have said this simple thing, old self, in any
    previous year.
But not to that one ritual flame—to that all-answering Heart
    abidant here.

S.S. to F.C. 29 March 1960

'Outcast and unprotected contours of the soul' is not *me*, but beloved *Belloc*. It must have been almost exactly three years ago, when I was in the vortex of struggling toward submission, that I came upon the following passage in Speaight's biography,* from a letter to K. Asquith: 'The Faith, the Catholic Church, is discovered, is recognized, triumphantly enters reality like a landfall at sea which first was thought a cloud. The nearer it is seen, the more it is real, the less imaginary: the more direct and external its voice, the more indubitable its representative character, its "persona", its voice. The metaphor is not that men fall in love with it: the metaphor is that they discover home. "This was what I sought. This was my need." It is the very mould of the mind, the matrix to which corresponds in every outline the outcast & unprotected contour of the soul. It is Verlaine's "Oh! Rome—oh! Mère!" And that not only to those who had it in childhood and

* Robert Speaight: *The Life of Hilaire Belloc* (London Hollis & Carter, 1957, p. 377).

have returned, but much more—and what a proof!—to those who come upon it from over the hills of life and say to themselves, "Here is the town."'

All that afternoon my mind had been pervaded by a sort of ghostly climatic disturbance—cloud conflictings and murmurous intimations of spiritual debate (if you know what I mean!—*I* do) as I sat here where I do now (it was a day of wild weather). Belloc's magnificent words settled it, once and for all. 'That's done it,' I said. My whole being was liberated. O that he could have known it, foreknown it when he came here twenty-five years ago. But I have been able to tell his daughter, Eleanor, and his grandson Dom Philip about it, which is something. So you see that the words have great significance. *Lenten Illuminations* is full of cardinal allusions, signal experiencings—every word is from the context of my living self.

You have put your unfailing finger on the one thing in *L.I.* which I'd felt uncomfortable about. The strictest autobiographical exactitude would have said, 'King's College Chapel,' since it was the only church in which I tried to say a prayer (in 1953-56). I remember kneeling alone in the choir stalls & saying one for George's career at King's; and feeling that the words went nowhere and came from nothing. 'Anglican churches' is, anyhow, too much of a particularization. My condition was that I had turned away from all churches, and from Our Lord (epitomized in *Faith Unfaithful*). One thing I can remember clearly—when staying at Rapallo I sometimes climbed the steep path behind Max's house to a hill-top church, and also went to a lovely little old one —S. Pantaleone—on the headland along the Spezzia road—and both produced a wistful awareness of devotion which I longed to share. I *knew* that they were different to Heytesbury church (in which I have never attended a service!). I have often asked my poor old self how much I would have been prepared to *give up* by becoming a Catholic. And the answer was always the same. Everything asked of me. How could it be otherwise (especially as I have got what I've always called 'my self-sacrificing complex'!). But at my age, giving up things worldly is no hardship. For years past I've felt like walking out on it all. I am, of course, not qualified to comment on the spiritual dangers of being addicted to the arts

& enraptured by the sublime & beautiful. But surely the arts, at their highest level, *have* been expressive of God in us. As to renunciation of the world, we have to decide *what* to reject, I suppose. One of my few maxims used to be, 'I believe in life, and will do my little best to prove it!' (by my poetry, I meant, & by refusing to become discouraged by 'the dirty devices of the world').

Ronald's *Pastoral Sermons* arrived yesterday—an enormous gain —all new except the dear *Window in the Wall*, and that has eleven added on.* My tubes have relented, and for the past two weeks my breathing has been almost normal, thank heaven. And I've been out of an afternoon, clearing encroaching ground ivy on the edge of the lawn, where crocuses have been abundant under the lime tree, & masses of primroses coming out now, & wild violets too, and lots of daffs everywhere, and also blue anemones. I wrote to the girls at the Notre Dame school, and received a rapturous reply from one of them. The F-h.M. was set for G.C.E. in 1954, & my son had to answer a question, 'What sort of man was George Sherston?' He replied—'As he happens to be my father I prefer to reserve my opinion'.

About your project of printing some lyrical poems, there would be no hindrance from the publisher. (Fabers publish my *Collected Poems*.) But I am sending you the only two I wrote last winter, and should, I admit, very much like *Rogation* to appear under the imprint of Stanbrook. It has been praised by Fr D'Arcy and other good judges. Eleanor Farjeon wrote that 'it is pure St Augustine'. I wish I could advise you about your selection. Such a book should be a designed sequence, shouldn't it?—possibly chronological. You ask for my 'terms'. There *are* none. How could I possibly take payment from you? My payment is the joy of being Stanbrook's poet. I am doubtful about including prose passages; but there might be things which would fit in. Of course there can be no question of copyright restrictions. In 1958 the boys at

* Ronald Arbuthnott Knox 1888-1957. The reference is to *The Pastoral Sermons* of Ronald A. Knox; edited, with an Introduction, by Philip Caraman, S. J. London, Burns Oates, 1960. This comprehensive volume incorporated an earlier series of twenty sermons on the Holy Eucharist, published under the same imprint in 1956 with the title, *The Window in the Wall*.

Marlborough printed a handsome 80 page selection—150 copies —which was heavily oversubscribed for.

I want to hear your final opinions of the Ronald Life. I have read a little at a time, as I do with anything that means much for me. Isn't the Invocation at the end wonderfully fine? He lent it to me in the typescript, and I made a copy of it—it was the beginning of the immeasurable instruction I have gained from his religious writings. He was the first—he and Katharine Asquith—to whom I told my decision. I have never ceased to be thankful that he had the happiness of knowing about it 'in time', and it did give him real happiness. Alas, that he went away before I could show him my true testament, *Lenten Illuminations*. I think its naturalness would have pleased him.

Sight Sufficient 15 December 1957

God, on the gloom divine wheretoward I pray,
You send no sign, no doubt-redeeming ray;
Nor manifest, for this unwisdom'd one,
The faith that blest his pilgrim path begun.

O purpose of my prayer, breath of my being,
Your inward light I share through sightless seeing;
Your love can but be told beyond blind thought
That knows your peace enfold believement brought.

S.S. to F.C. 14 April 1960

I have just made a copy of the first MS. of *Sight Sufficient* (to help unclamp) as it is a good example of how a poem clarifies itself from the first draft. (The pencilled scribble survived by chance.) It was wonderful the way it came right next morning—just hadn't got through when I was tired late at night. *Rogation* I wrote down without altering a word. What you say is just what I needed to be told. I needed to be reminded that subjective 'lights' are no proof at all of the reality of God's work in us. *Sight Sufficient* testified this, didn't it? The wonder is that one dares to say anything, when contemplating that infinite silence & stillness from one's human near-nothingness. Pray that I be advanced in selflessness. And objectivity—not easy for an almost entirely subjective writer and, I fear, character. And the old self is still there—that self which wanted to be used by God but failed to believe in its immortal destiny. The Faith broke that barrier down, in a ferment of emotion; but the hunger for proof of the presence is still there, and sometimes makes me feel that I can 'hardly wait to be dead', and really *know*.

I am specially grateful for your commentary on the Ronald biography. Evelyn Waugh is not a friend of mine—I last saw him in 1933. But E.W. does make it clear in the Introduction that he is only offering an *exterior* portrait. As you say, the man and mind and spirit so deeply precious to us are diminished to a character. I dare to say 'us' because he has spoken to me with a living voice, through his writings, as no one else has done. And how you will chuckle when I tell you that I once said to someone after an enchanting afternoon at Mells in 1955, 'I adore Ronnie; but somehow he seems, for me, to be behind a plate-glass window. I wouldn't dare to speak of *religion* to him!' (Of course it was I who was behind the plate-glass.) Unawareness again—and what a collossal (never *can* spell colossal—or parallel) ineptitude and 'satire of circumstance'—for he has been near to me every day for $2\frac{3}{4}$ years—a life line toward illumination in my crepuscular contemplations. And I am only one among thousands. We are told about his virtues and his idiosyncrasies—but where is his creative sanctity revealed in E.W.'s pages? Yet most people I have spoken to about it seem satisfied, owing to its being so readably written, I suppose. In a way he was a dual personality—the early incredibly brilliant and accomplished R. was always there, intermingled with the near-saint and incomparable expositor of alive religion. But in all that he was, he *gave* with both hands—spiritual help, scholarship, entertainment. The last time I was with him (5 July) he talked to me and Edmund Blunden for $3\frac{1}{2}$ hours with full enjoyment of seeing us—and almost made me forget how heartbreaking it was, that farewell.

A query from you—wherefore the epithet 'immaculate' applied to Patmore?* Heaven knows! I would certainly think 3 times now

* cf. *Siegfried's Journey* '(Freeman) began the after-dinner talk rather disappointingly for me by pinning the conversation to Coventry Patmore's

before using the word. I think I must have meant the *purity* of his versecraft and thought in the Odes, at their best; pellucid, perhaps, should have been the word. In 1918 I did not know *The Unknown Eros*, but have since much admired it—I think he is very much underestimated. By the way, I possess a copy of the rare privately printed edition of the first ones, most of which he destroyed. And before 1914 I used to play cricket at Heron's Ghyll, and once stayed there—with James Hope (Lord Rankeillour) —nephew of the old Duke of Norfolk, quite unaware that Patmore had lived there, & even less aware that I should some day be one with the Catholics—some from the Oratory at Birmingham—who played in Hope's XI. O the unawareness of worldly existence—one journeys *blinkered!* Yet mine now seems strangely coherent, almost as though arranged—and 3 years ago culmination came, release.

Yesterday evening I had a wireless treat—the Brahms B flat piano concerto—my favourite piano concerto, because the slow movement has such heavenly passages (it didn't quite leave the earth last night—only adequate playing). Some music *is* celestial, isn't it? Schubert did it, and Mozart, at the end (that D Minor Quintet) & bits of late Beethoven Quartets & Bach of course—by celestial I mean transporting, heart-stirring yet serene, as though the composer were overhearing & anticipating something angelic —it all has the same quality of finality, height, depth, breadth, and fulfilment.

Rogation 1959

Wisdom, remote from reason, mysteried Word
Shrined for reverberant precincts of the soul,
Above blind-led belief be held and heard,
Need of the nescient, radiate and enrol.

Indwelt redemption, doubted and denied,
Concord no sanctity could comprehend,
Mercy immeasurable and multiplied,

prosodial experiments. I have always found prosody a perplexing and unassimilable subject, and my appreciation of the immaculate author of *The Unknown Eros* was as yet insufficient.'

World watcher, armed and influent to befriend.
Hope of humility, resistless Rood,
Beyond our bodements bring beatitude.

S.S. to F.C. 14 November 1959
It means so much to me, to be in touch with Stanbrook, and the St Augustine page made me 'breathless' in an unbronchial way, by its beauty—such words, such exquisite printing, & such a superb gold capital! If my poems were in that type I should indeed be a proud poet.

About *Rogation*—it is, of course, packed with 'meanings'—some of them unperceived by me while I wrote it. Try to put it into prose! I told a friend that it is my idea of tabloid theology. But I *did* intend 'enrol' to signify souls finding the Faith (or finding *any* faith in the Word). The two final lines do not refer to the previous ones, but are the cry of the world-encompassed soul to 'where beyond these voices there is peace'—meant to evoke a picture of the imploring worshipper; 'resistless' has a double meaning—irresistible in power, and unresisting in merciful humility. Your dear nun said it is worth six treatises on prayer. I can only say that I know for certain that those ten lines, so spontaneous and unexpected, were the outcome of hundreds of hours of prayer.

S.S. to F.C. 28 January 1960
Your selection is excellent in perception, but I think I have improved the arrangement; and I hope you will approve of the three I've added. No need to ask Faber's permission. *Rogation, Deliverance,* & *Grace in me* are unpublished. The copyright of *Sight Sufficient* is mine. What to call the book is a problem. *The Path to Peace?* No introduction needed, I feel. I think *dating* the poems would add interest to the sequence for the perceptive reader. After copying out the tree lines I thought, with a sigh, how seldom the last line has come true for poor me. Too potent a metaphor for most of us, I suppose—too suggestive of that deceptive intruder, emotion. (Grace is bestowed stillness, isn't it?) But when writing such things I want to make them express the experience of those who cannot say it in poetry. The poet is an instrument being played on—it *happens* to him—in my case, has

often seemed to come from no preliminary process—and then one is just a dumb, dull creature for months on end. I pray for you all every night, and think of you as R.A.K. wrote—the interior peace of the enclosed Orders is the breath of the Church's life. Power-stations of prayer which make the materialism of principalities and worldly shows a fabric of unsubstantial unreality. I intend to visit Stanbrook in the summer.

Arbor Vitae 1959
For grace in me divined
This metaphor I find:
   A tree.
How can that be?

This tree all winter through
Found no green work to do—
   No life
Therein ran rife.

But with an awoken year
What surge of sap is here—
   What flood
In branch and bud.

So grace in me can hide—
Be darkened and denied—
   Then once again
Vesture my every vein.

S.S. to F.C. 14 March 1960
I had been aching to write to you; but thought 'I didn't ought to' in Lent. And now such a blessed surprise—your letter—after Fr Renehan had been to bring me sight sufficient. (My chest is much better lately, thanks to drier weather, I suppose.) I am sending a poem—the first since *Rogation*. One evening I felt a strong compulsion to produce something. But my mind only churned about, & nothing came through. The next afternoon I went out, in a

perishing cold wind, and picked the first—discouraged—daffodils (for my Communion table). That evening I felt the same poem impulse, frustrated at first; and then noticed how the buds were responding to the comfort of the room—and *there* was the idea for a poem, which popped out quite easily. I forthwith typed it out to send it to *The Tablet*—where you will see it this week, I suppose. I am pleased with the technique of it. You will notice how the shape of the words fits the meaning—the tight, staccato words in the first 3 lines, & then the softer sounds—and how the stanzas fit together—tight—life-locked—blest—befriended—and so on. Should we not put it in your sequence? It could come after *A Chord*. Along with your letter yesterday, arrived an envelope containing 13 letters from girls at Notre Dame Convent School at Liverpool. The F-h.M. is a 'set book' for the General Certificate of Education this year. They all congratulate me on winning the Cup, as though it had just happened (forty-nine years ago on 22 April!).

Unfoldment 1960

Tight buds of daffodil
Plucked where the wind blew chill
   In Lent begun,
Blessed by this well-warmed room
Unsheathe themselves, for whom
   The lamp's their sun.

So, when to prayer I turn
And my dark being discern
   Life-locked from Thee,
Unfold it as a flower,
That I may know Thy power
   Befriending me.

S.S. to F.C. 12 June 1960

Trinity Sunday: One of those peculiar experiences last night, when I sat up in bed for three hours, which seemed very much less, feeling compelled to attempt a poem, but until the 3rd hour quite unable to know what to say. What I muddled out then in

8 lines came through quite clear in 6 this morning. And appears to be fairly all right—theologically anyhow! And is recognizably my voice. 'Resolvèd requiem' might be queried, as an expression. But it *is* a reference to St Augustine's 'Until we rest in Him'. Tomorrow I will post your copy of *The Old Century*. You asserted that I am only coming to see Stanbrook. That is not so. I am coming to be with my friends—and it won't matter what we say. And I *am* aware that 'weaving shrouds and gathering lilies' isn't your main occupation. I have sometimes wondered how strenuous community life can be sustained without nervous and bodily breakdowns. That it can be is, I assume, the answer to anthropologists who say that religion is 'only an illusion'. What a tremor of anticipation I shall be in on the 25th. But shall arrive untired, thanks to good Brian. A story to make you laugh. A brewer came to Fr Gilbey for instruction. A.G. Any difficulties? B. None at all. A.G. How about the Trinity? B. *Plain as a pikestaff!*

A Prayer at Pentecost 1960

Master musician, Life, I have overheard you,
Labouring in litanies of heart to word you.
Be noteless now. Our duologue is done.

Spirit, who speak'st by silences, remake me;
To light of unresistant faith, awake me,
That with resolvèd requiem I be one.

S.S. to F.C. 22 June 1960

Brian hopes to be here by 10.45, and is a nippy driver in his little Austin Seven—but we may not arrive before 1.15, if then—it depends on how quickly we get through Cheltenham & Tewkesbury. There should be an hour of talk before Vespers (which will give me a chance to *rest* in uplifted taciturnity). I will try not to feel nearly 74. Am off to the Abbey this afternoon for some cricket anyhow!

Of course you can have *A Prayer at Pentecost* for the book. It seems to fit in perfectly as the final word to the 'litanies of heart', doesn't it? As usual, it emerged through a kind of instinctive process. The words, 'Master musician, Life' came into my head, and the rest came out almost mindlessly. 'Speak by silences' comes, of course, from the Carthusian's meditations, which I have read and re-read in the past year. I think it is one of my best 'condensations' —there really is a lot there, if you tried to put it into prose. It is just as if it had been given us to round off the sequence—and it somehow balances with *The Power and the Glory* (1925-60!) which now seems to me an effusion of complete ignorance of the real approach to God. I certainly wouldn't claim to 'hold invisible vastness' in my thought's hands now! But the search for God seems likely to reduce one to permanent speechlessness—'be still and see'. What should I amount to without those poems? What I *am* will vanish like a dream. But they will remain and be of some service to the living. What you say about their effect on you when read aloud—I suppose it is because they are real and direct and truly experienced. I have very seldom, if ever, produced the magic of words in verse (which seems to me some sort of spontaneous accident, or 'stroke of genius'). I think I score through absence of literary artifice, being an unprofessional writer. But poetry is a mystery.

Sydney C. Cockerell to F.C. 24 June 1960
Postcard reproduction of the Battersea Power Station designed by Sir Giles Gilbert Scott, showing its enormous smoking twin-chimneys. From the Worcester and Kew Advertiser:

'These chimneys are known to Londoners as Siegfried and Sydney. I can't think why. It is rumoured that Siegfried is about to be enlarged, and Sydney diminished or even demolished, owing to a transfer of power. It has long been suspected that Sydney, built quite 20 years before Siegfried, was out of date and no longer any good. The Government has appointed a group of lady engineers, known as the Stanbrooks, to investigate the matter. Their report is nearly ready and may fill the newspapers as early as next week—if they can find nothing more interesting to write about.'

F.C. to Sydney C. Cockerell Siegfried Sassoon's first visit to Stanbrook, 25 June 1960
About 1.30 the portress announced the arrival of 'Mr Sassoon and

Mr Butler'. Lady Abbess and I went immediately to Parlour I where you first met Dame Laurentia in 1907. We opened the sash of the grille-shutters to discover a tall, spare figure with the emaciated face of an El Greco saint and the pent-up energy of a hydrogen bomb, accompanied by a cherubic youth in his early twenties, rosy-cheeked and placid—a nice foil. I had half-expected to find S.S. looking very Byronic in an open-necked shirt as he appears in all the photographs I have seen save those in uniform. I was wrong. He was dressed in three shades of blue: that of his suit seemed so vivid as to be alive, yet it was soft as well; the cloudy deep-grey blue of his tie harmonized with the pale blue of his shirt, and threw into relief his eyes and abundant silver hair. But oh! was he nervous? Archie Wavell's letter to you in *The Best of Friends* had prepared me for the rapid, jerky, unfinished sentences which apparently characterize first meetings with S.S. Nevertheless, it was slightly nightmarish when, in an access of shyness and bewilderment, he confused the Abbess with ME, and nothing we did or said seemed to unravel the tangle. At the end of some minutes I began to doubt whether I was standing on my own legs, for Lady Abbess and I were knotted in some inextricable *pas de deux*. We simply could not free ourselves. Relief came with the arrival of an Extern Sister, who led the two guests to the dining room. How Lady Abbess laughed in the cloister as she said: 'Next time, you go alone!'

Go alone I did at 2.30 when they returned. In the twenty minutes before Vespers we mainly discussed the programme of poetry and prose which S.S. agreed to read to the assembled community after Vespers. It consisted of his satirical *Breach of Decorum* (at my request), *Sheldonian Soliloquy*, two prose passages from *The Old Century* (namely, his confession to Ellen Batty of having told a fib about Mrs Mitchell; and the three Sassoons' welcome to Aunt Lula at the Edingthorpe crossroads), and finally some of his recent religious poems. Much of his reading went unheard by the majority of his listeners. His speech was indistinct and slurred, he dropped his voice completely at the end of sentences, and although I ventured a protest twice, it had little effect. Yet one and all were enthusiastic. I think Dame Mary summed up the general feeling when she said that simply meeting him and watching the poet read his own poems was a memorable experience. He did it with such beautiful simplicity. Among the poems with which he concluded were *The Merciful Knight*, *A Flower has opened in my heart*, *Sight Sufficient*, the last section of *Lenten Illuminations*, and *A Prayer at Pentecost*, written only three weeks ago, and spoken with unforgettable feeling, head raised, eyes gazing into eternity. He seemed to gather his listeners up with himself, to associate them with his own burning desire to express the inexpressible, to leave behind the complex shadows cast by earthly existence and enter into the simple and direct truth of God.

There followed a few minutes of informal chatting and introductions, but by now it was close on 5 o'clock, and the tea which had been brought in at 4.30 must have been cold. All the audience retired, but the open parlour door revealed Dame Hildelith patiently waiting with a large wad of printing samples, anxious to discuss the lay-out of the proposed *Path to Peace*. However, before she came in at 5.30 we did manage to exchange a few ideas. S.S.'s shyness gradually fell away. He used his over-illustrative hands freely, raised them to heaven in frenzies of despair, dropped them to his sides weighted with woe, twirled them in a merry roly-poly, while the thin voice gathered strength, and he forgot the heat and his bronchial tubes, and concentrated only on the experience and gift of the moment. S.S. couldn't get over J.N.'s television talk. 'He sat there with his fat face beneath his Harrow black and white boater, telling the whole world, Lord, telling every one how frightened he felt—on television . . . telling everybody . . .' he moaned feebly. He informs me that Ian Davie is thirty-five, and the son of a doctor.

After half an hour's talk, Dame Hildelith joined us, and almost an hour passed in printing discussion. S.S. became the taut, critical connoisseur. No sooner had she passed a specimen of paper and printing through the grille to him than the strong, nervous, sensitive hands were testing texture, noting the watermark, colour, surface—and usually dismissing the sample with some short, devastating remark! He was always right too. He brought with him and would give it to us, but we refused to allow it, an exquisite little volume of his poems, twenty-two in number, engraved on copper by Charles Sigrist in 1934, the frontispiece being the work of Stephen Gooden. At one point, he exclaimed: 'You must get Sydney to let you see the Cardinal Bembo script. What has he done with it? It's one of the loveliest things in the world. I know it well, for I had his books in my house during the war. Has he gone and sold it?' There were moments even in the middle of printing, when he came back to poetry, quoting *Antony and Cleopatra* with something akin to ecstasy as he dilated on the necessity of poetry making an immediate and direct impact on the reader.

It was growing rather late and S.S. was obviously tired. Dame Hildelith was called away to another parlour and for five minutes I had S.S. ... no, not to myself. Brian remained to the end, standing sentry in respectful silence. S.S. was twirling an empty pipe. He asked if he might smoke. Repressing a 'What will THEY say?' I replied, 'Yes, of course'. So for a few minutes the virginal air of the monastic parlour was polluted with the delicious aroma of tobacco. I hadn't smelt a pipe since I sat beside Harry at home the night before I left home to enter Stanbrook. We rose and said goodbye.

S.S. to D. Hildelith Cumming 5 July 1960

If it is all right for the calligrapher, I would certainly choose the Millbourne Magnificat paper. The one you used for the carols would be all right, though to my mind a tiny bit too heavy. I would prefer no deckles at the side. I think that is all I need say—with a super blessing on your work added. You know what a joy the book is for me—the loveliest thing that has ever happened to my poems.

Yes, there were endless things we three could have talked about —and interior silence was foremost among them, as you say. (My suggestion that you can't quite remember was 'grace is stillness bestowed'—'from there where all surrenders come', as Hopkins wrote.) I humbly assume that the silences of the spirit are the ultimate quest of all dedicated religious. But I suppose that few, even of the elect, achieve the final *reality* of 'do nothing' contemplation. Perhaps it is like writing a real poem—one can't do it by trying. As I once told Sr Felicitas, I have had three special experiences of complete cessation of thought, accompanied by an emotionless state of serenity. But that, I suppose is only an outward symptom of grace, or even a form of what is called catharsis. If Life were a Master Musician only! More and more I am afflicted by the noisiness of life, and wonder how most people endure—and apparently enjoy—it! And how few of them are aware at all of the supernatural silences which surround their being—the mystery that is there for them with messages that use no human language and speak to the inmost shrine of sublimated self. . . . O dear, this won't do—I am getting out of my depth, and must make for the sea-shore of commonsense.

S.S. to F.C. 5 August 1960
Yesterday's cricket was rather spoilt by drizzle after tea, but we played on with a wet ball & were beaten by Mells, by 7 wickets. I only made 6, but withstood some fast bowling with confidence, and got out trying to hit a six. I am playing again tomorrow, and shall escape the Flower Show, which is all over the park, with a huge marquee & several tents, a pony gymkhana, and a caravan 'rally', whatever that may be. My two mares have been conducted to the other end of the park, where they are grazing peacefully with a flock of sheep, which include a horned 'Jacob sheep' which Jessica is fond of conversing with—it is very friendly. Has eyes like a goat, and goat-like feet.

6 August 1960 10.30 p.m.   Heavy rain here between 3 & 5 for the poor Flower Show, but the thunderstorms avoided Downside, though quite near. I returned rather pleased with my old self. We went in first, and I went in with five wickets down for 38. Christopher Hollis's youngest son, who has made two centuries for Stonyhurst got run out unluckily. Resolved to remain, I defended the stumps for forty-five minutes while 24 runs were added, of which I made exactly 1! The wicket was wet and not easy. Then got bowled somehow, and we were all out for 67. Stratton-on-the-Fosse won by 2 wickets, so quite exciting. Everyone was very pleased about the old gent remaining in so long, in fact they regard me as a prodigy-non-infant.

Yes; I must confess to being very nocturnal. I always did do most of my intensive writing at night—in the old days often until 4 & 5 in the morning. Now I have got in the habit owing to (like many people of my age) always waking up after 2 or 3 hours, so I put off getting to sleep as long as I can; and always do my devotional reading and praying after midnight. The mere fact of it needing an effort of will (though *nothing* could prevent me doing it) seems a good thing, and I always feel less tired at the end, and sometimes wonderfully refreshed.

Dom Hubert van Zeller to F.C. 12 March 1972

I forget when it was S.S. and I first met—round about 1955 and some time before he became a Catholic—but I remember the meeting was arranged, put off and arranged again, by Ronald Knox. 'You will find it difficult at first to know what he is talking about' Ronald warned me, 'but every bit of it is worth keeping.' On second thoughts it may have been earlier than 1955 because during the early fifties we had Cecil Burton, a onetime county cricketer, staying at Downside and coaching the First XI. Cecil Burton had been playing cricket at Heytesbury where he told me he had met a friend of mine who had sent me messages. 'A nice chap who must have been a good cricketer in his day—Sassoon, something Sassoon—and has known everybody who has ever played cricket. I hear he writes poetry.'

By the time he was received into the Church we must have known one another pretty well. When he started coming regularly to Downside on Tuesday afternoons to bat in the nets he invariably looked in on me at the stone-shed where I was carving. In spite of the three sculptors on his mother's side of the family, the Thornycrofts, he did not seem to be greatly interested in sculpture. Having puffed and blown on the cricket field, he puffed and blew—sitting crosslegged on the floor with his thermos and paper bag of cake-and-biscuit crumbs, while I worked and listened.

S: 'Why do you sculptor chaps wear knitted skullcaps when you work?'
H: 'To keep the stonedust out of our hair.'

SIEGFRIED

S: 'I shouldn't have thought in your case it was necessary. Forgive me, forgive me. However well one knows a man it is always poor taste to be personal. What I have never understood about twentieth century sculpture is why the figures always look so stiff.'
H: 'More stiff than Egyptian or Romanesque?'
S: 'Well they at least had their limbs in the right places and didn't look as if they had cramp. Greek and Roman sculpture, and neo-classical at its best, didn't make arms and legs stick

out at odd angles. (*Puff*) But of course I don't understand these things.'

H: 'Perhaps that's partly because today we want to escape from the obvious. Originality has become an obsession. And partly —but this is where I tend to lecture or become technical. . . .'

S: 'Do go on. I'm listening—for once.'

H: 'And partly on account of the modern respect for the material. In woodcarving we let ourselves be guided by the grain and the knots; in stone by variations of hardness; in alabaster by variations of colour. The material dictates.'

S: 'I should have thought (*puff*) that it ought to be the other way about and that the human being should be master of what he's handling. I know that in writing poetry I always have the last word. But then I know nothing—(*puff, puff*—) about sculpture.'

His shy, diffident, jerky manner, characteristic expressions, movements as well as words and facial contortions, suggested to me in equal parts a longing to get away and a longing to stop on and talk. After a bit of course the nervousness dropped away and the essential serenity was given a chance. When one got to know him well he was the most natural and unselfconscious person in the world, losing himself in his conversation and blithely unaware of time, telephone bells, interruptions, projecting the poet-image or creating an impression of any kind. When he had people staying with him, he used to bring them in to see me—Edmund Blunden and Ian Davie I remember particularly. I looked forward to his visits, and when there was no cricket to lure him over to Downside I used occasionally to go over to Heytesbury. I wish now I had gone over more often. Sometimes for these Heytesbury visits I would take two or three senior boys whose knowledge of books I knew would interest him. Siegfried was the perfect, if unexpected, host at these parties of young men. His vast knowledge delighted them, and he gave them an enormous tea. On one occasion during tea, he was so engrossed with what he was saying that he went on pouring into one of the cups long after it was full. When at last he noticed what he was doing, he rolled his head until it looked as though it might come off and said: 'Oh, I'm hopeless at this sort of thing—help yourselves to the stuff!' On another occasion while talking with great animation and at the same time signing a book of his poems which one of the boys had brought with him, S.S. was found to have written 'To Siegfried ... from Siegfried Siegfried' and beneath it the wrong date.

As characteristic as his clothes and way of talking was his car. He drove a car in the way that he rode a horse—at an uneven trot until lost in composition, and then at a smooth spanking gallop. The hood of this antiquated vehicle was secured, not altogether

He drove a car in the way that he rode a horse—at an uneven trot until lost in composition and then at a spanking gallop.

effectively, by a cross-hatching of what I took to be Sellotape, but which Dom Martin Salmon assured me later was a yellow adhesive plaster which retained its shine over the years and in all weathers. Anyway it glistened bravely in the evening sun.

You ask about what I knew of his spiritual life. Very little really. For someone as frank about himself in other directions—endearingly ready to talk about his literary life—he was curiously reticent about his soul. We talked about books *on* the spiritual life, and less frequently about spirituality in general, but hardly at all about his own experience of prayer. Whether it was I who urged him to read Dame Julian of Norwich, Richard Rolle, the *Cloud*, or whether he had been given these books by Ronald I do not remember, but I know he read them with all the delight of discovery. Especially Dame Julian. Since words meant so much to him it was interesting to me to find that he was not sidetracked by the style of the English mystics and was always more concerned with what they taught. But after a course of the classical authorities he would invariably come back to Ronald Knox who was probably his favourite author on spiritual subjects. I used to feel that Siegfried's was an extremely simple response to grace, and that he would be quite happy on a desert island—so far as his soul went—with the penny catechism and a children's prayerbook. 'I like Ronald's conferences to schoolgirls' he once admitted to me, 'just as much as I like his deeper books. Also of course it's great fun *hearing* him in everything he writes.'

Thinking back to our more serious conversations I seem to remember that there were more of them than I thought when I began this letter. The trouble is that with Siegfried in full flood it was difficult to come away with more than a cupful at a time. To change the metaphor he was like a juggler sending up a dozen glittering objects at once. He would toss them at you, and you'd be lucky if you caught a few before they fell, when others would already be in the air. I think he instinctively understood a lot more about the spiritual life than he was able to explain or willing to let on about. I never heard him say a single unkind thing of anyone. This is something one tends to say about one's friends who are dead, but I remember saying it during his lifetime and nobody had reason to doubt me.

When he was dying I was too far away to go. Also I was just out of hospital and had been forbidden to travel. I was devoted to him, as were all who knew him at all, and I miss him.

S.S. *to* F.C. St Gertrude, 17 November 1960
I need only say that I have prayed my best for this deliverance;

and for you who have suffered with her,* and must still endure the grievous loss. Words are poor things to offer, but the loving thoughts go with them. I *can*, anyhow, send you something—the six lines I wrote two weeks ago, a little step forward in expression of the contemplative quest.

> *Awaitment* November 1960
> Eternal, to this momentary thing—
> This mind—Thy sanctuary of stillness bring.
> Within that unredeemed aliveness, live:
> And through Thy sorrowless sacrament forgive.
>   Let me be lost; and lose myself in Thee.
>   Let me be found; and find my soul set free.

❧ F.C.'s request in 1959 for one or two lyrical poems had led to the compilation of *The Path to Peace* and its publication by the Stanbrook Abbey Press in November 1960. A sequence of twenty-eight poems traced the poet's journey from the dreamy pantheism of youth, through long years of seeking, to life 'breathed afresh' in the acceptance of Christian faith. The book has been displayed by the British Council as being one of the finest English typographical productions of that year, and has attracted the admiration of experts at various exhibitions throughout Europe and the Americas. The printer, Dame Hildelith, has written of it: 'The beauty of the book rests on the use of the best materials available: a superb type face, 20 point Cancelleresca Bastarda leaded 2 Didot points, used in complete accordance with the typographical principles dear to its designer;† every canon for the setting of poetry strictly adhered to throughout, and meticulous care in presswork. There are no pretensions to typographical novelty; even the setting of the highly swashed Contents page was determined by practical necessity—the centred setting because the deeply hanging figures could not be set in a column, and the free use of swash capitals and terminals to avoid the monotony of even line lengths.' ❧

* Dame Bernadette Plater, a nun of Stanbrook, died 15 November 1960.
† Jan van Krimpen (1892–1958), Dutch typographer.

S.S. to D. Hildelith Cumming 18 November 1960

The sun is pouring in at my tall windows, and the BOOK is standing upright against your framed Magnificat—its arrival concluding three weeks of solitude when no visitor came to my 'angel greeted door Or threshold of wing-winnowed threshing floor' (as D. G. Rossetti remarked). You must surely know what this book means to me and what a solace & delight to my uneventful existence. May it give you, who so beautifully made it, as much happiness as it brings to me. Of all my printed books it is the loveliest. Sr Felicitas will have shown you my All Souls poem (viz. *Awaitment*), which would have come in so well before the Pentecost one. I have wondered whether you could print a few copies for me to send to my friends who will have the book. But no hurry about that. You have still so much on your hands. When you have some more copies, could you post one to Edmund Blunden, The University, Hong Kong, as I want him to get it as soon as possible—& it takes six weeks to get there. My 'gift' to the Abbey is the best gift I could have made to my unworthy self.

S.S. to F.C. 22 November 1960

M.M. queries *Awaitment* as a name for the poem. It seemed to *me* right. 'Bestowment' implies the grace given rather than implored. If *you* think *Awaitment* right, I shall leave it. The dear one even asserts that there *is* no such word in the dictionary. For me, these lines have felt like a final release of what I longed to express. I wrote the last two lines first—they just came into my head while I was writing about All Souls, pulling to pieces my early poem *All Souls Day*, and saying how differently I would write it *now*. Next day my Muse kept on telling me I must add to it & I wrote the first three lines, but got quite held up by the fourth, and rubbed the three out in despair. Then 'sorrowless sacrament' arrived from nowhere, and I thought aloud 'that's done it', and the line emerged. How unfailing is your perception! That one word 'sorrowless' lights up the whole poem, the not quite expected felicity.

St Andrew a.m. I have just unpacked the special *Path to Peace*

& can find no adequate words for it. Has any more beautiful modern book been produced? I am most thankful to Sr Hildelith for the *Awaitment* page. It will be splendid if she prints it to go with copies of the book for the faithful. Of course I would like the duplicate *P. to P.* pages made into folders. There are many to whom it will be a revelation—the majority only know of me as 'a war poet' and through a few anthology poems. *Morning Express*, a mere verse exercise, goes on appearing in one school anthology after another.

5 p.m. S.C.C. really is a saddening spectacle—just being kept alive, with no inward consolation, after that so active & useful life of public service—a parable of mistaken reliance on material humanities which, as one grows old, *must* be put in proportion by the immaterial realities. A 'philosophy of life' is not enough—at the best it can only be stoical unselfishness & benevolence towards others. How many old people are reduced to the frivolity of desperation—their *solitudes* must be desolation—certainly 'going on being busy' is their only hope. Sydney, at 91, must still write to *The Times* to correct someone about something written about Ruskin or Morris or Hardy. And now can't even daydream through his old diaries. He has outlived his life, and even his precious possessions (so comforting to me here during the war).

> Ah, what avails the Worcester Sauce
> Which paid for Dyson Perrin's Missals?
> Sure, 'twould have been a wiser course
> To profit by St Paul's Epistles.
> The Perrins manuscripts are sold;*
> And Syd's invested in debentures.
> The gift he might have gained was told
> In different letters—Dame Laurentia's!

Well, well, watcher think of that for spontaneous combustion? But seriously, old age *should* be arriving at the *value* of things, shouldn't it? Browning's Rabbi Ben Ezra says it so well. One must go on being a sociable creature, concerning oneself with the active existence of others; but what matters most to me is what

* For more than a million pounds!

they deeply believe in—what they are willing to suffer & struggle for. This sounds priggish, but it is the truth. And the omnipresence of *Vanity Fair*!—what *can* one do about it?

1 December 10.20 p.m.   How lovely for me that I echoed St Gertrude in *Awaitment*. Others must have said it in much the same words. This afternoon I emerged in gum boots and terrific wind & rain, and posted the *P. to P.* to Hengrave, calling at the Presbytery in Warminster to deposit a bottle of 1934 Burgundy—*grand vin de l'infant Jésus*—to be raffled at the Bazaar, hoping it isn't the worse for damp air, as there are 3 inches of water in the wine cellar. One of the features of the house is a spring which rises in very wet weather and floods the enormous cellars. The pump doesn't act on the wine cellar, which still contains about 300 bottles, though I never drink anything now. Someone is playing a Brahms Intermezzo in B flat minor which I love. What depth of sadness there is in some of those late piano pieces of his. Max Beerbohm's library is to be sold at Sotheby's on 13 & 14 December. A depressing event—I was hoping it would have been preserved intact.

December 2, a.m.   Sun out! My visit will have to wait till the summer—May or June—as I am such a dormouse. But I hope for more than one.

S.S. to F.C. Eve of St Hilary 11 p.m. 13 January 1961

I am delighted about the unique copy of *The Path* for your brother. I received eight 'ordinaries' on Wednesday, and have sent one to Gordon Craig in the South of France—he is 89 next Monday. That adorable and greatly gifted man, when I sent him the prospectus in advance at once noticed the unique st in 'vast' in *A Prayer to Time* (there is only one other at the end of *Heart's Journey*), and applauded its 'merry inventiveness'—whom the gods love die young, applies to him. And did to his mother, whom I knew at the end of her life, and was enchanted by. One of the 'Specials' was bought by a grandson of Edward Clodd, the militant agnostic, who gave up visiting Hardy when he heard that he sometimes prayed (to Whom? the Immanent Will?). This man seems to be religious, but is an importunate collector of my 1st editions, like his grandfather, whom Meredith nicknamed Sir Reynard, because he always ran off with something—it was said that he purloined G.M.'s blotting-pad! Midnight; I must be less clod-like, warm up my hot water bottle, new cover—Cambridge blue—and be made a new man by Newman. 'My unchangeableness here below is perseverance in changing'—how wonderful that is.

St Hilary 10.15 p.m.   A hilarious interlude. Your letter must have affected my dream psychology to light heartedness! During a series of unusually happy absurdities I was having lunch with Tom Eliot (whom I haven't seen since he was brought here to tea in Nov. 1938, by Sir Bruce Richmond, who was 90 yesterday, bless him, and on whom I read an article by T.S.E. in the *Times Literary Supplement* at tea-time—mostly about T.S.E. and not very festive, though giving full marks to that great & genial editor) and someone else who was listening, much impressed, to him holding forth professorially about Yeats. His portentousness produced in me an excessive fit of the giggles—I was really convulsed with laughter, but T.S.E. orated on, quite oblivious, which made it funnier. I only record this because I have never giggled in a dream before. Sam B.'s* book—yes, expert reporting, but much padded out, it seems (I haven't read all of it, only dodged about with the index). I have heard a lot of it from Max himself—'O past, O happy life, O songs of joy!' All this posthumous Maxism gives me a heartache. I want *him*.

18 January 1961 10.45 p.m.   Another musical delight before dinner—Roger Quilter's settings of Herrick's *To Julia*. His music has a special quality for me which I call 'happy heart-ache'—'a latent pathos'. And Herrick's voice has it too, the gaiety and charm of transient things, and their fated brevity. I went through Herrick a few years ago, and found that not many poems stand out as his best. But the best are like no one else in freshness and 'country contentment'.

* Samuel N. Behrman, 'one of America's most conspicuous playwrights', according to *Siegfried's Journey*, chapter XXI. Siegfried Sassoon's friends can imagine his reaction to the glaring inaccuracies in the portrait of himself drawn by Mr Behrman in *Tribulations and Laughter* (Hamish Hamilton, 1972).

19 January 1961 noon Fr Hubert, to whom I sent an *Awaitment*, writes today: 'I have read your lovely verse over & over again. *It proposes the whole problem**—and that's why I like the title: we cannot bring about anything of ourselves—it has to be what God does—and it's *so* hellish when He doesn't and when one has to wait.' Encouragement—*premier con vintage*—château bottled. I love that strange man.

S.S. to F.C. 16 February 1961
It gives me a heartache thinking about S.C.C. and his touching words to you. If I could do anything to sustain him I would, but I feel helpless. O, that spiritual isolation—it is pitiful to think of him lying there with his memories—a tale that is told—and no belief in an unwritten sequel which will explain it all. Is it that people of tough fibre and strong preoccupation with human interests, activities and 'creatures', are more resistant to spiritual influence, less sensitive spiritually? An obvious remark—but somehow Sydney, with all his outside, extrovert interests, always struck me as a very uncompromising character. Are such people impervious to religious ideas? walled-in by worldliness, the worthy kind of it. I know that the great religious minds, and the deeply devout ones, are as tough as anyone. J.'s description of how faith came is grand evidence of how grace works beyond intellect. If only one could make the sceptics realize that such events are *facts*—more real than their materialistic 'realities'. However, it is not for me to argue with them. Years ago I used to assert that 'a single line of Blake is more powerful than 100 *Daily Mails*'. That was my point of view, and still is. But—as Ralph Hodgson heard a half-tipsy man remark in a pub—'Politics and religion apart, buses *are* safer than trams'. One mustn't live too much in the clouds. Money talks. It takes all sorts to make a world.

I will write what I can to S.C.C. The difficulty is that I don't know what to tell him about. I see no one that he knows. You are now my only link with him. Almost all the human and literary interests we used to share are 'upstairs in clockless rooms. . . . Me

* S.S.'s note: This fits in with what Fr Luke Harris wrote about the function of poetry in religion, doesn't it? By the way, David Knowles is elected to the Athenaeum Club under the special *honoris causa* rule, with Alec Guinness.

they did not foresee.' It isn't—as some of my friends probably think—that I am shutting myself off from life, but that my existence is restricted to the things that can really sustain me—most of what the outer world imposes on me is merely coped with as a duty. Last time I went to The Reform Club in 1955 (I resigned last year and saved 25 guineas a year) there wasn't a face there I knew, and only one of the old servants left. My life is rather like that now. The past is a back number—full of 'printer's errors' when one dips into it. Not for anything would I live it over again. But for what I have acquired in the past four years my life would be extraordinarily isolated and unpopulated. Blunden out in Hong Kong till 1962, and even he all tied up with minor literary interests. Geoffrey Keynes, totally taken up with his interests and activities. Dear Glen Byam Shaw, most understanding of friends, up to his neck in theatrical productions and never able to come here. Ralph Hodgson 90, & out in Ohio since 1938. Morgan Forster—O dear, I love him, but he is dreadfully antichurchdom & needs no help from me, living as he does in an apotheosis of adulation. This isn't a complaint, merely a statement of my situation, which is spiritual peace and plenty, unworthy of it though I be. And tiresome things are easily contended with, accepted and overcome. My great *gain* has been patience, and a fixed intention to be charitable towards others. In the past I had no rule of life to live up to. I have come to the conclusion that in human relationships it is sometimes virtuous to be *tough*. And I never could be, to my cost. As Shelley said, our whole life is an education of errors.

20 February 1961 a.m.   My only letter this morning is from Sir A. Lascelles, who says he can give me no idea of what *The Path* does to him: 'Nothing in literature, even in music or nature, has ever given me such a clear perception of beauty. Fifty years ago Arthur Symons wrote of Beethoven—"to have written this is as great a thing as to have built a cathedral, in which, not more truly, the soul shelters from its grief . . . nor was there ever a landscape of the soul so illuminated with all the soft splendour of sunlight."* That's equally true of yr. poetry and, had you never written another syllable, these poems would assure you a place

* The quotation is from Arthur Symons' *Studies in Seven Arts*, p. 218 in the edition of 1907 (Constable), long out of print.

among the immortals.' Good for dermatitis, anyhow, even if an overstatement on a large scale. I never know what to think when people exalt me to Parnassus, less than ever now, when all I've done that was any good is acknowledged as God's grace in the bundle of blundering animal unblessedness that I have been and still am, most of the time. (Upset my breakfast tray this morning & broke the sugar basin & butter dish, & have been mopping up milk and bits of glass.) Dear A.L. has insisted on getting me elected to his prestige Literary Society—a compliment, but I don't need it. Anyhow, it will compel me to stay with him, and he *is* the salt of the earth. NOW—cannot no letters in Lent be by-passed as part of vocation? Befriending a lonely poet isn't the same as correspondence. It is going about your Father's business, say I imploringly. I suggest a dispensation, humbly.

S.S. to D. Hildelith Cumming 17 June 1961

Yes, I got the *Time & Tide* review. I was thankful that the man had kept his hands off *The Path* as he could only have said something hurtful. The modern critics all say the same about me and find little merit in my mature poems. It has been going on since about 1935. *The Heart's Journey* in 1928 was received with acclamations, but all my old supporters have vanished. This morning I got one from the *New Statesman*, which says that I 'refused to write 20th century poetry, or live a 20th century life', contrasting me with Robert Graves, whom he applauds. He does, anyhow, concede that my verses are *human* achievements, though 'not poetic achievements at all'! I have long ceased to be upset by these clever poltergeists (what dear old T. Hardy used to call 'those clever people up in London', when they disparaged his poems, now quite the fashion with them). This 'critical world' doesn't seem to have any bearing on what I really am. The main trouble is, that all poetry now *has* to be intellectual, and they are utterly incapable of understanding my essential simplicity and naturalness. Meanwhile my poems are read & loved by innumerable non-professional people with literary taste and judgement, so all is well. I am fully aware of my limitations as a thinker and verse practitioner, but I had to be myself, and by 1920 I was too old to indulge in technical experiments. The strange thing about it is that my poems should have been liked by other good poets—Hardy, de la Mare, Belloc, Masefield, Blunden, for leading instance—(Edith Sitwell too, though *she* has cooled off, owing to my being regarded as old-fashioned!). I accept these intelligentsia disparagements as part of my pilgrimage, in which 'the world' seems to give me almost nothing to sustain me. Today 3 weeks I shall be rolling up to the Guest House in the local taxi—arriving about 4 o'clock—a personal path to peace.

F.C. to Sydney C. Cockerell: Siegfried Sassoon at Stanbrook, 8–11 July 1961

His letter had warned me that he was travelling by taxi from Heytesbury and would arrive at 4 o'clock on Saturday afternoon. However the afternoon wore on and there was no sign of our visitor. He was finally announced at 5.20, and after giving Lady Abbess a few minutes to greet him, I went to the parlour. The taxi had got into a traffic block and taken a false turning, so that although he had been on the road since 1.30 he had only just got here. He insisted on returning to Mrs Wilson's for tea, and promised to return at 6.30. I hoped that by then his fierce attack of nerves would have worn off. I never saw a handkerchief so twisted and tortured as his during that preliminary quarter of an hour. When he returned at 6.40 he was completely happy and at ease during the half hour we spent together before Compline, although he talked at such a rate that it was a strain to catch his words. What should we find ourselves discussing but that very picture of the Death of Chatterton by Henry Wallis which you had sent me so recently! Apparently Meredith was the artist's model. The time passed quickly with brilliant talk from S.S. who yet managed to be personal and human. He went off very happily to Compline, arranged to hear the Conventual Mass next day and to come to the parlour afterwards. But poets don't realize how closely planned a nun's time-table is, and so he arrived at 11.20 and I had to depart for Sext and None and dinner at 11.30. That hopeless waiting for him to come at the time arranged was typical of his stay. Dame Marcella meeting me pacing up and down the cloister within easy reach of the parlour day after day smiled and mischievously murmured: 'Alone and palely loitering?' On Sunday afternoon I asked him if he would talk to the little group who had worked on *The Path to Peace*—D. Hildelith who printed it, D. Joanna who painted the title page of S.S.'s special copy, D. Anne who wrote the capitals, and Sr Josephine who gilded the first poem. I arranged the session for 4 p.m. and asked him if he would meet the community after that and talk to us about anything. I suggested as a topic his friendship with Mgr Knox, but he recoiled from anything which touched him so nearly, and we finally settled on a ramble with poets he had known. He was prompt and turned up at 4. But it was at once evident that he was a victim of nerves again. He spoke at a terrific pace about Tomlinson, Eleanor Farjeon, and de la Mare. It was difficult to catch all he said, since he spoke through clenched teeth and slurred his words. At 4.45 we heard the gong sound to summon the community to the Large Parlour to meet him. I said to him teasingly, 'There goes your death-knell. We must leave this little parlour and go to the large one.' The effect was electrical. Up to then, the tray of cakes and tea had remained in front of him untouched. Now he started on the bread and butter, talking volubly all the time, and this time actually LOOKING at us, a thing he had so far avoided doing. I felt a little nervous of keeping the whole community waiting, but when I referred to it, he promptly seized a large chunk of cake. So I surrendered and waited in hope. We finally rose and made our way to the other parlour, where his reception of the rather formidable-looking assembly was characteristic and charming. He bowed very low and then raised his hands high over his head in a gesture of ecstatic welcome. We had taken the precaution of hiring a microphone and loudspeaker after the last experience with S.S. But I must admit that we might have saved ourselves the trouble, for in spite of it he was inaudible. Every time he inadvertently bent forward so that the microphone caught his voice, he backed away in alarm as if he had been stung by a scorpion. Most of us heard almost nothing. He talked of such interesting people too— Tomlinson, de la Mare, Hodgson, Bridges, Masefield, Drinkwater, Hardy. . . . But he did not use even his normal speaking voice, and he dropped his voice completely at the end of sentences. The concentration listening demanded was so great that I gave up and studied his head instead. He looked like some Old Testament prophet, very ascetical and world-weary. In certain lights he is an unmistakable Jew, and I thought how like his father he must be. At 6 o'clock Margaret Adams and her husband came to carry him off to their cottage—a pretty little Tudor house in a wood—about three miles away. Margaret did the gilding of *The Path*, and it transpired that her husband had been at one time in the same division as S.S. during the Great War. So they got on famously.

On Monday morning he came late as usual to tell me all about the previous evening. One would not have recognized the same man. He was youthful, laughing, excited, perfectly natural. That settles it, I thought. No more public addresses! He is much happier solo. Monday was lovely. By that time he was perfectly at home. 'I hope I shan't become TOO much at home,' he said laughingly. But as he smoked his pipe interminably in the parlour and nearly put his long legs through the drawer in the grille, I think he must feel at last as though he knows us. He had lunch here with our two Abbots and Father Pilkington from Westminster Cathedral. I am told that S.S. eats scarcely anything, but there was plenty of merriment and good talk. He drinks lots of tea, and when he has emptied the pot, he drinks the milk that remains in the jug! On Tuesday he was due in London for a dinner at the Garrick Club. So he planned to come up here as usual at 11 a.m. and catch the 12.55 train. He begged me to play to him before he went. He had heard the organ on Sunday and had loved it. He has of course studied it himself as a boy at Marlborough. He asked for Bach's great F Minor. So after Sext and None he went through to church, and while the community ate their dinner, I played goodbye to him. We avoided a goodbye in words. Instead I played Bach's *Nunc dimittis* by way of 'Go in peace', and his glorious F Minor which said better than any words could do, 'Thanks be to God'. I waved farewell from the organ to his distant figure, and so he departed. He wants if possible to return in September to fortify himself against the winter cold and loneliness.

I have given you no account of his appearance. He looked nice and shabby and used-to-us, if you know what I mean. He was no longer in the elegant suit he wore a year ago. He wore a blazer with brass buttons—in an attractive shade of blue—with grey trousers which had seen better days, and black shoes. And the 'pork-pie' hat he carried at one point was in brown, if I am not mistaken, and didn't really match anything. Which is as it should be! He can look amazingly young. His eyes are so innocent and luminous, and he laughs so delightfully. He has a habit of shooting rapid penetrating glances which take everything in, and he misses little. But there is a striking delicacy and sensitivity about all his comments and views of life or people, which make one say with conviction, 'Yes, I like him thoroughly, even though he is an oddity like most poets. They can't help it. They are made so.'

S.S. to F.C. 12 October 1961 10 p.m.

Here I am—convalescing from 96 hours in London (staying with the dear Lascelles, of course). It was all very good, as will transpire, but the social evenings are a bit too much for me, after a full day. Tuesday was the Literary Society. Several new people there, including the Duke of Wellington, whom I sat next to. I knew him forty years ago, when he was Gerry Wellesley, but had hardly seen him since. He was very agreeable and friendly, & we had plenty in common—even Ronald & Katharine, & there was general literary talk with Harold Nicolson opposite me, and Rupert Hart-Davis at the head of the table (being secretary), Sir A.L. president at the other end. What well stocked minds they all have! They make my own repertoire seem very small. I was dazed with fatigue, and had to say half my prayers lying down. On Wednesday there was a smaller edition of it—Sir A.L. entertaining H. Nicolson, John Betjeman, and George Sartoris—the latter a very nice quiet man, who greeted me by saying that *The Old Century* is one of his favourite books—he is a great-nephew of Fanny Kemble & her sister Adelaide Sartoris, the famous singer —and I love Fanny K. through her friendship with Ed. Fitzgerald. After dinner A.L. & Harold & J.B. did most of the talking—all in the thick of 'the great world', though the real Betjeman is quite a

simple soul. Talking about Rose Macaulay—a great friend of his
—Nicholson remarked that he 'couldn't understand a woman of
her intelligence becoming so interested in the Liturgy'. This evoked
a mild dissent from the Duke, who reads the Lessons in his estate
church, out of the *New English Bible*, he told me, when questioning me about Ronald's. Very confusing, a remark like that. How
much does he *know* about it? Humanists are a problem, aren't they?
One of mine died last Friday, a dear kind soul, but a bleak un-
believer, sustained by food and wine and bridge and the classics—a
sad stoic. He once said to me, 'after all, there's always one way out
—suicide!' One of the least uplifting remarks I have ever heard.

14 October 1961 10 p.m. Verdi's Requiem from Leeds
Festival this evening. A very fine contralto. But I wasn't in the
mood for it, and only like parts of it anyhow. Some imp caused
me to start being funny about my latter end—i.e. suppose I
became Sydneyish, and occupied my leisure by giving you elaborate instructions and suggestions about my Requiem, and exactly
where I want a magnolia tree planted in memory of me—no,
perhaps a bay tree would be better, and leaves from it must be
used to flavour the rice pudding on my birthday, etc. (My mother
did use bay leaves—did yours?) Apologies for frivolity. Luckily
for me I never feel any uncomfortable things about dying, and
seldom think about it at all as a personal event—though I pray
each night for preparedness of soul for the day of my death, when
it will be judged. Speculations & imaginations about what hereafter will be like don't seem worthwhile. Yet, there *is* the un-
answered question—how much—if any—of human memory
survives? Why should one want to remember the details, even of
happiness on earth? They are akin to dreams, anyhow. I suppose
the best thing to do is to say, 'I trust you, O God, and I leave it
all to you'. That's what *I* do; and meanwhile faith & works is all
that matters. Thus spake Zarathustra—I beg pardon—Captain
S. L. Sassoon, C.B.E., M.C., who knows about as much of
Eternity as a water wagtail.

S.S. to F.C. 25 October 1961
Dick de la Mare has asked me to unveil the Tablet to 'W.J.' in

St Paul's crypt—I dread the ordeal by publicity, but can't refuse the honour and labour of love.

1 December 1961   The de la Mare unveiling is on 18 December at 2.45. I am told that I need say very little—& not a lot of people likely to be there.

12 December 1961   Tomorrow there is an enormous sale at Sotheby's of MSS. and letters of writers. All R. Firbank's MSS.—dozens of them—which will be bought by Americans, as he is much the fashion, though so trivial. Edith Sitwell is selling all *her* poetry notebooks—I suppose she needs the money (I have got two of them which she gave me 30 years ago). And there is a MS. book of *Counter-Attack* (not attractive—partly printed poems stuck in) which I gave to a friend in 1919, who sold it, & it came up again & fetched £90, and will probably fetch more now. So there you have the world again—and what has it got to do with the *meaning* of poetry? Merely Mammon, & American universities & collectors.

10 p.m.   For the past ½ hour I've been in St Paul's crypt, as it were—rehearsing my remarks. But am unable to compose any set speech. How can one person represent thousands whom he delighted? I think I must make it quite intimate & unprofessional, & get away with it by being natural.

13 December 1961 10.15 p.m.   The only news today was that my MS. book fetched £400. It's a scrubby little notebook which I had at Craiglockhart—interesting only through associations—Wilfred Owen handled it, & Rivers, & it was sent to Robbie Ross to give to the publisher—and I added nine more afterwards. At this rate, what would they pay for my beautifully written manuscripts? How I dislike all this money-making in the arts. It has no relation to the glory of creativeness, & is ruled by fashion.

December 18th 1961
The unveiling of the memorial tablet to Walter de la Mare
By Siegfried Sassoon
in the
Crypt of St Paul's Cathedral

Notes of Siegfried Sassoon's Address

To be here as your representative is a great privilege. The task laid upon me is not an easy one. But I am sure you will forgive my inadequacies. And my words are nothing. All that matters is that we are here to pay homage and remembrance to the best-loved poet of his time.

But how am I to express it on your behalf? Apart from those nearest to him, there are some here who could speak more ably than I can. (Mention Bruce Richmond.)

You know—whenever I tried to think up what I was going to say here, I always found myself picturing him standing there watching me with an amused look on his face—just as he was thirty years ago in a photograph, which I treasure, in which he is handing me a silver medal—'presenting the Police-medal,' he called it.

He would not wish me to read an elaborate literary eulogy. Nor would you. So I decided to ask you to imagine me coming along here one afternoon with some uninformed young friend—pausing at the plaque—and being asked: 'Did you know him? What sort of writer was he? What was he like?'

Well, I would say, my association with him and his work began way back in 1910. I was looking through a poetry magazine called *The Thrush*, which had just been started. And there, among a lot of unrewarding minor verse, I came upon a poem which has haunted my head ever since:

All That's Past

Very old are the woods;
    And the buds that break
Out of the brier's boughs,
    When March winds wake,
So old with their beauty are—
    Oh, no man knows
Through what wild centuries
    Roves back the rose.

> Very old are the brooks;
>   And the rills that rise
> Where snow sleeps cold beneath
>   The azure skies
> Sing such a history
>   Of come and gone,
> Their every drop is as wise
>   As Solomon.
>
> Very old are we men;
>   Our dreams are tales
> Told in dim Eden
>   By Eve's nightingales;
> We wake and whisper awhile,
>   But, the day gone by,
> Silence and sleep like fields
>   Of amaranth lie.

Then for the first time I experienced the de la Mare magic of thought and cadence.

And two years later arrived *The Listener* volume, with all its felicity and freshness and immediate appeal—and a rhythmic flexibility which was a revelation to me. Above all that poem: ' "Is there anybody there?" said the Traveller, Knocking on the moonlit door,' which exemplifies his imaginative genius once and for ever.

Shyly I wrote to him from my obscurity and thanked him—and received, of course, a charming and courteous reply. Years afterwards he reminded me that it was the only time he had ever addressed me as: 'My dear Sir'!

After that, I suppose, I would advise my young friend to read *Peacock Pie* and *Henry Brocken* and *The Return* and the entrancing introduction to *Come Hither*. And all the rest would await him—and how many a masterpiece!

And then: 'What was he like?' ... Unlike anybody else, of course. But accessible and responsive to every one—treating all as his equals—ready, even eager, to learn from them—interested in the most ordinary things, though his mind dwelt so much on things intangible and visionary. And in all human relationships the homeliest of men.

I have known no one who could so stimulate and heighten one's perceptiveness. Absorbing and interpreting all that came his way, he could communicate his questing consciousness to others, sending them away with re-christened eyes.

In his later work there is a deepening awareness of the powers of darkness that pervade the world. But to the end he never lost that priceless gift: the essence of wonder. The wondering child was always in him, who was, indeed, the Laureate of childhood. No need for me to enumerate further the richness and variety of the output of that marvellous mind. But let it be remembered that, behind all his creative writing, though not always outwardly apparent, was *compassion*—compassion for all our creaturehood— and the will to promote human happiness. 'The principle of light' was in him and will continue to irradiate his memory.

Fare Well

Look thy last on all things lovely,
Every hour. Let no night
Seal thy sense in deathly slumber
   Till to delight
Thou have paid thy utmost blessing;
Since that all things thou wouldst praise
Beauty took from those who loved them
   In other days.

S.S. to F.C. 11 January 1962 10.30 p.m.

In the ordinary way I would have sent you an account of the unveiling; but on 21 Dec. the family invaded my seclusion, & of course the intense cold took a lot of contending with—much of the house being impossible to warm. Hester is still here, but George and Marguerite left on Monday—luckily, as that day the hot-water boiler nearly blew up, & even the cold water was cut off for two days, & I was nearly reduced to shaving with boiled Malvern water, which would anyhow have been a near link with Callow End. Last night the gale blew down a big beech on the lawn. It was a semi-copper, & the biggest tree on the estate. Amid all my exhausting distractions I have been thanking heaven that I got successfully through the de la Mare ceremony, so supremely important for me. And the bad weather just held off long enough to enable me to get there. I had a great struggle to compose my address & only got it on paper two days before the event. But after that I felt quite calm and confident. I went to the Lascelles on the Sunday afternoon (The Queen's secretary, Sir Michael Adeane there to tea!) and Ian came to dinner, & was a great success with Sir Alan. I had given them *Piers Prodigal*, and they at once ordered five more copies. Harold Nicolson came to lunch, & off we sailed to St Paul's—Tommy having arrayed me in his best funeral overcoat, which felt like a suit of armour, & much improved my appearance. Lots of chairs in the Crypt, but only about 150 there. No poets, except Ian & Leonard Clark & Sir G. Rostrevor Hamilton. Some not very good organ playing, & then the choir came in, & then the Dean & his clergy. Several very verger-like vergers, in different costumes—why do vergers always look lantern-jawed? After Ecclesiastes I emerged, and (having become confused in mind) was about to deliver my address, & had to be prompted by a verger to pull the cord! At the end I was much involved in hand-shaking & doing the polite, and about 20 photographers suddenly appeared like a party of poltergeists, letting off flash lights, which I endured as best I could. There was a very nice feeling about the ceremony—I felt that the people there really remembered him lovingly. As I was climbing the steps from the Crypt by myself, a humble little man joined me and said 'I must tell you that *A flower has opened in my heart* is one of my most favourite poems'—Wasn't that a nice finish-up? As we left the Cathedral Harold Nicolson said 'You looked magnificent while you spoke—like a Homeric bard'. Strange to think of my 23 year old self discovering *All That's Past* in that magazine, and reciting it in St Paul's 52 years later. And what he has meant for me in those 50 years! One of his last letters to me began 'Blessed Siegfried'. Blest indeed have I felt since Dick [Richard de la Mare] said to me 'You did it just as he would have wished'. Few episodes in my literary life have contained more significance.

S.S. to F.C. 16 February 1962
I spend a lot of time comparing my '60s with my '70s, and the '60s make a very poor showing. In '53 I thought I was being given a lift when they made me an Hon. Fellow of Clare. But it all faded away. I tried to make Cambridge a centre—but since Gwen Raverat & Frances Cornford died there is nothing there for me, except dear Alfred Gilby. 'O death in life, O strong destroyer Change!' as William Morris remarked. By the way, I only noticed the other day that 'They speak by silences' comes from *The Hound of Heaven*. Now *why* did Sydney make Francis Thompson write it out for him? What did it *mean* to S.? Just a fine poem, I suppose! By the way again, has anyone ever written a great poem *denying* Christ? An Agnostic anthology would be amusing, wouldn't it? T.H. I regret to say, wrote a queer poem called *The Wood Fire*—a man talking about how well these crucifixion crosses burn—'I buy them bargain-cheap from the executioners'—a really dreadful poem—but such was Victorian rationalism, and the resistless rood is still there, so say a prayer for dear T.H.'s soul. Swinburne's atheism, of course, was just *silly* stuff—no depth of thought was in him. T.H. *suffered* from unbelieving. He could not overcome the world. No thinker I. Merely one who has 'turned a stone' & 'started a wing'. Must now clutch heaven by the hem, as it is after midnight.

17 February 1962   I wish you were there to start the conversation! I have reached the last chapter of *Let Dons Delight*, read for the 5th time since 1938—Ronald's birthday tomorrow. The odd thing is that I enjoyed it so much before 1957, when the discussions about religion meant so little to me. I think the appendices were what I liked best, plus the cosiness of Oxford Common Room & the sense of the past, & the admirable characterization. I have got the Newman Letters, but they are still reposing on the library table with the Hopkins Journals which I only acquired lately. I seem to be reverting to my remote ancestors who in old age just spent the winter keeping the fire going in the dear old cave & meditating on the mobility of early manhood. What did they worship, I wonder? Probably the moon. And who knows what their contemporaries, the Corrigans, were adoring? Do you

believe in racial memories? Some of my hypnogogic visions have seemed like it, and many of them were oriental architecture. As de la Mare wrote, these things seem to belong to a separate order of experience & certainly aren't self-induced. But for some reason they have all stopped since 1959. The real ones were all connected with lying awake—would suddenly start in the small hours with extraordinary clarity. I suppose that at my age the whole mental apparatus becomes less active. Or does the peace of God put a stop to a lot of the nonsense? Some might assume that my serenity is indolence. But when set alight I am just the same as ever. But it has to be something that matters. And most things just don't. All I want to do is to help people spiritually. In the past I tried to be a benefactor with money and friendship. Not much of a success in most cases, mundane matters being what they are. But with J. I could say, 'What is faith? It is that which gives substance to our hopes, which convinces us of things we cannot see.' And for the first time, I really *did* help someone. There you have the whole thing in a nutshell!

18 February 1962   At 5.15 I was beside the graceful lime-tree on the edge of the lawn (the old English kind—large leafed). The last sunlight fell through loose clouds exactly on my circle of crocuses, as though exhibiting them for me. I always clear all the dead leaves away from them & the primroses, & have almost eliminated dandelions & other weeds, & grubbed up all the ground ivy. Five years ago there were less than 20 crocuses. Now there are at least 100. Gazing at them in thankfulness that it isn't 18 *January*, I said to my simple self, 'Your blessings have multiplied like the crocuses'. And there you have an epitome of my limited outlook on life in general compared with—say the Prime Minister, or my former friend Bertrand Russell, whose motto is 'The will—not to believe—but to find out'. Surely I am lucky in being able to regard a few crocuses as an annual event? and prefer them to 'the noise that men call fame'. Lots of sensible people feel like that, I know—I wish there were more of them. This morning I was reading Newman's sermon on Equanimity. How beautiful the passage at the end—'the Christian has a deep, silent, hidden peace, which the world sees not—like some well in a retired & shady place, difficult of access'. . . . I couldn't help feeling, not smugly I

hope, that the whole passage was very like my own condition, 'never less alone than when alone'. Scrutinizing the air-photograph of the Abbey at this moment, all summer-leafy as I have seen it, I try to picture you discovering all sorts of pre-Spring arrivals—have you many aconites?—none here alas. At 5.35 I turned on the wireless to hear the voice of Rumer Godden, who is doing a series of poetry for children—such a pleasant voice. She ended by reading de la Mare's *The Scribe*—one of his best. February's thrush—immortalized by Meredith—is Valentining me at eve. The thrushes here have never been the same numbers since the terrible winter of 1947, & the blackbirds far exceed them now. Sir Russell Brain (now made a Lord!) has sent me his privately printed poems. In one he says the wren is his favourite bird. I am inclined to agree with him. I was watching one this afternoon, pecking about on the fallen beech—one of nature's indomitable marvels. You can take it for certain that I shall come in June—and I *must* repeat my birthday visit—that blest and happy memory. But I suppose there are bound to be many people for the Church dedication feast. Shall I bring a bell-tent? Well, well. . . . 'Big Bill and me'd been boys together. My aunt had wed his cousin's father That kept the butcher's shop at Ripe And died of eating poisoned tripe.' And so good night.

S.S. to F.C. 12 March 1962 10.15 p.m.
The B minor Mass is entering its last half hour, but I have turned it off—and it's no use pretending that sounds coming out of a box are the same as being there, with great choral works. One of the things I'm always saying is that those who have never learnt to play an instrument are in a different category (or 'mouserie', a word de la Mare once coined in my presence) from those who have. Greatly as I rejoice in the enormous accessibility of music caused by wireless & the consequent increase in professional musicians, these glutted partakers in polyphony know nothing of the intensive experiencing of music which older people shared, when 'to go to a concert' was an event, and the little one heard made a memorable impression. Sydney in *The Times* again! Isn't he amazing? Ruskin gave two leaves from a 14th century

French missal to Hester's uncle, Charles Gatty. One of them is here, & the other in the Library at Downside. I learnt this from Philip Jebb when he saw mine. (C.G. left several things to Downside.)

About my little dental ordeal. On Friday I went to Odstock Hospital to see the specialist, Mr Wishart—very nice & we got on well (hospital a one storied army camp, put up by the Americans on the top of a hill). When I arrived my old car was boiling —something wrong with the water-pump. Stupidly, I unscrewed the stopper and a geyser flew up and scalded my left wrist rather badly. So I introduced myself by being bandaged up by a charming nurse, who asked me whether I am *the* Mr Sassoon. Today week I shall be only Mr Sore-Mouth, lying in a ward, and wondering how well I shall say my devotions, and probably still rather drowsy from the anaesthetic. The main operation is on Monday morning. I am taking Newman's *Sermons*, Belloc's *Selected Essays*, and Hopkins to sustain me, and of course Ronnie's *Gospels*. On 21 March all my troubles will be over. Yesterday afternoon I turned on Rumer Godden's poetry programme for children, and before long out came *Cleaning the Candelabrum*, perfectly read. And I exclaimed, 'What a good piece of vocal cadence verse!' I have sent her a photograph of the Candelabrum which George took ten years ago.

How I wish you could *see* George. I think his nature resembles mine in some ways, though his *mind* works in an entirely different way—exceptionally quick in absorbing & grasping ideas, & a born expositor, like Hester's brother Oliver, whom he takes after, mentally. He obviously resembles Hester's grandmother, Margaret Gatty, in his passion for being occupied, which her biographer laid stress on. From his earliest years he has been like that—would print & enlarge 100 photographs in a day, & kept a complete catalogue of all his negatives. His versatility of interests is a danger —all the old Gattys were like that except Julia Horatia Ewing, who stuck to her writing. George has a natural gift for writing, always lively & direct & never wastes a word. My great comfort is that he is benevolent & enjoys helping people.

S.S. to F.C. 27 March 1962 a.m.
Five nights in a 'Plastic & Oral Surgery Centre', but I could write 5,000 words about it with enjoyment! From the moment I got there there wasn't a thing amiss, & all was niceness & encouragement. On my return was a letter from a nephew of Helen Waddell —unknown to me—who is a master at Sherborne, saying that he is collecting her letters for publication. This in itself is nothing much. What does mean so much is that I had quite lost touch with her since 1954, when she became a complete invalid with pernicious anaemia & ceased to answer letters. When I applied to Constable's for her address (wanting to send her *The Path to Peace*) they refused to give it. I have *so* wanted her to know of my life transformed. She was one who could put life into people. I suppose she *gave* all of herself away to others.

I wish I could see Alec Guinness—he vowed to come & see me again, in 1960 when he came here to get hints about Lawrence for the Rattigan play. But one has to follow these busy people—their concerns prevent them from seeking one out. I shall be in touch with Stanbrook next Thursday, as Dame Agnes's friend, Mrs Sampson, is coming to see her and Hildelith, and is calling here on Tuesday afternoon. Hildelith sent me an account of her and her strange condition of super-Catholic enthusiasm, and yet not being a Catholic. She seems to have enormous vitality as a letter writer —slightly overwhelming! I was wishing I could send you something for mental recreation in your few times of release from work & duty. But could devise nothing except a MS. book of my poems, in which I accumulated *Sequences*. No one else, except H. M. Tomlinson, who died in 1958, has seen this book, which contains about 40 pieces that you haven't read. I feel doubtful about bombarding your mind with this collection, so lay it aside if you don't feel able to face it. But they will add something to your understanding of my blinkered ignorance before I found the fulfilment expressed in *Lenten Illuminations* and those others. There are a few others, sardonic epigrams and so on, which may entertain you. All I want now is to be enabled to produce just a little more, but it would be folly to force it. Why is it that, when by bestirring my craft I might write all sorts of things which might give pleasure, I go doggedly on for 17 months deliberately refusing to attempt anything until something *happens* which belongs to the sequence of religious experience? And what more *can* I say after *Awaitment*? Only a poem about Paradise, I suppose, and that Unknown Country which so haunted & pervaded the mind of Belloc in his greatest essays. (I re-read the *Portrait of a Child* the other day—surely one of the best lay sermons on Life?) Well, you have been warned of what will reach you on Thursday by Sampson Mail. And later on, your conclusions about it will be most valuable to me. On 12 April I have been roped in by Leonard Clark to give a reading in Sarum Close, to a collection of teachers he is shepherding for a week. Query: what will the toothless wonder's articulation be like?

> My muthic loving Thelf thith afternoon
> Clothed in the gilded Thurname of Thathoon . . .

Before a Crucifix April 1962 unpublished
When ultimate earned afflictions overtake me,
Lord, if it is Thy will to bend and break me,
    Grant sacramental purpose to prevail.
By Thine example, be this body broken;
Through Thee, some sacrificial strength awoken,
    Where life's illuminings no more avail.

S.S. to F.C. 16 April 1962
You will probably have perused the six lines I send. They slipped out quite unexpectedly last Saturday evening—the first attempt at verse since *Awaitment*. I am not able to judge whether they count as a *poem*. I only know that they have plenty of personal significance. I also know that I couldn't have written the lines *authentically* before my recent experiment in cross-bearing at Odstock (which was rather worse than I told you, physically). I realize that it is all quite obvious and unoriginal, couldn't be more so devotionally. But these little epitomizings of my Muse do sometimes re-illumine the obvious, as you know. And I am merely an instrument, it seems. To begin with, I was astonished

and delighted & offered it to our Lord with thanksgiving. Now, as usual, I am losing confidence & saying I can't possibly have produced a religious poem that is any good to anyone. But, in the context of *The Path to Peace*, it is the *one* testimony which is absent. So *might* be worth adding for that reason. And the prosody appears to be quite up to standard. It is for you to decide. All this nocturnal fuss about a few lapidary lines! But there seems something peculiar about my unproductiveness. Why do those few lines mean so much to *me*, even if they aren't good ones? All I've ever said since *Awaitment* was, 'please, before I die, "but once, O but one ray" '. And have said, over & over again, nothing vital *can* come except through real experience. O dear, am I in my dotage? I pray God that when I am really aged I shall not be exacting to others. And I sometimes think that if I can't be of active use I'd prefer to depart now. For I'm a bit weary of my old body, and I do hunger for the final revelation and summing up of what I've accomplished by that very mixed bag—my life. All I know is that my pilgrimage has ended as a man before a crucifix finding sanctuary, and asking to be ridded of his bibliography personality.

S.S. to F.C. 8 May 1962

I received the news of Sydney with thankfulness for his release. For some time past, the thought of him lingering on in that state has been burdensome and sad, and I felt that he too must be unhappy, though he put up such an indomitable performance. My only childish prayer now has been 'Let Dame Laurentia be looking after him'. That you have been given a sign to rejoice for is something I can only whisper to my candle-lit crucifix tonight. Behold I show you a mystery.

I am now able to think of him as he was in his prime; all the interests and admirations we shared; and all the benefits he brought me. His monument, of course, is the Fitzwilliam Museum—a really magnificent enterprise for the Arts. But his invisible monument is in the annals of his devoted friendships, tender yet astringent—brusque but adoring. How well I can remember his barking laugh, when he said of T.H. 'I told him he ought to stop waxing his moustache!' I suppose it is difficult for people so closely linked with constructive activities & organizings to achieve serenity in old age, unless they are religious-minded. Is it really one's duty to go on reading *The Times* until one has to do it with a magnifying glass? I shall use a minifying glass when I'm 80; and already find difficulty in reading it at all!

I agree with Dorothy Hawksley about Cockerell's testament of friendship being slightly unreal. A large part of my life has been given to acts and sustainments of friendship, fruitful & unfruitful, and I am loyal to them in memory. I have found that real friendships are proof against long separations and silences—one meets again after years, and it is just as though there had been no interval of time. Sydney's active correspondence was part of his need to be occupied and interested—his continual concern with the 'business of life'. It was methodical to a degree. And he *was* a connoisseur! (Did he give much solicitude to the undistinguished?) I dislike applying this cold douche of commonsense to our dear old friend. But there is something in it. In his prime—and his youth—he sought out the right people, served and looked up to them. In old age, I suggest, he discovered deeper & warmer sources of affection, through his need of sustenance. Well, well. Sir Sydney Conundrum did good things; and was wonderfully honest, wasn't he? He was my good friend for 47 years, and much of what mattered most to me, I shared with him.

I loved your Easter letter and particularly enjoyed the Ethiopian priest. I must admit that picturesqueness in religion does appeal to me, though I strive to be austere & don't get much chance to be anything else. I am delighted that Geoffrey Keynes's bibliography is providing entertainment. All that private printing certainly makes a good target for collectors, which has ended in a craving to be nothing at all except what my best work contributed. This afternoon I re-read Browning's *A Death in the Desert* for the first time for many a long year. And realized that I was reading it with new eyes. The background touches always appealed to me, but I understood nothing else. What was St John to me? (By the way, had he St Ignatius of Antioch in mind for the narrator?) It seems to me a bit diffuse, and even now I couldn't always follow his line of thought. And could a dying saint, even St John,

have said all that at once? But I love Browning more than ever
for having written it, though I don't suppose many people read
it. But there is nothing to touch the last lines of *Karshish*. What a
funny looking page. When I wake in the morning feeling all my
age, I sometimes wonder what on earth my midnight ramblings
amount to.

Compline May 1962 unpublished

Much weariness I plead, by daylong duties brought;
Much world-bewilderment from tired and troubled thought.
Now for my need, let child simplicity be sought.

Below the Crucifix I watch my candle shine—
I, O so earthbound, O so darkly undivine.
Light of our living souls, be lit this night in mine.

S.S. to F.C. 14 May 1962 a.m.

It must have been your commentary on *Before a Crucifix* which
caused *Compline*. I had felt that 'the former' was somehow
incomplete, but could find no way of amplifying it. I thought of
the last three lines while praying on 10 May, and added the rest
next morning. It satisfies me because it is what I have experienced
literally hundreds of times since 1957. And the two seem to go
together. Release from minor daily tribulations—and acceptance
of the meaning of ultimate suffering as grace. And it is all as far as
possible from *The Power & The Glory*, which was only an emotional glimpse of religious reality. Surely these two belong with
my testifyings?—though the significance for me of *Before a
Crucifix* will never be known to others; and some might laugh if
they knew that the way of the Cross only became authentically
understood by me—after years of lip service—through having my
teeth pulled out! But it *was* so; and this consciousness has been
deepened in me during the past eight weeks, so there is no nonsense about it. It is like wearing Tommy Lascelles' overcoat all
the time. Safe shall be my going.

Last night I dreamt that I was discussing something to do with
religion with a man, who said, 'I can only tell you that my

solicitors are Lex, Lex, and Lumen'. Can you beat that for a bit of Sassoonerie? I go on in solitude except that on Saturday I had four people to tea! The Custos of the almshouse, Canon Merriman & his wife—kind, homely people, typical Anglican country parson —he held a College living for years in Dorset; and the Colonel of the Black Watch & his wife, from the camp outside my wood. The Colonel was good value. Knew the Wavells, and was at Winchester with Archie John (and with him in Kenya when he was killed). Nothing now until next Sunday when I must preside at the Centenary Meeting of the Marlborough Literary Society— Dover Wilson giving a talk on *Othello*. Am still toothless, as my jaw refuses to revise its shape as required. I revisited Odstock, & was received with acclamations in the dear old Wessex Ward.

S.S. to D. Hildelith Cumming 3 July 1962

Those four days did me more good than I can say. Returning home was exodus from Eden; lovely though my own Eden is to look at, I found nothing awaiting me except letters about unwanted worldly affairs. At Stanbrook the world was well lost. Of course I will be glad to lend a hand with the Newbold nun's study of *The Path to Peace*. The Atherstone hounds used to go there—an attractive old mansion in a fine park. I've looked up my hunting diary, 1913–14, and found the following specimen of my early prose style:

'28 *November—Brinklow*. Found All Oaks & ran over the road towards Close Wood, but was headed & turned left-handed & was killed in a garden at Brinklow village. Drew Newbold Revel blank. Found a brace in Monk's Kirby Oziers & ran round Newnham Park (Earl of Denbigh—Feilding—7 daughters, one a nun) & killed after a bright 12 minutes. Found Copston's and ran nearly to Newnham where he was lost. Fell off when away from Copston's. Ditches round there very blind. Rode Cockbird. Home 6.15. Fine & mild weather.' Hasn't my life been a peculiar mixture? The blindness of the *ditches* was nothing to *mine*! Tell Felicitas that I have a lovely letter from Puck, & have replied in her own artless style, as best I could—she is inimitable—and ended, tactfully, with 'kind regards to your friend Mary'!—adding 'Hose-anna for the Hose'.

9 July 1962   'Externe Sampson' blew in just as I was starting lunch & not at my most luminous. She stayed 1½ hours; said she's seen you twice but was reticent about it. Talked about Vespers & Compline & the singing, & the dear externes, and the clothing, & the Belmont boys. Had called at Prinknash on the way. The only ghostly counsel I gave her was—be sure to *rest after meals!* Let us hope this will include resting in the Lord.

A youth from Balliol called on me on Saturday; he brought a friend who turned out to have been at Downside, in Fr Aelred's house, and quite won my heart by the way he talked—Robin Eyre, by name. The other very nice & lively, but R.E. seemed to have stability & graciousness of mind. Blunden & his Mrs are arriving today for two nights. Dennis Silk will come tomorrow & drive us to Downside for some cricket practice which will be the nearest I can get to sharing with beloved E.B. the essential fabric of my existence—'the thing at heart our endless own', as Meredith said somewhere.*

I read the earlier history of the Press with great interest, astonished by the amount of it there is, and it is such a good story. Dame Agnes's contributions, of course, are invaluable. How strange to think of her busy at her press work when I was only ten years old. An old boy has sent me his pamphlet about Rational Theism, which he believes to be the real right thing.† Says he was distressed by my becoming R.C. and can't understand how any educated man can believe in the Incarnation. Not being much of a reasoner, I can only wish him the best of luck in his rational relationship with the Supreme Being. He enclosed a printed list of how many million galaxies there are & suchlike astronomical headaches. To which my reply would be—'But how impudent of the mystics   To pay no heed to such statistics!' I felt tempted to write and advise him to read some P. G. Wodehouse, but refrained. I am fairly sure that the Almighty has a strong sense of humour. He must need it when contemplating All.

* George Meredith: *The South-Wester*
† Title of a novel by Henry James

A major event in my existence is on the way. Recently I came to the conclusion that I really must order myself a new mattress. Mine is more than 12 years old, and I've turned it round—and over—twice, owing to the hollows with wires sticking up, penetrative of my behind. I am always attached to old friends and objects with associations. But this seemed a case for severing connection with past life, and the new 'Slumberland' is expected shortly, and should last me until I set out for the galaxies gleefully.

S.S. to F.C. 13 August 1962

A spate of press cuttings reviewing the *Letters* to T. E. Lawrence* which includes some of mine, one of them reproduced in facsimile. Will send the book if you want it. Have also been asked to contribute to a TV programme about him (but will not be TVd!). My answer is, Let him be judged by what he was to others—not by his tortured inward self. The letters prove it. I suppose I've thought more about suffering than anything else since I returned from Odstock. People endure bodily suffering so wonderfully. Mental afflictions are harder to bear and rise above, aren't they?—more wearing to the spirit. One can be patient with pain, and distract one's mind from it somehow. But agonizing worry & anxiety & unhappiness—what doctor for that but from above? Suffering unjustly inflicted by circumstance—that seems the worst. To suffer for a cause or a purpose must be comparatively easy. Dear me, what a fountain of wisdom I am!

It is a comfort that you like *Compline*. As you say, it is nowhere near *Pentecost Prayer* in quality, but it is authentic expression, and satisfies me deeply when I say the last three lines. Perhaps I'll write another six lines before I'm 80! But my haunted and havocked self no longer exists. All things are now in proportion. 'The weariness of life that has no will   To climb the steepening hill' no longer applies. Such is my condition. My only problem now is, how to 'put it across' through my powers as a writer. My little poems just happen. Can't be done by trying.

Recently a good lady sent me a private volume of her poems—

---

* At Siegfried Sassoon's and Hester Gatty's quiet wedding on 18 December 1933, T. E. Lawrence had been one of the few guests.

quite good up to a point—all religious but with a strong flavour of Theosophy 'we need no creed or ritual' and so on. Can you tell me what 'There is no religion higher than Truth' means? Rather like *Nihil vero veritas* above the front door at Weirleigh. The only Theosophist I ever knew (closely connected with Mrs Besant & Krishnamurti) was so silly & 'phoney' that I wiped Theosophy off the list for ever. He occupied Robbie's rooms at 40 Half Moon St for several years, an amiable man & an osteopath. Dear old Miss Burton (Robbie's housekeeper) thought him absurd. His room was full of Buddhas and Egyptian things, & he crystal-gazed. I asked her once 'What's Mr Fleming doing up there now, I wonder?' 'Praying to that blooming 'awk, I expect,' she replied. She was glorious. Julia came in yesterday while I was having dinner, carrying her prep book. 'What are you learning?' I asked. 'Rithmetic'—adding, 'I'm learning the Cattykizzum too.' 'O,' said I, 'so you're learning your Pussyism too, are you?' And a flower opened in my heart.

S.S. to F.C. 19 May 1964

What you call my 'high jinks' in London *are* in that category, but I sometimes feel that they are 'the high that proved too high, the heroic for earth too hard' (Browning). I am submerged by a spate of admirable worldly, literary, & artistic gossip, and have to distribute my vitality in every direction. *Literary* admiration no longer means much to me. My best work was an attempt to do service to God, and I give it back to Him always who gave me my little talent and aspiration. I partook—yes, partook—in discussions about the reviews of Hassall's life of Rupert Brooke, and Hotson's 'Mr W.H.' The latter, I'm sure, was the romantic friendship of a young man, quite blameless. And I am equally sure that the sonnets were written in youth. They *couldn't* have been written when he was writing the plays of his maturity. It is creatively and sequentially impossible. The nicest person I talked to was David Cecil's sister, the [dowager] Duchess of Devonshire—really refreshing give & take, & all in common. I also liked Veronica Wedgwood, whom I met for the first time. We talked a lot about Frances Cornford—her cousin—whose poetry she much admires. Anyhow 'twas determined, dared, and done. And on Saturday there was the Hunt Pony Gymkhana in the park, in perfect weather—a most happy scene—about 100 ponies & riders, and I presented rosettes with old world courtesy and conversed with a legion of locals. I had a nice letter from Alec Robertson about his programme with a *Prayer at Pentecost* in it next Sunday. By the way, Fabers have written asking if I want to add anything to the reprinting of *Collected Poems*. I *don't* want to. Seems somehow wrong.

S.S. to *Alec Robertson* at the BBC 15 May 1964
Dear Robertson,
  I was wondering about your Pentecost programme. I didn't much want to record the poem—seemed a bit obtrusive, and very difficult to do, except on one's knees. Poems like that can't be done by trying. And anything in the nature of devotional verse is incredibly difficult—everything having been said over and over again by the enlightened. But a thing like *Awaitment* just *happens*. It emerged as though dictated.

S.S. to F.C. 5 August 1964
Except for my three days in London, July was a marathon of monotony. Not that I mind monotony much, especially in fine weather. At the Lit. Socy. dinner I sat next to J. Betjeman, who is a kindred spirit & almost *too* stimulating. Next day David Jones came to lunch with the Lascelles—ulta-sensitive. I talked to him alone for $1\frac{1}{2}$ hours, & worked hard. He was a private in the 15th R.W.F. & wounded at Mametz Wood. His Battn. relieved ours after my day out bombing the Prussian Guard. Have you tried to read him? Fr Sebastian (Moore) specialized in *The Anathemata* —quite beyond me. *In Parenthesis* is an important war record. But doesn't reach me like *Undertones of War*. That afternoon 6–7 I was conveyed to 2 cocktail parties! At the Austrian Embassy I shook hands with Prince Schwarzenberg, but it was very loud & boring, & we only stayed 15 minutes. The other was quieter, daughter of Mrs Willie James who used to entertain King Edward. Two drawing rooms plastered with priceless Impressionist paint-

ings. I took refuge in a cosy chair, until Sybil Cholmondeley pounced on me protectively. By the way, Rupert Hart-Davis came to lunch on Saty. On his way he went into a book shop at Petersfield. The first book he pulled out (a Somerville & Ross) was inscribed by *me*, to my old Company Commander E. J. Greaves, in 1916. ('Old man Barton' in the *F-h.M*.) Can you beat that?

Proven Purpose 18 September 1964
Because I have believed, I bid my mind be still.
Therein is now conceived Thy hid yet sovereign Will.
Because I set all thought aside in seeking Thee,
Thy proven purpose wrought abideth blest in me.
Because I can no more exist but in Thy being,
Blindly these eyes adore; sightless are taught new seeing.

*A Prayer** in Old Age* 23 September 1964
Bring no expectance of a heaven unearned
No hunger for beatitude to be
Until the lesson of my life is learned
Through what Thou didst for me.

Bring no assurance of redeemèd rest
No intimation of awarded grace
Only contrition, cleavingly confessed
To Thy forgiving face.

I ask one world of everlasting loss
In all I am, that other world to win.
My nothingness must kneel below Thy Cross.
There let new life begin.

S.S. *to* F.C. 24 September 1964
This is the first sheet of a new note paper pad; so I hope I am turning over a new leaf. You will see by the dates under the two

---

* S.S.'s first draft called it 'Orison'

poems that I had a bit of luck after I wrote to you. Both were produced in the usual unprepared & tentative way—as though I were watching myself doing it—a tired man, late at night. Both times I made a few alterations next morning, which made all the difference. I must leave it to you to decide whether they are up to standard. First thing in the morning I feel that the *Orison* is only a sort of Salvation Army hymn. Last thing at night I feel it is the one thing I've wanted to say since *Awaitment*. Devotional verse is so difficult to judge as *poetry*. I wrote *Proven Purpose* in 12 lines, but realized that it has more weight in six.

The arrival of T & Y at 1 o'clock yesterday was an acute contrast to completing my poem. I am still recuperating after being put through it by the good old predators. There is absolutely nothing wrong with them except that they collect experience instead of absorbing it. Y is the difference between a typewriter and sensitive handwriting.

Immediately after they left, a little man called on me, humbly asking me to autograph *Collected Poems*. I talked to him for an hour, & he told me the whole story of his '14 war service. He enlisted at 17—in the Worcesters—& was in all the worst places as a private, & wounded twice. The Somme, Mouchy-le-Preux in Arras battle, & Passchaendale. Said he had lived with me for years, in the *Sherston Memoirs*, and never said a word amiss about it—understood everything! I had a curious feeling that he was a kind of offshoot of E.B. whose *Undertones* he also knows backwards—and he has the same beaky nose—the same look in his face while he speaks of that war. E.B. would have delighted in him. This really moving experience contrasted so strangely with T and Y. His name was Saxty—very odd one. I gave him half a bottle of Champagne to drink Sherston's health in, & he went away enchanted. A really wonderful little chap—I loved him. And a typical exponent of wry front-line humour. He had worked as a commercial traveller, selling vacuum cleaners, Nylon stockings etc., but is now retired. Thus *real* humanity returned to replace bleak humanism.

Sister Peggy is indeed a discovery to rejoice in. I sent a batch of *Path to Peace* offprints for her and Sister Tottie to share, & received the lovely letter I enclose. I told her that I had only lately realized that *Faith Unfaithful* was an affirmation of light unrevealed to me, though at the time it seemed darkest night. It *is* so, isn't it? Lord, that I may see—and know—beyond this mortal darkness—my nightly prayer. Yet, to believe *is* to know, isn't it? And to feel that one couldn't go on without Him is assurance of safety. And it isn't feeling, it is *being*. Am I waxing pietistic? Must resort to my Newman book, which always affords me an overcoat of enlightenment & recollectedness. And the little candle which changes the room to a sanctuary of stillness (& not *silliness*, I hope!) Lawks, how lucky I am!

Hoping for a favourable verdict. I want to have the luxury of hosanna from HQ!

S.S. to D. Hildelith Cumming 22 October 1964

It is a kind of relief to hear that Margery Sampson is at rest. I always said that she would pass out at the wheel of her car. As you say, she was very generous, but wholly reliant on outwardness and insubstantial substance. Tell Felicitas that I am pondering her list of poems. But the whole thing pertains to *her* mind, and I rely entirely on her judgement and intuition. No hurry, anyhow. This autumn has been one of the loveliest I've known here. The limes & beeches are yellowing, and it all looks like a mellow aquatint.

The other day I heard Grieg playing my beloved Schmetterling on an old piano roll. He played it with extreme rubato, and it was enchanting. It has occurred to me that you might perhaps run off a few copies of my two new poems. Ian Davie thinks *Orison* should be *Prayer*—more natural. I repeat these poems again & again, & they sustain my soul. Sybil Cholmondeley is coming to lunch next Tuesday, so I'm going up in the social scale. She is very nice, & I shall enjoy showing her everything. David Cecil came to tea, which I delighted in. His biography of *Max* has arrived. He has done it beautifully. There is a photograph of his sister Dora, the Anglican nun who I loved so much—the only really holy person I knew then. She knitted an exquisite coverlet for George's cot. She died in 1940. It was a case of clutching heaven by the hems—& how I clutched!

S.S. to F.C. 24 November 1964

How I wrote those two poems is a mystery—must have been the result of staying at Stanbrook which always puts new life into me. Aelred Watkin, to whom I sent them, wrote today that *A Prayer in Old Age* is 'one of the most beautiful and true poems I've ever read'. (Loud blushes.) The BBC has invited me to speak for six minutes in a 'feature' about the Battle of the Somme, which I declined to do. I am weary of being a war writer. Much prefer Dame Ninian's mother reading *The Old Century* & William Plomer reading the H. Vaughan sonnet in a programme at Hereford Festival, which he mentioned. The *Complete Memoirs* went up from 14 to 357 in the first half-year, but *The Old C.* only sold 44. *F-h. M.* about 3,000 in the 6/- edition. Anyhow I got £236 from Faber's for the various editions—a sort of old age pension.

S.S. to D. Hildelith Cumming 1 January 1965

On Monday midnight, after a very tiring family Xmas, I was suddenly taken queer in the head & tummy, & on my way to the bathroom fell down in a sort of faint & lay there for some time in the freezing passage. The family was down in the library, but I managed to crawl back, & was able to re-heat my hot water bottle an hour later, and was none the worse next morning. It was a hemmeridge [*sic*] from my ancient duodenal ulcer, and I am now having a glorious rest-cure, exploiting the event for all I'm worth, and living on superb invalid diet. I hadn't had a day in bed since I had my teeth out in March '62 owing to saving the staff trouble, & feel much revived already, & shouldn't be surprised if I wrote a poem! Hester is fussing after me all the time. It was providential that she was here. It was a horrid experience.

S.S. to F.C. 15 January 1965

The disturbance of my duodenum has been a major benefaction. Hester's presence is providential and the volcano in the kitchen is now an olive grove of affability. Even the iceberg Hania has thawed and is a maid of honour to 'Madame'. Meanwhile I sit here firmly declining to 'get well', though I am quite capable of getting up & going downstairs. The rest has done my mind all the good in the world. My main occupation continues to be gazing at the bed-spread which Max's sister Dora (the Anglican nun) made for George, though too beautiful to use. Hester got it out of my wardrobe cupboard, & it is being used for the first time. It is woollen multi-coloured squares, seventeen by twelve—how many is that?—and not one alike. Max used to choose the colour schemes for her. I never tire of contemplating its endless varieties, a labour of love indeed, and more meaningful than most of what the world has to offer me in prestigeful poppycock. Dennis's baby daughter lay on it last week, staring stolidly up at me—14 lbs of adorable infancy. I have read almost nothing since the accident, & skim through *The Times* like feeing the doctor for a nauseous draught. I dutifully perused the *T.L.S.* article on Eliot, a sensible summing-up. I don't think he & I could ever have fitted in with one another. The few times I met him, in the 1920s, I found him too professorial for my impulsive immaturity of mind, & I couldn't make head nor tail of *The Waste Land*. Anyhow, he was there to put us all in our place. But what will *his* place be, in fifty years? Ask me another.

18 January 1965 p.m. It is strange, isn't it, to compare the ebbing away from life of Winston, with that other world event, Pope John's passing? *This* is an orgy of publicity and popular self-expression—*That* was an immense response of love and reverence for a holy man. Winston deserves all the homage he receives, of course—nationally and internationally. But O, the ruthless impact of the world on that overdue death-bed (he has been longing to die for the last 2 or 3 years, I've been told by those who know). *Is* it civilized, this pandemonium of reporting & besiegement of his home by Press and Public? Think of Tennyson, dying peacefully at Haslemere in 1892—all England emotionalized by it, but everything serene & dignified. I verily believe they would televize his bed-room if they could! Could anything more exemplify the blatancy of the age we exist in? But there it is—he enjoyed the fierce light that beat upon his earned renown, and this is the climax. Let us hope it will be a fine day for the funeral. And that seemly solemnity will prevail in Westminster Abbey,

in spite of the TV cameras. (As I stood by T. E. Lawrence's open grave, a man tried to photograph the coffin. I knocked the camera out of his hand, God forgive me!)

S.S. to F.C. 18 February 1965

Hester departed a week ago, having stayed longer than I needed, as I was quite fit to fend for myself, though I feel rather old for my age, and *joie de vivre* is in abeyance. Not increased by the news of dear Dame Agnes in hospital. *Please* let me know how Lady Abbess finds her in that ward. Can only hope and believe that her light is shining for those around her, the brave old darling. It is easy enough to suffer lovingly, but to love someone else's suffering is terribly difficult. Your splendid quotation from de Chardin is much the same as what I read lately by the gentle Carthusian in *They Speak by Silences*, & I'd been meditating a lot on the problem of accepting suffering in the right spirit. I feel that I have everything to learn about it, in my spiritual self (poor little thing). I know that it does one more good than prosperity. But have never been able to find joy in sorrow! I suppose it is one of the top things in the task of faith—to believe that God knows what He is doing when the world's behaviour seems blind and brutal, and one's impassioned pygmy fist is clenched cloudward and defiant. Not that mine is now. I just say the one word, Love, and am shriven. *Amor vincit omnia.* Ain't I a Latinist? Must light that candle. Did you see *Everyone Sang* on the back page of *The Times* on the day of Winston's funeral?

S.S. to F.C. 11 March 1965 p.m.

On Tuesday I was reading Ronald on the Problem of Suffering,* and it all seemed as sound as a bell, and I said '*Me*, by all means, and I'll take it and offer it up; but when it comes to others I'm in the consommé and can't bear it!' And then dear old Armitage came in and took me to Warminster for a hair-cut, much longed for, as I'd been cutting it myself since the autumn, and the good

---

* A series of six Lenten addresses on suffering, under the general heading of 'The Cross of Christ', included in Ronald Knox's *Pastoral Sermons*.

hairdresser divulged that he'd been Laurence Whistler's corporal in the Rifle Brigade, & spoke of him with affection—knowing somehow that *I* knew him. And then Armitage took me to his house & we watched Cheltenham Races on TV with rollicking excitement, & a friend of his won the 4 mile race, and the problem of suffering was properly put in its problematical place. But it remains in my mind; and I have thought often of how darkly I endured tribulations in the past, with nothing to sustain me except my determination to get my writing done despite them. Anyhow I *did*. But not with any kind of Xtian submissiveness—angrily demanding what had *I* done to deserve it, which I now know to be *most* unsound theologically and spiritually.

Have not heard from Puck since 12 Dec. I was slow in picking up after my 6 weeks in bed, but these dry sunny days since the Ash Wednesday blizzard have done me good, and I get out a bit after lunch instead of dozing in the library. By the way, *The Times* has already begun fussing about my 80th birthday. The assistant-editor wrote to Edmund Blunden saying they would like me to write 2 long articles of 'recollections' and be interviewed. I could as well write 39! and am averse to the interview. (They must think it is this year, I suppose.)

I find the new liturgy very incompatible with contemplativeness! And long for the Latin. But it is obviously an act of unity with the congregation, so good for me. (Latin is said at the early morning Mass.) How *does* the new liturgy affect the Choir? I simply can't imagine doing the St George's act in Stanbrook Chapel, which has been like nothing else in the world for me—even Downside's majesty.

S.S. to F.C. 28 July 1965
Tommy Lascelles & Colin Fenton were here for week-end 9–11 July, intensive entertainment, though I love them both. And the next one, Haro Hodson, who does those clever drawings for *The Observer* and knew Max—delightful character & High Church—but age cannot keep pace with youth. The result has been 10 days of bad digestive discomfort, rather misery. I lie on my back, listening to the rumblings of dyspepsia, that naughty

nymph, and am unworthily wishful of evading all the world asks of me—never low-spirited, but incapable of much effort. I am set free, and ten stomachs couldn't interfere with my steadfast serenity. The way is growing very wearisome, but—I often tell Mary 'how long will it be before I share your liberation in the world of light?' Probably another ten years or more!

Our new parish priest has arrived, and makes a very good impression. Irish, but minus an accent. Like Fr Hubert, I rather bemoan the vernacular doings, but O how tired I get of standing up almost all the time. Can hardly hear myself meditate! We even have to sing a hymn during the Offertory. But I suppose it is very good for everybody.

S.S. to F.C. 25 October 1965

Our new parish priest, Fr McCarthy, is a *great* acquisition. Came to tea last week and we got on famously. I feel I can be spiritually intimate with him, and he is deeply interested in my repertoire among other things, and entirely kind and unsolemn. Calls me 'the Abbot of Heytesbury'. I must look up the Hopkins-Bridges Letters again—as you say, splendid reading. Yesterday after tea I read through Pater's essay on Pascal. Goodness knows what I got from it—except awareness that it must have meant nothing at all when I perused it in my early twenties. Anyhow I *do* know the difference between Jesuits & Jansenists now, and *have* learnt the spiritual meaning of the word 'grace'! Have *you* read the *Pensées*? But I always enjoy Pater's prose—the stately sentences and cloistral consonances—it always leaves me wanting to compose spoof Pater. I could write an Imaginary Portrait about a pensive personage pilgriming to an Abbey you wot of—'he was to recollect in after years, with a sense almost of *hyperaesthesia*—no other word is available—the ultra-mundane, yet intimate—experience of inclusiveness—the comely comportment of the externe sisters—the demure alertness of the emparloured dames' etc. Meanwhile—about the anthology—... I was thinking last night how nice it would be if Ian Davie could drive me to Stanbrook for a night or two. Dear Mrs Wilson will probably have to feed me on scrambled eggs. There is so much I can't discuss with you in letters.

S.S. to F.C. 19 January 1966

I must scribble a hasty bulletin about my weary bones. I have had a dozen treatments of massage, electricity, & heat lamp. The old boy who massages me is a dear. He was, as a boy of 18, in the same Division as me in 1917, in the West Surreys, so we go over all the ground together, remembering the good things & people, and deploring the insanity of it all. I continue to spend the afternoon on the library sofa, still much reduced in vitality & have lost weight. My main comfort lately has been Fr Hubert's lively autobiography*—a fascinating story of ups and downs—and all the Benedictine background so appealing to me—and some very revealing sidelights on Ronald, whose make-up he analyses with much sympathy and perceptiveness. So for once I've found a book I *want* to read!

S.S. to F.C. 26 March 1966

You ask about Edmund Blunden. He was elected to the Professorship of Poetry at Oxford. Got double the votes of his American adversary, Robert Lowell (a poet I've never perused). There was a lot of newspaper publicity. He will now be recognized properly as what he is—the most distinguished figure in English Letters—a fact obscured by his long absences from England. *The Times* gave him a big headline this week for his lecture on Wordsworth to the Royal Society of Literature, and his election was widely acclaimed. So, for once, an exceptionally modest man is given his due.

I, too, often ask whether things are worth while, for the keyword to my present existence is passivity. I submit to 'the long littleness of life'† dutifully, but the central me dwells elsewhere.

---

* Dom Hubert van Zeller *One Foot in the Cradle* John Murray 1965
† cf. Frances Cornford on Rupert Brooke:

> A young Apollo, golden-haired
>   Stands dreaming on the verge of strife,
> Magnificently unprepared
>   For the long littleness of life

What Newman calls 'the accidents of life' no longer interest me, and like the late lamented Cleopatra I have immortal longings in me. The busy-mindedness of people revolves around me, and I conform to it obediently. But, O dear, I say to myself, if only things would stop happening! Not that much does happen to my seclusion. I just go on being told that I am a war poet, when all I want is to be told that I am only a pilgrim and a stranger on earth, utterly dependent on the idea of God's providence to my spiritual being. But the game goes on, so I must put my pads on and make my way to the wicket. The wicket—O please, dear St Peter, don't delay too long in opening it to me!

S.S. to F.C. 17 May 1966

This is only a reportage, to let you know that I saw an extremely nice surgeon in Bath this afternoon, and—to my great relief—he has arranged for me to go into the nursing home on Friday for preliminary tests and, all being favourable, I will have the operation on Monday. My condition has become such a nuisance, I am longing for a *vita nuova*.

S.S. to F.C. Lansdown Nursery 25 May 1966 9.45 a.m.

Op was at 8 yesterday; I came to about 1, 100% thankful. About 5, Mrs Watson, the superb anaesthetist & sweet lady, came to vet my breathing. When asked for my reactions to the Op. I replied, without a moment's hesitation, 'Elementary, my dear Watson!' an obvious crack which she took as a sign that I was on the mend. Mr Glaser, the surgeon, like a second Dr Rivers, a really beneficial presence, was in this morning, and I gave him a few minutes' tutorial about Max, whom he only knows through his broadcasts. All the people here simply couldn't be nicer. On Sunday I had a surprise visit from Dennis and Diana. He was playing in a Charity Match on the County ground. Went in first & made 20, & then popped up here to see me. George came to see me on Monday afternoon and was a great comfort. He has realized that I am his second self, though so far behind him in scientific ability and intellectual quickness. Glen [Byam-Shaw] rang up on Monday evening from London to say that he will come and see me on Friday, a major blessing, as I've not seen him for almost 2 years, and of all my old friends, Glen is the one who never failed me in sympathy & understanding.

It is now 11.45 & there have been several visitations, including the therapeutist, a jolly soul called Joy Lewis, who has given me breathing instructions and is still observing the condition of my chest, which is affected by the Annie Sthetic operations. Now a bit of the world. A fortnight ago Charles Causley (a good poet who came to Heytesbury House twice ten years ago about broadcastings) wrote on behalf of the Literature Panel of the Arts Council, saying they want to celebrate 80th birthday appropriately, and could I suggest anything. As a result, he & the Arts C. secretary came to see me on 14 May, a pleasant but ultra-talkative & tiring afternoon, even with George's admirable social assistance. They urged me to let them print a few poems—150 copies—same sort of thing as was done for David Jones's 70th recently. After demurring a bit I decided that the only thing I could do would be to let them have the eight from *Sight Sufficient* to *A Prayer in Old Age*. I sent them to Causley who replied rapturously.

Extract from *The Stanbrook Abbey Press*: Ninety-two Years of its History Written and Illustrated by the Benedictines of Stanbrook 1970

'The press's contribution to the eightieth birthday celebrations was its first calligraphic book—*Something about Myself*, a cat story composed by Mr Sassoon at the age of eleven, which appeared in a volume written and illustrated for his mother, entitled *More Poems by S. L. Sassoon*. The dedication is 'For Mamsy from Siegfried'. On one of his visits to Stanbrook Mr Sassoon had read this one afternoon to a group of nuns in the parlour, whence came the happy inspiration to print it as a surprise for his birthday. The text was written out and illustrated in two colours by Margaret Adams. It was reproduced entirely from line blocks and printed on handmade paper with a white cover embellished with a cat printed in gold leaf. The fly-leaf bore the inscription: 'Homage on his eightieth birthday to Siegfried Sassoon, poet, warrior, and fox-hunting man, who even to serene old age has kept the heart of a child.'

S.S. to D. Elizabeth Sumner, *Abbess of Stanbrook*
Heytesbury House, 9 September 1966

My dear Lady Abbess,

Among the bewilderingly gracious gracious and numerous tributes I have been awarded, none is nearer to my heart than the exquisite and adorable one from beloved Stanbrook. Sitting this morning with a stack of still unopened letters and telegrams I opened the parcel and was amazed and delighted beyond expression. It is indeed a wonderful postscript to *The Path to Peace*. All I can do now is to send in double quick time the Arts Council *Octave* of which 100 copies were brought to me yesterday by the two secretaries, and can send more copies if needed for those unable to subscribe. I think Charles Causley's Foreword is excellent in delicacy and good sense. I felt a bit shy in giving them these poems for their purpose—their spiritual significance being what it is for me. But it will make them a little better known and the production is a lovely one, isn't it? I almost dreaded the impact of all this acclamation which has exceeded my expectations. But I have prayed to be enabled to see myself as I truly am, and to be beyond it all in the sanctuary of Him who is my final refuge and rest.

With love and gratitude to you all
Siegfried

Autograph letter from John Masefield to Siegfried Sassoon
Telephone: Clifton Hampden 277   No date.
Burcote Brook   Abingdon

Dear Sassoon,

I have this morning received the gracious, kind, and noble gift of your deeply felt poems.

I have read them through, with reverence, thinking that

nothing like them has come here for two centuries: and that they mark the beginning of a movement deep and great indeed.

You have ever led the way: and all your readers will learn some of this brief book by heart, and each will think his choice the best.

I thank you for sending the book, & hope that you will receive many glad letters from its readers.

John Masefield

Edward Lindley to Siegfried Sassoon

153 Coleman Avenue,
Wednesfield,
Wolverhampton,
Staffs.
31 January 1967

Dear Sir,

I have just read again my subscriber's copy of the 80th Birthday edition of *An Octave*, and I know that I must tell you not only of the pleasure but also of the great inspiration the reading and re-reading of these poems has been to me.

When my father was killed at Passchendaele leaving my mother with six children, the eldest nine years old, and we suddenly became poor indeed, the first questionings, doubtings, revoltings began to form indistinct and uncertain though they were in the mind of one who, as the elder brother, strove to tend and look after the younger sisters, and so to help an often tired and bewildered mother.

I was soon to meet you in your *Everyone suddenly burst out singing* and in the war poems. I remember especially the 'only one who remembered' (the cowardly swine whom the officers praised) was the mother with the white hair! And I remembered when I read it, the telegram and the letter (which my mother read proudly to us) about my father's death.

And so I hated war and the waste of it. And so I denied that there was a God.

Since then tentatively and by slow steps only, I have come back nearer to God. Since then I have grown ever more strongly to be aware of the stupidity, the waste and the absolute wrong of war. Always you have influenced my living and my thinking.

And now, as ageing a little, I turn more and more towards my God comes your *Octave*. And now I know that I must be lost, losing myself in God, that I may find myself; may find my soul set free; I know that my nothingness must kneel below the Cross that there new life for me may begin.

An Octave came to me because I was a glad and willing subscriber to the 80th birthday of one whom I have always admired, for his *Fox-hunting-Man* through to *Sherston's Progress* as well as for all the poetry I have read. It came to me at a critical time in my own life and in my own progress, and its influence is profound.

I cannot tell you just how profound this effect has been, I have not the words—the art (how often I have wished I had). I can only say humbly and in gratitude: 'Thank you, Sir, very much indeed'.

Yours sincerely,
Edward Lindley.

S.S. to Edward Lindley, 8 February 1967

Dear Mr Lindley,

Does it surprise you to hear that your letter has given me as deep contentment as any that I have received about my poetry? You see, those eight poems are something apart from any others I have written—and have, for me, an ultimate significance. That they should have brought you the spiritual aid you tell me of is indeed a wonderful reward. . . .

I feel as strongly as ever about the madness of war. And the 1914 war seems to be more insane the further it recedes in history. I can understand how you, in your boyhood, reacted against Religion. I felt rather like that myself about the attitude of the Churches. And could not realize that Christ was being recrucified all the time and everywhere. (The second war was, anyhow, a crusade against a Satanic organization, wasn't it?)

May your faith grow ever deeper and more defending is the prayer of yours sincerely

Siegfried Sassoon.

S.S. to F.C. 11 October 1966

The pussy cats have enchanted all the few who have seen them (Blunden agrees with you about *The Old Century* voice being perceptible). The loveliest tribute *The Old C.* has yet received. My own best has been Masefield's letter. That truly religious man believes, I think, in a future resurgence of spiritual activity in this disordered world. God bless him for believing it; and for saying what he does to imperfect me.

The homage of the world is the antithesis to my inward existence, which knows what wordly adulation is worth, and how little to be relied on. An innocent youth wrote recently that he is convinced I am the greatest writer in the world (from New Zealand). A touching letter—so simple & unaffected. Another young man wrote, only yesterday, that I am to him what Hardy must have been to me. Such tributes are worth having, aren't they, even if I don't deserve them. *Your* comment on Masefield's letter is Stanbrook encouragement *in excelsis*. But I must try not to be a portentous portent. Hermits must be humble. I can't claim to have *enjoyed* the celebrations. It was just something to be got through as defensively as possible. With a 'well earned' 80 to my credit, I returned to the pavilion, and all the members 'stood up' to me. Taking my pads off in the dressing room I asked God to help me to see it all in proportion to its true value. He alone knows what those eighty years have been worth, and I don't desire to be an acclaimed celebrity—I want only to continue a common sense Christian. My answer to the world's passing homage is the *Octave* poems. For they matter to me more than anything else, knowing that 'this is the victory that overcometh the world, even our faith'.

S.S. to F.C. 3 January 1967

To my astonishment and joy I received this letter from Fr Hubert. I have heard nothing further of his bodily condition, and fear he is making light of it in his usual wonderful way, and sending that *light* to me for my comfort—as indeed he did. Fr Aelred called in yesterday on his way back to the Abbey from Grayshott, and did me a world of good, as always. Fr McCarthy comes every Friday morning at 11.30, and we have lovely talks. He is a major blessing and makes up for all the solitudes and long littlenesses. Rupert's knighthood has given 1967 a good start. He is much more of a knight than most of them—a knight errant, in fact. The MS. books etc.—What will their *ultimate* destination be, I wonder? Not Texas University, I hope! All those 'literary remains' of mine seem so redundant now. Literary executors must do their duty. But I am only interested in my Spiritual executor, who will make quick work of it—dare I assume—without regard for prestige or reputation. The strange thing is that I feel no timidity at all about that Assize. Only *awe*. Am I wrong to be so trustful and so childlike? My present retreat from the world that wearies me is re-reading *Framley Parsonage*! (It was Ronald's favourite Barset book.) I find it better than ever. He seems so absolutely sure of his characters and the construction of the story. And they are all completely alive and convincing. And I love the Victorian humdrumness and homeliness. St Albert the Great's *Cleaving to God* has been a book at bed-time lately. Have also read some of de Chardin's *Pensées*—a very different cup of tea—consoling at times, but too scientific and cosmic for me on the whole. Anyhow, *you* aren't. A thing I've meant to ask of you. Can you tell me of the most easily obtainable edition of *The Dream of the Rood*?

S.S. to F.C. 9 July 1967

Since last autumn's upheaval it has been almost as if the clocks had stopped—my own pensive clock continues to tick, though the strike isn't working. So the weeks slip away, and I get through the empty days automatically, much slowed down physically, and bothered all the time by minor digestive discomforts. Spiritually, I am become completely acquiescent. I accept my deprivations as inevitable, and am permanently thankful for my central peace and 'sightless seeing'. But tiredness is pervasive.

Sherston's Progress

I nearly always saw myself engaged in doing something for the first time. All this, I suspect, has been little more than the operation known as the pilgrimage from the cradle to the grave. I am one of those persons who begin life by exclaiming that they've 'never seen anything like it before', and die in the hope that they may say the same of heaven. As regards being dead, however, one of my main consolations has always been that I have the strongest intention of being an extremely active ghost. Let nobody make any mistake about that. It has been a long journey. And my last words shall be these—that it is only from the inmost silences of the heart that we know the world for what it is, and ourselves for what the world has made us.

From his tall-windowed Wiltshire room, in the year 1967, on the first day of September, his favourite month, the poet went 'To stand with those white presences delivered through death'. At 8 o'clock on that evening of golden sunshine with its hint of frost, as the cricketer put away his bat and the huntsman shook out his mulberry coat, Captain Siegfried Loraine Sassoon, CBE, MC., alias George Sherston, quietly fell asleep.

Falling Asleep 1919
Voices moving about in the quiet house:
Thud of feet and a muffled shutting of doors:
Everyone yawning. Only the clocks are alert.

Out in the night there's autumn-smelling gloom
Crowded with whispering trees; across the park
A hollow cry of hounds like lonely bells:
And I know that the clouds are moving across the moon;
The low, red, rising moon. Now herons call
And wrangle by their pool; and hooting owls
Sail from the wood above pale stooks of oats.

Waiting for sleep, I drift from thoughts like these;
And where today was dream-like, build my dreams.
Music . . . there was a bright white room below,

And someone singing a song about a soldier,
One hour, two hours ago: and soon the song
Will be '*last night*': but now the beauty swings
Across my brain, ghost of remembered chords
Which still can make such radiance in my dream
That I can watch the marching of my soldiers,
And count their faces; faces; sunlit faces.

Falling asleep ... the herons, and the hounds ...
September in the darkness; and the world
I've known; all fading past me into peace.

INDEX

Abel's Blood, 93
Acceptance, 140
Adams, Margaret, 211, 243
Adeane, Sir Michael, 218
Aftermath, 24
Again the Dead, 116
Ah, what avails the Worcester sauce, 203
Alliance, The, 37, 159
All That's Past, 215
Alone, 103
Anathemata, The, 232
Ancient History, 93
And God the Father (Boja d'un Dio!), 121
An old and weather-beaten beech, 50
Another Spring, 154
Apocalypse, 30
Apollo in Picardy, 162
Apologia, 146
Armitage, J., 238
Arts Council, the, 41, 243
As I was Walking, 29
Asking, An, 130
Asquith, Katharine, 102, 181, 184
At Max Gate, 137
At the Grave of Henry Vaughan, 105
Augustine of Hippo, Saint, 19, 39
Awaitment, 201, 202, 232
Awareness of Alcuin, 139

BBC, 84, 86, 169
Balding, Ian, 98, 107
Bank of England Literary Society, 123
Bartók, Béla (1881–1945), 112
Batty, Ellen, 18, 50
Baudelaire, C. P. (1821–67), 36
Beerbohm, Sister Dora, 235, 237
Beerbohm, Max (1872–1956), 66, 136
Before a Crucifix, 224, 227
Before Day, 62, 87
Befriending Star, 138
Behrman, Samuel N., 205
Belated Discovery, A, 45
Belloc, H. (1870–1953), 66, 134, 181, 224

Bernard, Saint (1090–1153), 19
Best of Friends, The, 34, 192
Best of It, The, 152
Betjeman, Sir John, 212, 232
Blake, William (1757–1827), 95
Blunden, Edmund, 15, 20, 23, 137, 151, 157, 185, 198, 207, 229, 234, 239, 241
Blunt, Wilfrid Scawen (1840–1922), 68
Brain, Lord Russell, 221
Breach of Decorum, A, 106, 192
Brontë, Emily (1818–48), 140
Brooke, Rupert (1887–1915), 173
Browne, Sir Thomas (1605–82), 98, 98
Browning, Robert (1812–89), 55, 166, 203, 226, 227
Bunyan, John (1628–88), 32
Burton, Cecil, 196
Burton, 'Dame' Nellie, 231
Butler, Brian, 190, 194
Byam Shaw, G. A., 207, 242

Carroll, Lewis (1832–98), 22
Catherine of Siena, Saint (1347–80), 19
Causley, Charles, 243, 244
Cecil, Lord David, 102, 235
Change of Garments, 119
Child at the Window, The, 126
Child's Faith, A, 77
Cholmondeley, Dowager Marchioness of, 233, 235
Chord, A, 166
Christ and the Soldier, 81
Churchill, Winston (1874–1965), 237
Claridge Gallery, 26
Clark, Leonard, 218, 224
Cleaving to God, 248
Clodd, Edward, 204
Cloud of Unknowing, The, 200
Cockerell, Sydney C. (1867–1962), 33, 68, 127, 136, 144, 174, 191, 203, 206, 219, 221

Cohen Joseph: *The Three Roles of Siegfried Sassoon*, 35
Collier, Florence ('Puck'), 126, 228
Come Hither, 152
Compline, 227
Conclusion, 30
Contention, The, 162
Convent of the Assumption, 39, 108
Cornford, Frances (d. 1960), 68, 157, 173, 219, 231, 241
Corrigan, D. Felicitas, Letters to Sydney C. Cockerell, 191, 209
Corrigan, Mary (d. 1965), 240
Cory, William Johnson (1823–92), 160
Counter-Attack, 24
Country Life, 136
Court of Death, The, 51
Craig, Gordon, 156, 204
Craiglockhart, 23, 214
Cranford, 168
Credo, 148
Crosland, T. W. H., 63
Cumming, D. Hildelith, Letters to, 57, 103, 131, 193, 194, 201, 202, 208, 210
Cunard, Lady, 106

Daffodil Murderer, The, 67
Daily Herald, the, 25
D'Arcy, Martin, S. J., 183
Davie, Donald, 111
Davie, Ian, 139, 193, 198, 218, 235, 240
Davies, D. Josephine, 210
Davies, W. H. (1871–1940), 157
Day-Lewis, Cecil (1904–72), 121
Death-Bed, The, 24, 80
Death in the Desert, A, 226
de la Mare, Walter (1873–1956), 98, 112, 137, 152, 158, 160, 214, 218
Deliverance, 173
Devonshire, the Dowager Duchess of, 231
Devotion to Duty, 94
Donne, John (1572–1631), 26, 104
Doubt, 58
Dowland, John (1563–1626), 57
Dream of the Rood, The, 248
Dug-Out, The, 89

Earth and Heaven, 28
Elected Silence, 125
Elegy, 90
Eliot, T. S. (1888–1965), 48, 122, 123, 205, 237
Emblems of Experience, 158
Epitome, An, 167
Euphrasy, 135
Everyone Sang, 24, 92, 238
Example, An, 136
Eyre, Robin, 229

Faith Unfaithful, 168
Falling Asleep, 249
Fare Well, 217
Farjeon, Eleanor, 183
Farm Philosophers, 69
Fenton, Colin, 102, 239
Field, D. Anne, 210
Fitzwilliam Museum, 225
Fleming, Edward, 231
Food of the Gods, The, 147
Forster, E. M. (1879–1970), 207
Four Quartets, 123
Fox-hunting Man, The, 189
Framley Parsonage, 248
Francis, John (1780–1861), 16
From inexperience I was wont to claim, 146

Garrick Club, 91, 102, 211
Gathorne-Hardy, Robert (1902–73), 145, 153
Gatty, Charles, 222
Gatty, Jessica, 206, 220
Gatty, Margaret, 222
Gatty, Oliver, 144, 222
Gilbey, Mgr. Alfred N., 190, 219
Glaser, Mr, 242
Godden, Rumer, 221, 222
Goodbye to All That, 79
Gosse, Edmund (1849–1928), 22, 56, 60, 65, 109, 143
Graves, Robert, 63, 79, 112, 208
Guinness, Sir Alec, 206 footnote, 223

Hambleden, Lady, 107
Hamilton, Sir G. Rostrevor, 218
Hardy, Florence, 136

INDEX

Hardy, Thomas (1840–1928), 24, 27, 132, 204, 208, 219, 225
Harris, Luke O. C. R.: article in *Clergy Review*, February 1961, 206
Hart-Davis, Sir Rupert, 91, 212, 233, 248
Hassall, Christopher, 66, 231
Hawkins, Phyllis, 135
Hawksley, Dorothy, 226
Hawthorn Tree, The, 82
Heart and Soul, 127
Heart's Journey, The, 38
Hebgin, D. Scholastica, 101
Heinemann, William Ltd, Copyright Dept, 92
Herbert, George (1593–1633), 103, 155, 161
Herrick, Robert (1591–1674), 205
Heytesbury House, 176
Hodgson, Ralph (1871–1962), 126, 207
Hodson, Haro, 239
Hopkins, Gerard Manley (1844–89), 47, 194
Hound of Heaven, The, 219
Human Bondage, 161
Humbled Heart, The, 163

Ignatius of Antioch, Saint (c. A.D. 107), 226
I have no need to pray, 23
I have seen Christ when music wove, 83
Imperfect Lover, The, 96
In a Great Tradition, 174
In Parenthesis, 232
In the Church of St Ouen, 84
In the Churchyard, 50
Into Hades, 157
Invocation, 88
I Stood with the Dead, 24
It is rumoured of God Almighty that He has made us, 100

Jackson, Stanley, 17, 47
Jamieson, D. Joanna, 210
Jebb, Eleanor, 182
Jebb, Dom Philip, 182, 222
Jeremiah, 22, 35
Joan of Arc, 56

John XXIII, Pope, 237
Jones, David, 232
Julian of Norwich (1342–c. 1416), 200

Kew Gardens, 29
Keynes, Sir Geoffrey, 207, 226
King's College Chapel, 182
Knowles, David, 206
Knox, Ronald A. (1888–1957), 101, 175, 184, 185, 188, 196, 200, 219

Langland, William (1330–1400?), 32, 37
Lansdown Nursing Home, 242
Lascelles, Sir Alan, 103, 107, 207, 212, 218, 227, 239
Last Judgement, A, 28
Last Meeting, The, 79
Last thing at night, in solitude serene, 171
Lawrence, D. H. (1885–1930), 123
Lawrence, T. E. (1888–1935), 141, 230, 238
Lehmann, John F.'s review, 24
Lenten Illuminations, 15, 28, 178ff.
Lindley, Edward, 63, 64
Lindsay, Robin, great-nephew of Helen Waddell, 139, 223
Litany of the Lost, 113
Literary Society, The, 208, 212
Little enough you've learnt, 35, *to face*, 128
Little, Dom Francis, 177
Liverpool University, 110
Lovers, 96
Lowell, Robert, 241

Macaulay, Rose, 213
Making, The, 37, 152
McCarthy, Nicholas P., 240, 248
McLachlan, D. Laurentia, 144, 169, 174, 225
Margaret Mary, Mother, 39, 168, 175, 202
Marina, Princess, 107
Marlborough Literary Society, 228
Marsh, Edward (1872–1953), 40, 65, 66

Masefield, John (1878–1967), 66, 244, 247
Meeting and Parting, 125
Memoirs of a Fox-hunting Man, 31, 78
Memoirs of an Infantry Officer, 75
Memory, 70
Merciful Knight, The, 111
Meredith, George (1828–1909), 116, 138, 205, 229
Merriman, Canon, 228
Messenger, The, 141
Montaigne, Michel E. de (1533–92), 159, 161
Moriarty, D. Mary, 192
Morning-Express, 24, 203
Moore, Henry, 168
Moore, Dom Sebastian, 177, 232
Morris, William (1834–96), 219
Morrison, John, 107
Mystic as Soldier, A, 85

National Book League, 57
Nativity, 106, 108
Need, The, 143
Neighbours, 176
Newman, John Henry (1801–90), 38, 167, 220, 222
New Statesman, 156, 208
Nicolson, Harold (1886–1968), 91, 212, 218
Norris, John (1657–1711), 125
Notre Dame High School, 189

Observer, the, 20, 28, 239
Octave, An, 41, 243, 245
Ode for Music, An, 64
Odstock Hospital, 222, 223
Old Century, The, 18, 33, 45, 46, 50, 51, 52, 54, 77, 247
Old Huntsman, The, 21, 23, 41
One Foot in the Cradle, 241
One Who Watches, 109
On Poetry, 27, 29, 40, 104
On Scratchbury Camp, 144
On Some Portraits by Sargent, 99
Orpheus in Diloeryum, 59–61
Oundle, 128, 129, 144
Owen, Harold, 25, 26, 93
Owen, Wilfred (1893–1918), 18, 21, 23, 26, 41, 75, 86, 87, 214

Pascoe, Sister Peggy, 234
Passing, The, 48
Past and Present, 124
Pastoral Sermons of R. A. Knox, The, 183
Pater, Walter (1839–94), 162, 240
Path to Peace, The, 187, 201, 202, 204, 207, 210, 223, 228, 234
Patmore, Coventry (1823–96), 185
Paul's Cathedral, St, 214
Pepys, Lady Rachel, 107
Perrins, Dyson, 203
Philpot, Glyn, R. A., 26, 168
Piers Prodigal, 218
Pilgrim's Progress, 32
Pilkington, Canon Ronald, 211
Pitter, Ruth, 157
Plater, D. Bernadette, 201
Plomer, William, 236
Pontifex, Dom Dunstan, 177
Pope, Alexander (1688–1744), 45, 97
Portrait of a Child, 66, 224
Pound, Ezra (1885–1972), 122
Power and the Glory, The, 28, 106, 108, 227
Praise Persistent, 132
Prayer at Pentecost, A, 190, 193
Prayer in Old Age, A, 233, 236
Prayer to Time, A, 98
Premonition, A, 113
Proven Purpose, 233
'Puck' (Florence Collier), 126, 228

Quail, Elizabeth, 236
Quilter, Roger (1877–1953), 205

Rabbi Ben Ezra, 203
Rankeillour, Lord, 186
Raverat, Gwen, 219
Reconciliation, 219
Redeemer, The, 75, 76
Redemption, 134
Reeves, J., 147
Remembered Queen, A, 176 footnote
Renehan, Joseph, 188
Renewals, 39, 164
Resurrection, 38, 130, 131
Retreat from Eternity, 149
Revisitation, 115

INDEX   255

Rhymed Ruminations, 33
Richmond, Bruce, 205, 215
Rivers, Dr William Halse (1864–1922), 20, 23, 114, 115, 214, 242
Road to Ruin, The, 33
Robertson, Alec, 232
Rogation, 186, 187
Rolle, Richard (1300–49), 200
Ross, Robert (1869–1918), 90, 91, 168, 214
Rossetti, D. G. (1828–82), 202
Rothenstein, William, 26
Russell, Bertrand (1872–1970), 133, 220

Salmon, Dom Martin, 175, 199
Sampson, Margery, 223, 229, 235
Sartoris, George, 212
Sassoon, Alfred Ezra, 17, 46
Sassoon, George, 34, 125, 144, 156, 182, 183, 217, 222, 242
Sassoon, Hester (1905–73), 34, 126, 217, 230, 236, 237, 238
Sassoon, Theresa G., 16, 168
Sassoons, The, 17
Saved by unnumbered miracles of chance, 89
Saxty, J., 234
Scratchbury, 176
Scale of Perfection, The, 42, 177
Scribe, The, 221
Sea of Life, The, 48
Self-Epitaph, 155
Sequences, 34, 37, 130, 169, 223
Seymour, Richard, 167
Shakespeare's Sonnets, 231
Shaw, G. B. (1856–1950), 169
Sheldonian Soliloquy, 100ff.
Shelley, P. B. (1792–1822), 207
Sherston's Progress, 20, 32, 33, 84, 88, 114, 124, 248
Sic sedebat, 35
Siegfried's Journey, 33, 83, 86, 89, 90, 91, 97, 99, 109, 113, 124, 174, 185
Sigfrid, St, 47
Sight Sufficient, 184
Silk, Dennis, 229, 237, 242
Sitwell, Edith (1887–1964), 48, 157, 209
Sitwell, Dom Gerard, 42, 177

Some say, my dear Dame Hildelith, 131
Something about Myself, 52, 243
Sparrow, John, 101
Stanbrook Press, 201, 229, 243
Sumner, Dame Elizabeth, Abbess of Stanbrook, 41, 192, 209, 244
Sunday Telegraph, 24
Sunday Times, 86, 111
Swinburne, A. C. (1837–1909), 55, 154, 219
Swinnerton, Frank, 145

Tablet, The, 189
Tasking, The, 149
Teilhard de Chardin, 238, 248
Tennyson, Alfred (1809–92), 237
Teresa of Avila, Saint (1515–82), 19
Terry, Ellen (1847–1928), 204
There is an organic connection, 122
The sage, and the beetle at his feet, 122
They are all gone into the world of light, 104
They Speak by Silences, 238
They were not true, those dreams, those story books of youth, 73
Thomas, David, 79
Thomas, Dylan (1914–53), 150, 151
Thompson, Francis (1859–1907), 219
Thornycroft, Sir Hamo (1850–1925), 16, 47
Thornycroft, Sir John, 16, 144
Thorpe, Michael, 91
Thoughts in 1932, 110
The Thrush, 215
Time and Tide, 208
Times, The, 144, 238
To a Childless Woman, 93, 94
To Any Dead Officer, 86, 87
To my Brother, 78
To the Wild Rose, 49
Tomlinson, H. M. (d. 1958), 146, 223
Traherne, Thomas (1637–74), 156
Trial, The, 155
Trollope, Anthony, 248
Tupper, Martin F. (1810–89), 123

Undertones of War, 232
Unfoldment, 189
Unknown Eros, The, 186 footnote

van Bruyn, D. Marcella, 209
van Krimpen, Jan (1892–1958), 201
van Zeller, Dom Hubert, 173, 196, 206, 241, 247
Vaughan, Henry (1622–95), 27, 28, 33, 93, 104, 136, 156
Vidler, Canon Alec, 93
Vigils, 33, 123
Visitant, The, 150

Waddell, Helen (1889–1965), 139, 140, 167, 223
Waste Land, The, 237
Watkin, Dom Aelred, 175, 236, 247
Watts Exhibition, The, 51
Waugh, Evelyn (1903–66), 185
Wavell, Major Earl (killed in action in Kenya, 1953), 144, 155, 167, 192, 228
Weald of Youth, The, 59, 61, 62, 65, 66, 70
Wedgwood, Dame Veronica, 231

Weekend Stroll, 69
Wellington, Duke of, 212
Wells, H. G. (1866–1946), 147
What Hope for Poetry?, 121ff.
Whichcote, Benjamin (1609–83), 156
Whistler, Laurence, 239
White, T. H. (1906–64), 126
Wilde, Oscar (1854–1900), 91
Wilson, Mrs Doris, 209, 240
Wilson, Dover, 228
Wirgman, Helen, 62, 66, 69, 70, 105
Wirgman, Theodore B., 69
Wishart, Mr, 222
Wodehouse, P. G., 229
Wood, D. Agnes, 229, 238
Wood Fire, The, 219
Woolf, Virginia (1882–1941), 69, 149
World Without End, 142
Worst of It, The, 153

Yeats, W. B. (1865–1939), 122, 205
Young, Andrew J. (1885–1972), 157

OHIO UNIVERSITY LIBRARY

Please return this book as soon as you have finished with it. In order to avoid a fine it must be returned by the latest date stamped below.